# ISLANDS OF TURMOIL

## ELECTIONS AND POLITICS IN FIJI

BRIJ V. LAL

# ISLANDS OF TURMOIL

## ELECTIONS AND POLITICS IN FIJI

BRIJ V. LAL

ANU
THE AUSTRALIAN NATIONAL UNIVERSITY

E PRESS

Asia Pacific Press at
The Australian National University

# ANU

## E PRESS

Co-Published by ANU E Press and Asia Pacific Press
The Australian National Unversity
Canberra ACT 0200
Email: anuepress@anu.edu.au
Website: http://epress.anu.edu.au

National Library of Australia Cataloguing-in-Publication entry

---

Lal, Brij V.
Islands of turmoil : elections and politics in Fiji.

Bibliography.
Includes index.
ISBN 0 7315 3751 3
ISBN 1 920942 75 0 (Online document)

1. Fiji - Politics and government. 2. Fiji - Social
conditions. 3. Fiji - Economic conditions. I. Title.


996.11

---

Editor: Bridget Maidment

Publisher: Asia Pacific Press and ANU E Press

Design: Annie Di Nallo Design

Printers: University Printing Service, The Australian National University


Cover photo, *Nukulau Prison*, is copyright and used with permission (www.fijilive.com).
Author photo by Darren Boyd, Coombs Photography.


First edition © 2006 ANU E Press and Asia Pacific Press

For the people of the Fiji Islands

There is a dawn at the end of the darkest night

# Contents

# Abbreviations

| | |
|---|---|
| ALTA | Agricultural Landlord and Tenant Act |
| ALTO | Agricultural Landlord and Tenant Ordinances |
| BP | British Peteroleum |
| CSR | Colonial Sugar Refining Company |
| FAP | Fijian Association Party |
| FLP | Fiji Labour Party |
| FNP | Fijian Nationalist Party |
| FPC | Fiji Pine Commission |
| GCC | Great Council of Chiefs |
| GEA | General Electors Association |
| GVP | General Voters Party |
| NFP | National Federation Party |
| NLTB | Native Land Trust Board |
| PANU | Party of National Unity |
| SVT | Soqosoqo ni Taukei ni Vanua |
| UGP | United General Party |
| USP | University of the South Pacific |
| WUF | Western United Front |

# Preface

Fiji is a bit like Churchill's Russia, a 'riddle wrapped in a mystery inside an enigma.' Here is an island nation, easily the most developed in the South Pacific, with a talented multiethnic population that would be the envy of many a underdeveloped nation, the hub of regional transportation and communication links, the home of international diplomatic, educational and aid organisations—it has everything going for it. And yet, despite this good fortune, it is strangely prone to debilitating self-inflected wounds that hobble its prospects and dent its future. The two military coups in 1987 and the attempted putsch in 2000 have strained race relations, damaged the economy, infected public institutions with the virus of mismanagement and failing accountability, nurtured religious intolerance and periodic acts of sacrilege against non-Christians, disrupted improvements to essential infrastructure, education and social and medical services, and led to a mass exodus of some of its best and brightest citizens.

This indictment may seem harsh, for on the surface things look normal. Despite all the temptations, inducements and provocations, Fiji has not descended into a bloodbath of the type common in other developing regions. There are no unmarked mass graves, no long knives in the night. Certain institutions—the judiciary, for instance—bravely continue to uphold the rule of law despite intimidation and subversion through political interference. The press is free. But the overwhelming sense in Fiji is of the essential fragility of things, the sense that things could go wrong at any time. The almost daily reports of verbal exchanges between the military leadership and the government about who is the ultimate custodian of the national interest underlines the point. As I write this (October 2005), the Fijian Minister for Home Affairs informs the media that the Commander of the Fiji Military Forces and his family need protection because not all the ammunition stolen from the army has been returned and rogue elements continue to roam the land. And the government is contemplating passing legislation to give traditional chiefs immunity from prosecution 'for certain kinds of activities', such as trying to 'resolve disputes in volatile situations' however illegal that activity might be. I suppose it is not so much whether things are not as bad as they ought to be or could have been. It is, rather, whether things could be, could have been, much better.

Why is Fiji prone to periodic political turbulence? What is its source and how can it best be resolved? I address these issues historically by focusing on the last two decades of Fiji's post-independence life, including the period since George Speight's attempted putsch in 2000. These years, full of drama, chaos, anxiety and apprehension, capture the essence of the conflict in Fiji, its roots and routes, the issues that inflame public opinion, the rhetoric that is used to mobilise support in the electorate for particular political purposes and the end to which that support is put. There are various ways of charting the contours of a country's political evolution. Here, after the introductory survey chapters, I use elections to measure the tone and temperature of political discourse in Fiji. I choose elections as the vehicle for my analysis because it is during elections, more than at any other time, when deeply held views and contentious issues are brought to the fore, when the public gets engaged, however briefly or fleetingly, with major public issues of the day, when the limits of political parameters are truly stretched and tested and exposed, and when politics is at its rawest.

The fundamental cause of Fiji's problem, I argue, is its obsession with race, with its entrenchment in the political process and in public policy. The inevitable result of this preoccupation is that every issue, every concern, is seen through the prism of ethnic, as opposed to national, interest. Ethnic fears and prejudices are cynically exploited for political purposes during elections. The appeal to ethnicity and ethnic identity is fostered through a racially compartmentalised electoral system in which two-thirds of the seats in parliament are elected on racial rolls, and the remaining on open non-racial rolls. The logic of the system is for political parties, which are essentially racially based, to consolidate their own ethnic constituency and wrest enough numbers from their opponent's to win power. Divide and Rule. When political competition is equated with ethnic competition in a zero-sum struggle, the potential for conflict and tension increases dramatically.

Not only electoral politics but public memory is racially archived as well. Fiji citizens entering or leaving the country are required to state their 'race' on the arrival and departure cards. They are required to declare their race when taking out a driver's licence or opening a bank account. The government has adopted a race-based affirmative action policy in favour of the indigenous Rotuman and Fijian communities, and there is a 'blueprint' to promote Fijians in commerce and industry where their success is unremarkable (though slowly growing). The penultimate year of secondary education is fee-exempt for Fijian students but not for children from other ethnic groups. Fifty per cent of all the taxi licences are now reserved for the indigenous community, and the higher echelons of the public service are dominated by them as well. Schools which are designated 'Fijian' receive special government subsidy, but not non-Fijian schools, even though in many cases over 50 per cent of their students are indigenous Fijians. In short, race stares at you in most areas of the public sector. Ratu Sir Kamisese Mara, Fiji's first prime minister, often said that race was a fact of life in Fiji. If present policies continue, it will become a way of life for its people. The reality, of course, is that race is one among many and perhaps more important facts of life such as unemployment, poverty, urban violence, collapsing infrastructure, corruption in public life, misuse of public office. The list is endless.

There are other causes of tension as well. Among the most important of these is land. By law, native land—some 83 per cent of the total land area of Fiji—is held in inalienable right by the indigenous Fijians. In the 1990s, the government transferred all the former Crown Land to the Native Land Trust Board with the result that now nearly 90 per cent of all land is in Fijian ownership. On the other hand the bulk of the commercial farmers, particularly in the sugar industry, are Indo-Fijians. To the Fijians land is more than a commodity to be disposed of in the market place or a simple commercial proposition. The attachment to land is deep, almost mystical, as a source of pride and identity. Not all the land is cultivable. And in recent years, the Fijian population itself has increased and demanded the termination of leases when these expire. The Fijian predicament is understandable, but so, too, is the dire situation facing the Indo-Fijian community. The 30-year leases which they acquired in the late 1960s began expiring in the late 1990s, with the landowners refusing renewal, or renewing them on terms favourable to themselves. Forced off the lands on which they have lived for generations, the evictees, unskilled and often unlettered, start a new, uncertain future while their formerly productive farms decline or revert to bush. The nation suffers, and the anguish of eviction is deep.

Another source of conflict is about who should be allowed the rein of political leadership in Fiji. Fijians, though not all of them by any means, insist that national leadership should be in Fijian hands. Without that, Fiji will know no peace. Fijian interests should be paramount in Fiji. For their part, the Indo-Fijian community insists that ideology, not primordiality, should form the foundations of Fiji's political system, that the state should be race-neutral in its obligations and responsibilities to its citizens. The Fijian view that they can trust only their own leaders derives from the political culture of the twentieth century that encouraged the three races to entrust their future to their own ethnic representatives. Their high ranking leaders, sometimes even paramount chiefs, were also their political leaders, people of towering personalities and overarching influence, trained by the British to assume power when Fiji became independent. But they have all moved on, and no clear successor of broad influence and authority is clearly visible. Many aspiring Fijian leaders are embroiled in local and regional issues. Moreover, they—and Indo-Fijians' leaders, too—lack the experience and cross-cultural skills to provide the kind of leadership needed for a divided multiethnic nation like Fiji.

There was a time, long gone now, when the two major communities had little in common. Fijians lived a subsistence lifestyle and Indo-Fijians were in the commercial agricultural sector. The opportunities for interaction between them were limited—and discouraged by the authorities. But in recent decades, modernity and the challenges and opportunities of globalisation have perforce fostered closer interaction. I cite two examples from popular culture to illustrate this point. Bollywood movies, which once attracted an exclusively Indo-Fijian audience, are now so popular with Fijians that some of the films are dubbed in Fijian. This would have been unthinkable a decade ago. And rugby, once a mystery game to most Indo-Fijians, is now followed by them with great knowledge and passion. When Indo-Fijian grandmothers go 'ga-ga' over Sevens' maestro Waisale Serevi, it is time to take notice of change. There are many other such examples of cross-cultural intersections and insurrections which pervade the daily life in Fiji.

The unity, imposed by the colonial government and nurtured by paramount chiefs through the course of the twentieth century, is now becoming frayed. This was once a taboo subject, but it is now the topic of public talk. There are many reasons for this. The absence of paramount chiefs at the helm of national leadership is one. When they were alive, the chiefs' wisdom and guidance were seldom questioned or questioned only in hushed tones. The effects of modern education have undermined the traditional ideology that the business of government is solely the business of chiefs. More and more Fijians are living in urban and peri-urban areas, exposed to all the challenges and opportunities which urbanisation brings. There is now in Fiji a large and growing Fijian middle class, filling the gap left by departing Indo-Fijians, which is much more firmly enmeshed into the modern economy than ever before. Fijian women and men selling root crops, vegetables, fish, crabs, prawns in urban stalls or on footpaths or along highways in large numbers could not have been imagined a decade ago. Money economy has penetrated the Fijian households and the Fijian hinterland in profound, life-altering ways. Traditional institutions are coming under increasing pressure.

Social and economic fragmentation in the indigenous community is also accompanied by greater and very public debate about power-sharing and redistribution of power among the Fijians. Western Fijian dissent and demand for appropriate representation in national decision-making to reflect the contribution their region makes to the national economy has long been well-known. Gold, pine, sugar and tourism are all located in western Viti Levu. But there are other sources of friction and dissension as well. The eastern provinces rose to ascendancy in the late nineteenth and early twentieth century and consolidated their hold as the century progressed, to the quiet disappointment of their former rivals. In the 2000 putsch, no attempt was made to hide the fact that the rebels had, as one part of their agenda, the restoration of the primacy of the Kubuna confederacy. George Speight spoke of Ratu Sir Kamisese Mara in insultingly disrespectful terms and demanded his resignation.

These internal debates will continue to influence the pattern and direction of Fijian—and national—politics, now more so than in the past. For long, the fear of Indian dominance was an important factor propelling the political unity of the Fijians. But that fear has been declining as Fijians realise the power—military and civilian—they have in their hands and as Indo-Fijian population continues to decline through as lower birth rate and emigration. It is projected to be 37 per cent of the national population in the next few years. This demographic shift has important implications for the way politics will operate in Fiji in the future. It seems inescapable that the future directions in national politics will be determined by the interests and impulses of the indigenous community.

Many essays in this volume appeared in different incarnations over a period of years, written in different moods for different purposes and audiences. They have been revised or otherwise amended to give the book structure, intellectual coherence and narrative flow. They are my attempt to decipher the patterns of a recent past of a country to which I am inextricably linked both emotionally and intellectually, and in whose recent public life I have played a minor role. The essays, then, speak from a position of active interest and concern, not from disinterested, detached observation. If this volume contributes to a more informed debate about Fiji's recent past and prognostications about its future, especially in Fiji itself, it will have achieved its purpose. *Et res non semper, spes mihi semper adest.*

## Afterword

Since this book was written, an election has taken place (May 2006), Fiji's tenth since independence. I discuss this election in Chapter 10. After the elections, a multi-party government came into existence. This experiment has raised the hope among the people of Fiji that a new beginning towards more inclusive, non-racial politics may be on the horizon. But it is too early to tell.

## A note on sources

In different forms the essays in this volume began life as talks and seminar presentations and articles published in *Pacific Studies*, *The Contemporary Pacific*, *Journal of Pacific History* and *Asia Pacific Viewpoint*. They have, for the most part, been inaccessible to ordinary readers and observers of political developments in Fiji. I hope that this collection will rectify this.

## Acknowledgments

My grateful thanks to Maree Tait at Asia Pacific Press for her support and to Bridget Maidment for editing this manuscript with care and skill. In the Division of Pacific and Asian History of the Australian National University, Oanh Collins helped with the preparation of the manuscript. The Division itself supported my research on contemporary Fijian politics for which I will always remain grateful.

I am also grateful to readers and scholars who have over the years provided me with information and insight into Fiji politics. I hope that they will accept my heartfelt gratitude collectively. Padma has been my 'partner in crime' for more than thirty years. Her support and encouragement have been indispensible.
Brij V. Lal
Canberra

# 1

# The road to independence 1874–1970

Some basic facts first. Fiji Islands, covering some 1.3 million kilometres of the South Pacific Ocean, lie between the longitudes of 175 and 178 west and the latitudes of 15 and 22 south. Most of Fiji's population lives on the two major islands of Viti Levu and Vanua Levu. Its total population of 772,655 (1996 census) comprises 394,999 Fijians (51.1 per cent) and 336,579 Indo-Fijians (43.6 per cent), with the remaining 41,077 coming from other ethnic groups (5.3 per cent). Nearly half of the population now lives in urban or peri-urban areas, a significant increase over the previous decade when 39 per cent lived there. Interestingly, now over 40 per cent of indigenous Fijians live in urban areas. Tourism is the main foreign exchange earner for Fiji, followed by the garment industry, sugar, fisheries, gold and such niche products as mineral water. More recently, remittance from Fiji residents working abroad has become an important contributor to the national economy. Fiji became a British Crown Colony in 1874 and attained its independence in 1970.

Fiji's self-image at the time of independence was of a three-legged stool. The three legs were the indigenous Fijian, the Indo-Fijian and the European communities. Each of them was seen as distinct and separate in their culture, history and economic position, largely homogenous in their own internal social and cultural configurations, but interlinked to the overarching national structure, making their unique contribution through their own separate compartments. The Fijians provided the land for economic development, the Indo-Fijians provided the labour and Europeans the capital. Since the contribution of the three groups was deemed to be equally valid, none alone (except the indigenous Fijians, but more on that later) was to enjoy privileges and rights greater than others. Equality of group representation, irrespective of population size, was to be the basis of political representation. The colonial government positioned itself as the neutral, benevolent, disinterested arbiter of conflict between the three main groups. Edward Said's observation is apt: 'the rhetoric of power all too easily produces an illusion of benevolence when deployed in an imperial setting' (1993:xix).

This was a comforting metaphor for a complex, conflicted reality. In truth, none of the three ethnic groups was homogenous. Religious and cultural divisions racked the Indo-Fijian community, along with class. Europeans feared being swamped by part-Europeans with whom they were grouped together for voting purposes. Class and regional differences divided the Fijians, as they do today. There was no equivalence—or balance, to use the colonial vocabulary—between Indo-Fijian labour on the one hand and European capital on the other. Nor, it has to be said, was colonial rule as benevolent as its champions argued. The metaphor served the interests of the colonial officialdom, but did grave disservice to Fiji's complex history, for which the country is still paying a heavy price. It is to the evolution of that complex history that I now turn.

The foundations of modern Fiji were laid when it became a British colony in 1874.[1] Reluctantly acquired, Britain expected Fiji to become economically self-sustaining in the quickest possible time. But the conditions for rapid economic development were absent. European planters, numbering around 2,000 in the mid 1870s, were insolvent. Indigenous Fijians were dispirited and restless, having lost one-third of the population to an epidemic of measles accidentally introduced from Australia. To make matters worse, large parts of fertile Fijian lands were being claimed by European settlers and speculators.

Fiji's first resident governor, Sir Arthur Hamilton Gordon, promulgated a set of policies that settled Fiji's future for more than a century. He instituted a system of 'indirect rule' designed, he said, to 'seize the spirit in which native institutions had been framed, and develop to the utmost extent the capacities of the people for the management of their own affairs, without exciting their suspicions or destroying their self-respect' (see, among others, France 1969; Legge 1958; Chapman 1964). To that end, he formalised a council of chiefs to advise him on Fijian concerns and problems. The council, entrenched in the 1997 constitution, retains its status as the supreme advisory body to government on matters affecting the Fijian community. It nominates the president and vice president, and its nominees in the Senate enjoy the power of veto over all legislation affecting Fijian land, customs and customary rights. While the Council continues to enjoy broad respect, some of its activities in recent years—approving a constitution and then lending support to those who wanted it abrogated—and its apparent manipulation by politicians have tarnished its image.

Gordon's land policies ensured that 83 per cent of all land remained inalienably in Fijian ownership, under the correct that, without land, the traditional Fijian society would collapse and suffer the fate of other dispossessed communities in the Pacific islands. Today, as Crown land (Schedules A and B—either not claimed by any landowning units or whose owners had died out) has come under the jurisdiction of the Native Land Trust Board, more than 90 per cent of all land in Fiji is now owned by the indigenous community although it has to be said that large portion of it is unsuitable for agriculture.[2] Gordon decreed that the Fijian people should be freed from the pressures of commercial employment and allowed to progress at their own pace in their own traditional surroundings, paying tax in kind rather than cash, and tending to their subsistence lifestyle in their age-old fashion. For nearly a century, the Fijians had their own separate court system, their own provincial administration, native regulations and strictly observed schedule of work in the villages. Their isolation from the mainstream of colonial society was almost complete.

Gordon's policies were well-intentioned, but over time they became encrusted in orthodoxy (see France 1969; Thomas 1990).[3] A once-fluid situation, represented by dynastic wars and warring chiefdoms, was frozen by fiat, uniform codes and customary practices imposed on a diverse and complex society where none had existed before, and certain cooperative regions were rewarded in leadership and political status over others. Chiefly hierarchy and privileges (such as the *lala*, offering the first fruits of the land to chiefs) were entrenched and enforced with law. Gordon had intended for his policies to be reviewed after 25 years, enough time, he felt, for a distressed community to achieve some stability. But when the moment came, officials baulked and the opportunity for review and reform was missed. Sadly, Fijians watched uncomprehendingly, cocooned in their subsistence sector, as the world around them changed and moved on and the tentacles of a capitalist economy spread.

From the very beginning, Fijians were led to believe that in the colony their interests would be 'paramount'; and the phrase 'paramountcy of Fijian interests', mistakenly attributed to the Deed of Cession, was often invoked throughout the twentieth century both by the Fijians themselves and by European settlers to block political change. But the phrase was originally intended to be used in a protective sense. That is, in the management of Fijian affairs, the government would give 'paramount' importance to the views of the Fijian people and their leaders. Over the course of the twentieth century, particularly as independence loomed, the phrase came to acquire another, more assertive, meaning—that, in the broader scheme of things, Fijians would enjoy rights and privileges over and above those of their fellow citizens. The view came to be asserted that only Fijian political control could ensure the paramountcy of Fijian interests.

To solve the problem of capital, Gordon turned overseas. Having seen the success of plantation economies in the Caribbean and Mauritius—he had been governor of Trinidad and Mauritius before coming to Fiji—he chose the plantation economy as his preferred mode of economic development, and sugar cane as the plantation crop. He invited the Australian Colonial Sugar Refining Company to extend its operations in Fiji, which it did in 1882, and remained there until 1973, dominating the economic life of the colony and in the process exercising preponderant influence on its affairs (see Moynagh 1981). To work the plantations, Gordon imported Indian indentured labour. Between 1879, when emigration began, and 1916 when it ended, more than 60,000 men and women and children arrived in the colony (see Gillion 1962; Lal 2000b). When their five-year contracts expired, the government encouraged them to stay on. Most did. Out of the experience of indenture emerged a new society, more egalitarian, enterprising and driven by desperation, seeking, as W.E.H. Stanner puts it, 'peaceful seepage into every opening left unclosed and a tenacious defence of every position once occupied' (1953:179). Isolated, struggling, self-absorbed and vulnerable, the Indo-Fijian community was just as caught up in its own internal affairs, adjusting to the requirements of their new adopted homeland, and just as myopic about its long-term interests as the Fijian community.

Indentured emigration was sanctioned by the Government of India on the broad understanding that the indentured labourers who decided to settle in the colonies would enjoy rights equal to the other British subjects there. Europeans and even some colonial officials disputed the spirit of the undertaking and questioned its application to Fiji. But the historical record is clear. The assurance of equality was periodically reinstated.

The whole tenor of the correspondence between India and the colony shows that it was on this condition that indentured immigration in Fiji has been allowed in the past, and any measures leading towards lowering the political status of the immigrants or reducing their economic freedom would, in our opinion, involve a breach of faith with those affected (Lal 1997a:6).

Throughout their political struggle in the twentieth century, Indo-Fijian leaders would continue to cite the principle of parity in support of their cause.

After the end of their indentures, the freed Indians settled on leased land, and continued to work mainly in the sugar industry as growers and mill workers, as did their descendants for several generations. The community diversified and grew, outnumbering indigenous Fijians in the mid 1940s, in the process spawning publicly aired and politically charged fears about 'Indian domination' (see Gillion 1977; Mayer 1973). But while remaining on the land, the Indo-Fijians established schools, often without government help, seeing education as the way out of the vagaries of life on leased land. In time, most settlements had a primary and even a secondary school whose students over the years filled the junior ranks of the civil service, and from the 1950s onwards, the professions as lawyers, doctors, nurses and accountants. Fijians, too, had their own schools—with longer histories, and government support—but their educational success was limited. Cultural factors, emphasising group solidarity and the virtue of subordinating individual interests to communal interests, rural isolation and poor educational facilities played their part.[4] Moreover, Fijian leaders actively discouraged 'academic' education for ordinary Fijians. The few opportunities for higher education were reserved for people of chiefly rank. As the starkest example of this, the Great Council of Chiefs declined to offer a university scholarship to Rusiate Nayacakalou, a commoner who later emerged as the most brilliant Fiji-born social scientist of the twentieth century. Nayacakalou completed his university education on a private scholarship given by an European business house, Morris Hedstrom (Firth and Tarte 2001).

If the disparity in the educational opportunities for the two communities was one problem that would haunt Fiji in the future, another was the monoracial character of its schools. The Queen Victoria School (opened in 1907) was exclusively Fijian while most schools in the sugarcane belt were predominantly Indo-Fijian by virtue of population distribution. Multiracial schools were mostly Christian and set up in urban areas. The children of the two communities, then, attending their own racially oriented schools, and firmly tethered to their own cultural ethos and values, had few opportunities to acquire knowledge of each other's culture and language, and of the deeper impulses which drove them. And yet, students from these schools would be called on later to play a vital role on the national stage, a task for which, because of their cross-culturally limited education, they were spectacularly ill-suited. It is no wonder that Fiji has faltered in its post-independence journey. The tragedy is that little is being done even now to rectify the situation. On the contrary, government policy, through special subsidies and grants, provides inducement for Fijian children to attend predominantly Fijian schools even though in many urban areas mixed schools are the norm.

The minuscule European population occupied the apex of the colonial social and economic pinnacle. They dominated the retail and wholesale commerce of the colony, owned copra plantations and shipping companies and occupied a pride of place in colonial administration. They had their own racially segregated clubs and exclusive voluntary associations and schools. In the twentieth century, they began to move to urban towns and centres. The community was not homogenous, though, with fine lines of demarcation differentiating the various nationalities that comprised it. Europeans of all hues saw themselves as superior to part-Europeans who, for electoral purposes, were grouped with them. In the late nineteenth and early twentieth centuries, some prominent Europeans, dissatisfied with the policies of the local government, tried to have Fiji annexed to New Zealand, but when that alternative failed, they agitated for a privileged place in colonial politics (Lal 1992). Paramountcy for Fijians, parity for Indo-Fijians and privilege for Europeans—these three conflicting ideas informed the political discourse in colonial Fiji.

From the very beginning, the electoral system in Fiji was race-based.[5] The colonial government saw this as natural and desirable. In part, it reflected its own interests: with the three communities locked in their own separate compartments, the colonial government could play the role of impartial referee. The government did little to encourage the communities to forge common, multiracial links among themselves. Europeans were accorded elected representation in 1904, Indo-Fijians in 1929 and indigenous Fijians in 1963. Before then, Fijian representatives in the Legislative Council were nominated by the Great Council of Chiefs. Each group had equal representation irrespective of population size. Under the Letters Patent of 1937, which remained in force until 1963, the three communities had five representatives each.

Three of the five Indo-Fijians and Europeans were elected by their group and two nominated by the governor, while all five Fijians were nominated by the Council of Chiefs.

This arrangement was frequently questioned after World War II to make the political representation more accurately reflect the demographic, social and economic changes sweeping Fiji, as well as Whitehall's commitment to gradual self-government for the colonies. Specifically, advocates of constitutional change wanted elected representatives to be more directly involved in policymaking. This demand for constitutional change was led not by Indo-Fijians, but by a group of Europeans. Their goal was not the removal of racial representation; they wanted that maintained. They wanted the system of nomination abolished for everyone, including the Fijians. Fijians were opposed to the extension of election. Why, they asked, change the system of government when that system was working satisfactorily? A democratic system of government did not suit the Fijian people (see Lal 1997b). A universal franchise would be open to abuse and corruption and manipulation by selfish individuals. Chiefs were the natural leaders of their people and it was un-Fijian to trust critical decisions to commoners. Fijian fears about the security of their rights were exacerbated by the rapid increase in Indo-Fijian population. The Fijian Affairs Board asked Whitehall to take a firmer line with Indo-Fijian politicians and others misguidedly agitating for constitutional reform. Colonial rule had been good for the Fijians. It had preserved their social and cultural institutions—their way of life. They therefore saw no need for change.

Indo-Fijian leaders disagreed. They accepted that the rights and privileges of the indigenous community should not be questioned. Minority rights should be protected, but, as A.D. Patel, the Indo-Fijian member of the Legislative Council, put it in 1946, minority communities had 'also to appreciate and realise the fact that you cannot expect or hope for privileges and rights in excess of those enjoyed by the majority'. He continued to argue for a non-racial common roll form of voting, which he had pursued since the late 1920s, and would continue to do throughout his political life. Common roll, he believed, was the only way forward for a racially divided society, the only way 'a common denominator of a political outlook will be developed' (Lal 1997a:29). But he agreed that a common roll could not be introduced unless everyone accepted the idea. His plea fell on deaf, nay, hostile ears.

Lack of consensus about the pace and direction of constitutional change suited the colonial government, placing it in the position of not

7

having to take a stand or propose initiatives on controversial political issues. Privately, though, its views were deeply divided. Among many there was sympathy for the Fijian position and a marked antipathy for Indo-Fijians. There was a sympathetic understanding of the Fijian predicament, leavened with a good deal of adulation of, and romanticism about, the Fijian way of life (see Roth 1953). Moreover, many felt a moral responsibility for a people who had ceded their islands voluntarily, had pledged total loyalty to the Crown, and had shed blood for the cause of the Empire. The fact that Fijian leaders looked to Britain for guidance, after having reposed complete trust in her institutions and policies, increased the sense of obligation and responsibility correspondingly. The government had little understanding of the cultural and social impulses that drove the Indo-Fijians, for whom colonial rule was not the solution but the cause of Fiji's problems. Remembering the hardship of indenture and acts of petty discrimination their forebears had endured, they saw little of value but much to criticise in colonial rule. And they were not averse to airing their grievances outside the colony and seeking external alliances for their cause, much to the irritation of colonial officials.

There was an Indian problem, many agreed, but it could just as easily have been labelled a 'Fijian problem'. As Governor Grantham told London in 1946, 'apart from the relative growth in population, it might be better termed the Fijian problem, since it is rather a question of raising the Fijian so that he is able to hold his own with the Indian in the modern world, than holding back the Indian so that he does not outstrip the more easy-going Fijian' (Colonial Office document 83/252, cited in Lal 1997b). Fijian interests should be protected, the Commissioner of Labour told the Legislative Council in 1946, but the Fijians had 'reciprocal obligations to the other races in this colony to recognise their economic and political aspirations and facilitate their attainment'. The Europeans and Indo-Fijians had made their contribution to the colony 'and they are entitled to be admitted into full membership of the colonial family'. Yes, there were divisions and distinctions, but the 'interests of the three races are not as so many independent threads, but strands which are interwoven into one economic fabric which are interwoven into one economic fabric; and each strand is essential to the strength of the whole' (Colonial Office document 83/252, cited in Lal 1997b). To those who invoked real or imagined promises to the Fijian people, the governor replied candidly

[t]he obligation of the government to the Fijians can be stated comprehensively in a few sentences; we must preserve all that is good of their culture, but not outworn customs and ways of life; we must give them the opportunities and the means to expand that culture; we must protect them from exploitation and disease; and

otherwise so govern and lead these people as ultimately to achieve their full integration into the political and economic life of a composite society comprising all the races of the colony (Legislative Council Debate, July 1946).

In the 1950s, questions that had been shelved or brushed aside began to resurface with the appointment of Sir Ronald Garvey as governor. Garvey, an old hand in the Pacific, was independent-minded, self-confident and acutely aware of the local realities. He wanted to move the constitutional train along because he was convinced that

[f]airly steady progress is being made [towards common citizenship]. Both colour and social barriers are being broken down and the desirability and, indeed, inevitability of unity is taking shape. It is a policy which I constantly preach myself and it is having its imperceptible effect throughout the whole community (Colonial Office document 1039/9).[6]

In 1954, Garvey asked the Great Council of Chiefs to consider directly electing three of their five representatives to the Legislative Council to give the Fijians an experience of electoral politics. He told the chiefs that the 'chiefly system on which so much depends should march with the times and should not ignore—for too long—the modern trend of democracy'. To those who invoked the Deed of Cession in support of gradualism and permanent paramountcy of Fijian interests, Garvey responded with characteristic but unprecedented bluntness. He said in 1957

[s]urely the intention of this Deed, acknowledged and accepted by chiefs who were parties to it, was that Fiji should be developed so as to take a significant place in the affairs of the world but that, in the process, the rights and interests of the Fijian people should be respected. To read into the Deed more than that, to suggest, for instance, that the rights and interests of the Fijians should predominate over everything else, does no service either to the Fijian people or to their country. The view, for the Fijians, would mean complete protection and no self-respecting individual race wants that because, ultimately, it means that those subject to it will end up as museum pieces. The Indians are equally eligible to have their interests respected. By their work and enterprise, the Indians in Fiji have made a great contribution to the development and prosperity of their country, and to the welfare of its people. They are an essential part of the community and it is unrealistic to suppose that they are not or to imagine that the position of Fijians in the world today would benefit by their absence (*Fiji Times*, 15 October 1957).

Governor Garvey approached the Colonial Office in 1956 with fresh constitutional proposals. His ultimate goal was common Fijian citizenship, he said. Perhaps his most radical proposal was a 'multiracial bench' of four members, one each from the three main racial groups and one to represent 'other races', such as Chinese and other Pacific Islanders, all of them elected from a colony-wide constituency. This was the first time that such a proposal had been made. But Garvey was not supported by his more cautious, conservative officers who argued that the concept of a multiracial bench would be opposed by the Europeans and Fijians who would see the proposal as 'the thin end of the wedge' driving to a common roll, and paving the way for reforms far too radical for the colony to bear. Furthermore, would not members not elected by their own group be seen as the puppets of those who elected them? Garvey was undaunted, saying that 'if we are aiming at a growth of a consciousness of Fijian citizenship overbidding differences of race and religion, I think it has considerable merit' (Garvey to Sir Thomas Lloyd, 11 Febuary 1956, in Colonial Office document 1036/10).[7] Maintaining the *status quo* was no solution to Fiji's political problems.

Garvey's proposal was discussed by the old colonial hands in London—the 'back room boys', Garvey called them derisively—who raised all the usual arguments about the need for Whitehall to 'keep a firm grip of the initiative', and act 'just in advance of pressure, but only just' (Colonial Office document 1036/10, file 33). The racial factor could not be discounted lightly. 'It is true that constitutional advance does not wait upon a country's demand, but the circumstances of Fiji are rather special and to go too fast would...play into the hands of the Indians' (Colonial Office document 1036/10, file 77). 'If there is no pressure for a change, we should be the last to stimulate it' (Colonial Office document 1036/10, file 77), was the advice of one colonial officer. Predictably Garvey's motive was questioned. Was he actuated by the desire to end his term of office by 'some significant advance'? The Secretary of State replied to Garvey's proposals on 20 March 1956

[i]t seems very unwise to do anything to encourage it [constitutional reform] to grow more quickly unless we have some fairly clear idea where we are going. In some respects Fiji is a very difficult proposition from the point of view of constitutional advance. We are all, very naturally, inclined to think of such advance in terms of British institutions, leading in the direction of an elected assembly, universal adult suffrage, the party system, the vesting of executive power in unofficial Ministers and so forth. Yet we are learning by experience elsewhere that the traditional British pattern, however suitable for places of a certain size, is difficult to work out in small territories, even where there is a homogenous and relatively well advanced population; it is still more difficult to apply in such a place as Fiji, where race means more than party, and where a dilemma is created by the numerical preponderance of the Indians on the one hand and our obligations to the Fijians on the other. It may

well be that what we ought to aim at in Fiji is some form of constitution different from the traditional pattern. In this connection you may like to look at the enclosed document about another of our problem areas—Mauritius—not because the ideas which are being tried out there are necessarily all applicable...but as an illustration of the fact that new ways are being sought to establish forms of democracy and of representative institutions in places where the conditions favourable to the 'Westminster model' do not exist (Sir Thomas Lloyd to Garvey, 20 March 1956, in Colonial Office document 1036/10).

Garvey was disappointed but not surprised. The fears of the floodgates were, in truth, groundless, he said. In taking the initiative, he reminded the Colonial Office, he was 'not playing with a scorpion's tale' (Garvey to Sir John Macpherson, 14 October 1956, in Colonial Office document 1036/10, file 33). His modest proposals would have resulted in 'some quickening of interest in a direction where we are failing to make progress even though we are far better equipped than many who have raced ahead of us'. If Fiji were to wait for integration to take place at the local government level, before proceeding to any constitutional change, 'we shall have to wait a long time for progress in that direction'. When recommending the appointment of a commissioner to advise on constitutional matters, Garvey said he was not thinking of anyone entirely unfamiliar with Fiji. He had in mind Sir Arthur Richards, now Lord Milverton, a widely respected former governor, who had, with Sukuna, engineered the creation of the Native Land Trust Board.

By the late 1950s, Fiji hardly resembled the place in had been at the beginning of the decade. The working class, increasing in size and visibility, had begun to organise. A series of lightning strikes in the 1950s, culminating in the December 1959 riots, shook Fiji. A crippling strike in the sugar industry was in prospect, after a peaceful interlude of nearly two decades. The population was increasing rapidly and becoming better informed about events in Fiji and overseas, thanks to a thriving print media and the advent of the radio. Fijian soldiers were returning to Fiji after four years of service in the Malayan jungles, where they had gone to fight the Chinese communist insurgency. Two major commissions of enquiry were under way, one by geographer O.H.K. Spate into the economic and social problems facing the Fijian people (Spate 1959), and another by Sir Alan Burns into the natural resources and population trends in the colony (Burns et al. 1960), both recommending a fundamental change of direction.

The government could no longer afford to stall or stonewall. In his budget address to the Legislative Council in 1960, the new governor, Sir

Kenneth Maddocks, tested the waters by suggesting the need for constitutional reform, hoping that the next election (in 1963) might be held under a new Letters Patent (Letter from Maddocks to H.P. Hall, 17 January 1961, in Colonial Office document 1036/612). The aim was to pave the way for a ministerial system of government—initially to be called the Member System—under which unofficial members of the Legislative Council would be invited to undertake supervisory roles for government departments, contribute to policy formulation and oversee its implementation, all under the principle of collective, cabinet-type responsibility. The proposal was intended to be the first step towards full internal self-government.

The government's constitutional proposals were debated during the April 1961 sitting of the Legislative Council, the motion introduced by the Acting Colonial Secretary. His tone is almost pleading, begging European and Fijian members to have an open mind on reform. For the first time, the government was taking the lead, somewhat along the lines Garvey had envisaged in the 1950s. The Colonial Secretary asked the members to 'try and establish for ourselves a long term objective'. The winds of decolonisation were moving closer to the Pacific. Samoa was on the verge of independence and Fiji could not afford to be indifferent. 'I know it would be nice to consider Fiji in a vacuum and isolated and do as we wish, but unfortunately we cannot'. He continued

> ...we are part of the world and there are forces moving which, whether we like it or not—and I know many of us do not like it—are going to have a profound influence on us and on our future. We need to consider these forces; what they are and what steps are necessary to meet and mould them to our ends. We want to do it in our own unhurried time. We do not want to wait till the forces are built up against us and we have to do things as a matter of urgency. Let us think ahead, see what is coming, be ready for it and do all that we have to do in our own time, and by our own choosing...do not let us forget the forces outside. It is no good forgetting them; they are there and they are real (Legislative Council Debate, April 1961).

By 'forces out there', the government meant the pressure from the United Nations' Committee on Decolonisation, which watched developments in Fiji closely, much to the irritation of the colonial government as well as Fijians and Europeans.

During the same legislative council debate, the Colonial Secretary responded to those who maintained that the majority of the people were satisfied with the *status quo*. He is worth quoting at length.

Almost everything starts with a minority. Minorities have a way of growing, and when minorities have a popular idea, any government that ignores such a minority does so at its peril. A minority can be likened to a small stream. It is there, something quite small and water is soft. It can be used for many purposes. If you dam the stream the waters build up behind the dam so you build a bigger dam, but one day you cannot go on and the burst comes. We do not want a burst here. What we want is to look together into the future and be sure that this stream of ideas, this minority perhaps, this thing called democracy is not dammed up or held back but is guided to our purpose. We want no burst dam (Legislative Council Debate, April 1961).

Unsurprisingly, the Indo-Fijian members supported the motion while European members opposed it. But what mattered more now than ever before was the reaction of the Fijian leaders. As in the past, Fijian opinion was not solidly against change. Although the majority opposed the motion, they did so for differing reasons. Among those who remained unconvinced of the government's policy was Ratu Kamisese Mara, the ascendant Fijian political leader and Fiji's first prime minister. The government's policy was ill-conceived and ill-timed, he said, because it ignored the spirit and implications of the Deed of Cession and the special place of the Fijian people in their own country. The chiefs had ceded Fiji 'to be part and parcel of the United Kingdom', in the same way that the Channel Islands and the Isle of Man were integral parts of the United Kingdom. That special relationship was recognised in the title Fijians used to refer to the Queen: *Radi ni Viti kei Peretania*, the Queen of Fiji and of Great Britain. Ratu Mara urged caution and advised a gradualist approach. Constitutional development should follow, not precede, social and economic integration. Ratu Penaia Ganilau another high chief and future governor general and president of Fiji, agreed—no constitution, no matter how good, would work unless 'we have a common background of accepted principles'.

The government listened politely, knowing that it had no alternative but to take the lead, but also aware that it must avoid embarrassing the Fijian members. It sought to allay their fears without compromising the principle of constitutional reform. The government denied that its proposals detracted from the promises of the Deed of Cession, and assured the Fijian leaders that it would entrench provisions safeguarding the native ownership of land as well as others that touched on customary matters. To the argument that social and economic integration should precede political reform, the government argued that 'unity does not have to grow from the bottom. In fact, when there are present communities speaking different languages, having different religions, living mostly in a different economy and having different customs', unity 'can spread downwards'. Suva was not doing anything that London itself had not adopted as official policy. The Colonial Secretary reminded the Legislative Council that as early as 1943, the United Kingdom had pledged itself to 'guide Colonial people along the road to self-government within the British Empire', adding that 'it is no part of our policy to confer political advances which are unjustified by circumstances or to grant self-government to those who are not yet trained in its use'. For Whitehall, though, the latter qualification had out-lived its usefulness.

In 1963, Fiji got a new Letters Patent that provided for an enlarged Legislative Council, consisting of 19 official and 18 unofficial members (see Meller and Anthony 1968). The three main communities had six members each—the principle of parity was preserved—four elected from racial rolls and two nominated by the governor. Property qualification for voters was abolished, and for the first time, a universal franchise was extended to the Fijians. The following year, the membership system was introduced. The issue after 1963 was not if self-government and independence would come to Fiji, but rather the terms and conditions upon which they would be acceptable to its various ethnic communities.

By the mid 1960s, the political landscape of Fiji had altered dramatically. Fijian fears, alluded to above, had intensified. The industrial disputes of 1959 in Suva and in the sugar industry in 1960, aroused, or, rather, reinforced, the threat of Indo-Fijian domination. The calls for reform in the Fijian system of administration, for traditional structures to be loosened to enable greater personal enterprise among those Fijians who wanted it, for the natural resources of the country to be used in an economic way for the benefit of the country as a whole, for the system of Fijian Administration, which had kept the indigenous community isolated from the mainstream, to be liberalised, startled a people used to gentle counselling, flattery and effusive praise for their traditional way of life. Their leaders expressed their anger, and London listened. 'I see no future in the Burns recommendation that the Fijian administration should be wound up as soon as possible', wrote Julian Amery, the Parliamentary Under-secretary of State for the Colonies, in 1960. 'The Fijians are determined to resist any move in this direction. They realise that whatever its defects the tribal system does provide a leadership capable of defending the Fijian communal interest against what they regard as the Indian threat. Without their chiefs they would be leaderless' (Amery, 'Report on Fiji', in Colonial Office document 1036/612).

Still, Fijian leaders realised that they could not go on resisting whatever constitutional proposals the government presented. And so the Fijian Affairs Board, the executive arm of the Great Council of Chiefs, presented their views in a document that subsequently came to be known as the 'Wakaya Letter'.[8] In it, they stated their preconditions for constitutional reform. Addressed to Nigel Fisher, the Parliamentary Under-secretary of State for the Colonies, the letter reminded the Crown of the special significance of the Deed of Cession for the Fijians. It was the Fijian view that 'the possibility of severance of this link with the Crown—a link forged in a spirit of mutual trust and goodwill—should never be contemplated' (cited in Lal 1992:189). Before any further constitutional changes were considered, the letter stated, the terms of the relationship, which they mistakenly likened to the relationship between Britain and the Channel Islands, should be clarified and codified. The letter went on

> ...there would have to be a precise restatement of the guarantee on Fijian land ownership. We visualise that the native land trust legislation should not be changed or added to without the prior consent of the sovereign and the agreement of the Council of Chiefs. We also stand by the expressed desire of the high chiefs in the preamble to the deed of cession that Fiji should be a Christian state and that therefore no constitutional or administrative changes should take place that would deviate from that intention. The provision of the Fijian affairs ordinance that all legislation affecting Fijian rights and interests should be referred to the Fijian Affairs Board or, on the recommendation of the board, to the Council of Chiefs, should be retained and likewise the governor's direction to the Public Service Commission to work towards a balance of the races in the civil service (cited in Lal 1992:189).

If these concerns were addressed, the letter concluded, the Fijian chiefs would consider contemplating further constitutional changes.

The letter was a powerful negotiating tool, designed to extract the maximum concession from Suva and London. The Colonial Office was sympathetic to Fijian concerns but firm about the need not to ignore the interests and concerns of the non-indigenous communities. The government in Suva privately assured the Fijian leaders that the special position of the indigenous community would be safeguarded, and not placed under 'the heels of an immigrant community', in the words of Governor Derek Jakeway, who was himself, in the mid 1960s, active behind the scenes helping the Fijians to organise politically.

Europeans, used to a privileged position, felt threatened about their place in any future constitutional arrangement. The Suva riots, multiracial in character and overtly anti-European in intent, had shaken them as never before. Alone, they knew, they stood little chance of maintaining their disproportionate representation in the Legislative Council; and they had few friends in places where it really mattered, such as Whitehall. Hence, they sought closer alignment with the Fijian leadership. Understandably, it was an alliance of mutual convenience. The Europeans needed the political protection the Fijians could provide, and the Fijians, appreciating the Europeans' vulnerability, knew they could count on European support against the Indo-Fijians. This alliance of interest against the threat of a perceived common enemy would last the rest of the decade and, indeed, well into independence. It was formally institutionalised in the Fijian Association-backed Alliance Party that emerged in early 1966.

The Indo-Fijian scene was energised by the return to the Legislative Council, after the absence of more than a decade, of A.D. Patel. Patel, Indian-born but a Fiji resident since 1928, was a leader of unequalled intellectual brilliance—a Gandhian at heart, a fierce and fearless critic of colonial rule and an untiring advocate of common roll (see Lal 1997a). He united the usually fractious Indo-Fijian community and formed Fiji's first political party, the Federation, in 1963. Two ideas lay at the heart of Patel's political vision. One was independence, or at least a large measure of internal self-government, eventually leading to independence. If Samoa and the Cook Islands, small, vulnerable and resource-poor, could become independent, why not Fiji, he argued? Independence was a matter of time, Patel believed, not if but when it came, and he wanted Fiji to be prepared for it.

The other idea was common roll. He had been its advocate from the beginning. Communal roll, which Fijians and Europeans wanted, would be ruinous for the country.

> Of all the people, Indians are bitterly opposed to communal representation because they have seen its painful result in the course of time. It may not be very serious now, but as time goes on, once people get used to the idea of racial separation, racial attitudes harden and people start thinking in racial terms and racial interests which leads not to one nation but, in the course of political developments, it leads to claims of several nations (A.D. Patel, cited in Lal 1997a:189).

'Communal roll', he continued, 'symbolised divided loyalties, and inhibited the formation of secular parties, with success in politics depending on reflecting communal interests and prejudices. Compromise will be rendered difficult and relative party strength may be frozen for long periods because a party can grow only with an increase in the size of the community upon which it is based'. On the other hand, common roll would 'encourage the citizens to organise political parties along national lines and in the long run compel everyone else to think in terms of his country rather than a particular race, community or religion'. It was 'only through making one nation out of Fiji that we can achieve the sort of future we want for everybody' (Lal 1997:192).

The passion with which Patel pursued the idea was reciprocated by the passion with which its opponents—which included all Fijian and European leaders—rejected it. The system of communal representation was well established in Fiji; it had worked well, they argued; a system of guaranteed racial representation produced no fears of any one group dominating others; it realistically accepted the differences of culture, language, custom and religion. These two positions illustrate the two contrasting, even diametrically opposed, visions of Fiji; and they have continued to haunt Fiji's subsequent political history. Indeed, in many ways, they lie at the heart of the political problems besetting Fiji today.

In July 1965, Whitehall convened a constitutional conference, and invited the elected representatives of the three communities to London.[9] All the established positions were expressed, with Europeans and Fijians agreeing only to limited internal self-government and the Indo-Fijian delegation hoping for a final blow to colonial rule in Fiji. Important advances were made. The Legislative Council was expanded to include 36 members: 14 Fijians (9 elected on communal roll, 3 on multiracial cross-voting and 2 nominated by the Great Council of Chiefs); 12 Indo-Fijians (9 communal and 3 cross-voting); and 10 Europeans (7 communal and 3 cross-voting). The system of cross-voting was seen as a limited concession to common roll in which multiracial electorates voted for seats reserved for candidates of different races. The Fijian and the European delegation were delighted with the outcome, and for good reason: the Europeans' privileged position was maintained, and the Fijians had, for the first time, got two additional seats. Fijian-European solidarity was consolidated.

The Indo-Fijians were disappointed. They had lost parity with the Fijians (see Lal 1992). The communal roll had been maintained, their plea for at least partial introduction of common roll falling on deaf ears. And the Indo-Fijian community was now more isolated than ever, electorally segregated from the other communities. The Fijian roll, for instance, was expanded to include all the other Pacific islanders and the European roll opened up to accommodate the Chinese. Why should the Chinese be on the European roll when they had culturally less in common with Europeans than the Indo-Fijians, Patel asked, but to no avail.

17

He accused the Colonial Office of not playing a fair mediating role at the conference (preoccupied as it was at the time with the crisis in Aden), by not persuading the Fijians and Europeans sufficiently enough to accept at least partial common roll by effectively capitulating to combined European and Fijian pressure. I am presently investigating the thinking of the Colonial Office, so can only provide a tentative assessment of the subject, but my overwhelming impression is that London had a deep sympathy for the Fijian people and was concerned not to let them end up in a secondary position in any future political arrangement. Their rhetorical advocacy of Westminster democracy was secondary to their sensitivity to Fijian feelings. London also had a prudent appreciation of its dependence on Fijian security forces to maintain law and order.

Nor did everyone in London share the vision of Fiji as a cohesive multiracial nation, although most hoped for at least some movement in favour of non-racial politics. Julian Amery reported confidentially to the Colonial Office in 1960 that 'The Fijians and Indians are more distinct as communities than Jews and Arabs in Palestine, Greeks and Turks in Cyprus or even Europeans and Bantu in South and Central Africa' (Colonial Office document 1036/11). Understandably he did not add that London itself was partly responsible for this unfortunate state of affairs. It was 'impracticable to think in terms of a single Fijian nation or of a common roll at any rate for the foreseeable future', he advised. The concept of a 'single multiracial community as the goal towards which Fijians and Indians alike should strive' was illusory, he added. 'The Fijians will no longer accept this; and the more we lay the emphasis on multiracialism, the more suspicious they will become that we plan to sell them out to the Indians'. Indeed, Amery recommended setting up a separate system of administration for Indo-Fijians, as a counterpart to the separate administration for the Fijians. In view of this, a non-racial vision for Fiji was doomed from the start.

In September 1966, fifteen months after the constitutional conference, Fiji went through another election, for the first time on party lines: the Indo-Fijian-based Federation Party and the Fijian Association-backed, nominally multiracial Alliance Party launched in 1966. Both parties won in their constituencies, the Alliance winning two-thirds of the Fijian communal votes and the Federation a similar percentage among the Indo-Fijians. After the elections, Ratu Mara became the Chief Minister. The 1965 constitution had produced the result both Suva and London wanted, and it seemed there was no urgent reason to review the constitution that the Federation Party had accepted under protest. The new government jettisoned the bipartisan approach of the past. Patel feared that unless the constitution was reviewed, the entire Indo-Fijian community would be consigned to the wilderness of frustrated and possibly endless opposition (Lal 1997a). And so, on 1 September 1967, the Federation Party walked out of the Legislative Council in the middle of an Alliance attack on the motion it had introduced rejecting the constitution and demanding a new one that was based on more democratic principles.

The ensuing by-election was fought in an intense atmosphere of great bitterness and tension (see Anthony 1969; Norton 2004). When the Federation Party won all the Indo-Fijian communal seats, and with increased majorities, too, many nationalist Fijians threatened violence, bringing the country to the edge of a crisis. But cooler heads prevailed and emotions subsided. Nonetheless, the message was clear—the 1965 racially unbalanced constitution would have to be re-examined, and the wishes of the Federation Party could not be ignored. Nor, on the other hand, could Fijian views be discounted. The battle lines were clearly drawn. Apprehending the gravity of the situation, Governor Jakeway urged Mara and Patel to resume dialogue. They did in August 1969, as representatives of the two parties met in Suva under the chairmanship of Ratu Edward Cakobau for a series of confidential discussions to identify areas of agreement and disagreement between them.[10] In an atmosphere marked by cordiality, the leaders talked frankly and freely about their concerns and fears, stating their views about the constitution and possible ways out of the current impasse. A.D. Patel, who died a month after attending the first meeting, pressed his case for common roll and immediate full independence. After his death, Patel was succeeded by Siddiq Koya, also a lawyer by training, who proved less doctrinally or ideologically committed to common roll, and who was more conciliatory and pragmatic. Mara's relations with Koya were more cordial, as they never had been with Patel. Mara had the measure of Koya, where he feared Patel's guile.[11] Influenced by a wider and deeper knowledge of history, particularly of the Indian subcontinent, raised at the dawn of Mahatma Gandhi's struggle against the British, philosophically committed to the idea of a non-racial society to the point of stubbornness, Patel was not one to give in easily. Koya, on the other hand, accepted the reality on the ground and sought to work pragmatically within its parameters and constraints where as his predecessor had sought to change them, to alter the terms of the debate.

In the confidential discussions between August 1969 and March 1970, common ground was reached on many issues. To allay Fijian fears about their rights, the Federation Party proposed an upper house, the Senate, where the nominees of the Great Council of Chiefs would have the power to veto any legislation that affected specific Fijian interests. It also proposed to go into independence without election to avoid the acrimony that an election campaign would inevitably entail, because it felt that Ratu Mara, then widely popular, was the best leader to be at the helm to effect a smooth transition to independence, and because the Federation Party itself was diffident about the broad acceptability of its own leadership.[12] In truth, they acknowledged that all the power was on the other side, and that they would have to accept the role of opposition for a long time into the future. There was also the hope that by making concessions and adopting a moderate stance, space might be created for racial reconciliation and harmony and for genuine multiracial politics to emerge.[13]

On one issue, though—the composition of the legislature and the method of election—the two parties disagreed. The Federation Party presented its case for a common roll, though without the conviction or authority of the past. Predictably, the Alliance opposed the idea, while promising an open mind on common roll as a long-term objective. Both parties decided to defer the issue to the impending constitutional conference in London, with the Federation agreeing that, in the event of an impasse, it would accept a formula 'approved and settled by the British Government'. Lord Shepherd, Minister of State for Foreign and Commonwealth Affairs, who went to Fiji to witness first hand the progress and the authenticity of the local negotiations, was clearly delighted by the Federation's concessions—as, of course, was the Alliance Party. He insisted that the consensus be formally recorded. The consensus was that 'if no agreement was reached and circumstances remained as at present, it would be necessary that the constitutional instruments for independence should reflect, subject to any formal changes arising from independence, the provisions of the existing constitution' (Foreign and Commonwealth Office file 32/571). That is, the same constitution that the Federation Party had rejected in 1965 as 'undemocratic, unjust and iniquitous'. In their quest for an orderly transition to independence, the party leaders had sacrificed their long-held principles for political expediency. As they saw it at the time, a smooth transition to independence was their primary aim, with the hope that things might change for the better in the future. They did not.

The penultimate conference paving the way for Fiji's independence was held in London in April 1970. Words spoken at the opening session at Marlborough House by both parties alluded to racial harmony, nation-building, common future, gratitude to the United Kingdom and close links to the Crown, trust, mutual understanding and goodwill.[14] The political turbulence that had accompanied the enactment of the 1965 constitution seemed a distant memory. Shepherd queried the over-representation of the Europeans, which Mara justified as a reflection of their contribution to the economy. He did not say—did not need to say—that the Europeans invariably voted with the Fijians, and that their disproportionate numbers in parliament was a guarantee of Fijian political dominance.

On common roll, Mara was adamant: it was nothing but a ruse for Indian domination of Fiji. Fijians would never accept it. 'These fears are like the devil. Many people can prove that there is no devil, yet they are fearful of devils' (Transcript of pre-London talks in Suva:94). The Federation Party presented its case for common roll, and expected Lord Shepherd to impress on the Alliance the need to make at least some token gesture towards accepting it. The Alliance refused and Shepherd proposed that acceptance of common roll be a long-term objective. NFP Secretary Karam Ramrakha objected, but officials in London and Suva both knew where party leader Koya stood. For him, it was a long-term objective too. To break the impasse, Shepherd resurrected the idea of a Royal Commission to look into the method of election after independence. Mara and Koya endorsed the proposal. In 1975, a commission was appointed with Sir Harry Street as chairman, and recommended moving away from communal roll to a system of proportional representation.[15] But by then the Alliance was firmly in control, and refused even to debate the report in parliament. National Federation Party cried foul, but one is left with the impression that its leaders, with a few exceptions, did not mind the Alliance's about-face on its Marlborough House commitment. The Indo-Fijian population growth was slowing down, and many saw guaranteed racial representation to be in the community's long-term interest.

The final constitution was in its most fundamental aspects an extension of the principles and values that had underpinned the 1966 constitution. It preserved the *status quo*. Fiji was to have a bicameral legislature with an appointed Upper House (Senate) and a fully elected Lower House (House of Representatives) of 52 seats, with 22 each reserved for Fijians and Indo-Fijians and 8 for the general electors (Europeans, part-Europeans, Chinese and others). Of the 22 seats reserved for the Fijians and Indo-Fijians, 12 were to be contested on communal (racial) rolls and the remaining 10 on national (cross-voting) seats. This meant that candidates themselves were required to be Fijians, Indo-Fijians and general electors, but they were all elected by registered voters. In the House of Representatives, then, Fijians and Indo-Fijians had parity. The general electors' privileged position was also preserved: though they comprised only 4 per cent of the population, they had 15.4 percent of the seats, compared to Fijians and Indo-Fijians who had 42.3 per cent of the seats each. General elector over-representation was accepted, indeed advocated, by the Fijian leaders, who knew from experience that the general electors would support them, as they had invariably done in the past. In the 22-member Senate, the principle of Fijian paramountcy was explicitly recognised by giving the 8 nominees of the Great Council of Chiefs the power of veto over legislation specifically affecting Fijian interests and privileges.

The independence constitution, then, represented continuity with Fiji's racially divided past. It was based on the assumption that 'race', or ethnicity, was, and would long remain, the most important determinant of political behaviour of the people and that Fijians would control political power if they remained united and voted solidly as a racial group. But Fiji was changing rapidly. New forces of modernity and globalisation were altering the fundamental social and political structures of society, reducing the relevance of race in everyday life. The gulf between the public culture constructed on the pillars of communalism and the realities of everyday living was growing.

Two days before Fiji became independent on 10 October 1970, Sir Robert Foster penned his last despatch as governor of Fiji. In it, he tried to capture the mood of the moment, the sometimes-tumultuous events which had led to it, and embroiled it in conflict and tension, and offered his prognosis on what the future held for the young nation. 'Seldom can a country have prepared for independence with such aplomb', he told London. The diverse people of Fiji 'do not yet think of themselves as a nation' (Foreign and Commonwealth Office file 32/606), and Julian Amery's words about the differences between the two communities, written a decade ago, still retained some salience. Foster commented on developments which had facilitated the smooth transition to independence: the sobering effects of the 1968 by-elections, and the conciliatory posture of Siddiq Koya and his warm relations with Mara.

The future looked reasonably bright. But in his despatch was the suggestion of dark clouds on the horizon. The land problem—not ownership but leasing arrangements—remained as intractable as ever.

Time had been bought by setting up a committee to examine amendments to the Landlord and Tenant Ordinance. 'But a solution to the land problem is no nearer. I doubt whether the problem will ever be solved without far more radical changes in the system of land tenure than Fijians have hitherto been prepared to contemplate' (Foreign and Commonwealth Office file 32/606). The second major problem, unresolved at the conference—shelved, to be confronted after independence—was the electoral system. 'A calm search for a just solution to the problem of representation has in the past proved virtually impossible; feelings ran far too deep for that. One is therefore bound to regret that in effect a time bomb will lie buried under the new constitution, and to pray that it may be defused before exploding. The two parties have however publicly committed themselves to an act of faith that must give reasonable ground for hope' (Foreign and Commonwealth Office file 32/606).

Prescient words. There was reasonable hope—all that could be hoped for—as Fiji took its first steps into its independent future.

## Notes

1  Since this is a largely well-known story, detailed bibliographical reference is not necessary. For a general overview, see Lal 1992.
2  For a discussion of land issues, see Lloyd 1982 and Kamikamica 1997.
3  Pointing out the gulf between official rhetoric and the realities on the ground has been the hallmark of most revisionist historiography on Fiji.
4  See, for instance, the Fiji Education Commission's report (Government of Fiji 1969) for an analysis of reasons for Fijians' poor academic performance.
5  For a succinct summary of this, see Ali 1980.
6  A fuller treatment of Garvey's views is forthcoming in the Fiji volume in the British Documents on the End of Empire series, scheduled for publication in 2006.
7  Full details in Lal 1997b.
8  Reproduced in Lal 1992:189.
9  See House of Commons cmd Paper 1783/1965. Also Davidson 1966. More recent analyses are in Norton 2002, 2004.
10  A copy of the confidential proceedings is in my possession.
11  For Mara's assessment, see Mara 1997.
12  See Foreign and Commonwealth Office file 32/405.
13  I base this on correspondence with Karam Ramrakha, a key player in the NFP at the time of the negotiations.
14  Proceedings in FCO 32/572.
15  'Report of a Royal commission appointed for the purpose of considering and making recommendations as to the most appropriate method of electing members to, and representing the people of Fiji in, the House of Representatives' (Parliamentary Paper 24/1975).

# 2
# Continuity and change 1970–87

On the surface, calm and goodwill characterised race relations and political life in the post-independence years. Development proceeded apace as new jetties, wharves and roads were built; modern amenities such as electricity, piped water and paved roads reached remote villages in the islands. More and more people of all ethnic groups and social backgrounds streamed towards cities and urban centres in search of employment or better education for their children. Elections were held periodically; the sanctity of the ballot box was respected (partly, as it turned out, because one party was regularly returned to power and because the *status quo* was not threatened); and parliament served as the principal, and much respected, forum for political debate. On the surface, things looked fine, but forces were at work that would undermine this ostensible calm.

An important feature of the final constitutional negotiations in London was the agreement between the Alliance and the National Federation Party (NFP) that the method of election would provide only for the first House of Representatives elected after independence, in 1972. The electoral system thus was set up to be an interim solution. In their joint statement of 30 April 1970, both Mara and Koya agreed to appoint a Royal Commission that would work out a permanent electoral system for Fiji's plural society. A Royal Commission was appointed in 1975, with Professor Harry Street, Sir William Hart and Professor Sir Keith Lucas as its members (Parliamentary Paper 1975/24). In its report, the Commission accepted the importance of ethnic factors in Fijian politics and recommended the retention of communal seats with the same weight to counter racial fears and to provide reassurance and a sense of security to ethnic minorities. But it also suggested that racial reservation for the 25 national seats be removed, turning them into common electoral roll in five constituencies 'with no restriction of race or religion for either voters or candidates'. It further suggested that election for these seats should be on the basis of single transfer vote. This careful formula attempted to reconcile the particular ethnic interests of the different communities with the urgent necessity to forge a sense of nationalism that transcended ethnic loyalties.

The Alliance Party rejected the recommendations on the grounds that they were not binding and that in any event the constitution, of which the electoral system was an integral part, was a permanent arrangement. Broadly interpreted, the Alliance stance was correct, but in relation to the provisions for altering the electoral system, it was in conflict with the Joint Statement of 1970. It appeared to be at variance with the position Ratu Sir Kamisese Mara had adopted at the 13th Plenary Session of the London Constitutional Conference, where he had argued that the Commission's findings 'would be taken into consideration and then become part of the constitution otherwise its recommendations could be subject to the whim and fancies of any Parliament' (Parliamentary Paper 1975/24). This had been the understanding of the NFP leadership, which pointed out to the Royal Commission that 'both sides to say the least would accept the recommendations of the Royal Commission on moral grounds if nothing else'. By 1975, Mara had shifted his stance because the 'interim arrangement' had preserved his party's advantage as the 1972 elections clearly showed. The issue was not tested on the floor of the parliament, but the rejection of the recommendations was a foregone conclusion given the Alliance's preponderant majority.

The Alliance's stand contradicted the view of the British representative at the constitutional talks, Lord Shepherd, who held that the 'constitution is a living creature, subject to growth, susceptible to change; it is a sign of life, vigour and maturity to be ready for change when change is required' (Legislative Council of Fiji 1970:19). The Alliance was clearly not ready for change. The NFP leadership had also learnt a bitter lesson. As Ahmed Ali put it, 'their wish was meaningless and the expected flexibility of independence had proved elusive; the rigidity of the colonial era still held sway; the old arguments against total rejection of common roll persisted despite expert advice' (Ali 1980:180). The Alliance's new position marked the end of the 'honeymoon period' between Koya and Mara and the beginning of bitter relations between the two that would culminate in Mara's vow in 1977 not to work with Koya again. Koya's own position within his party was considerably weakened by his inexplicably close relationship with Mara not bearing fruit. His political days were numbered.

The constitution continued to be a controversial issue. Many Fijians still appeared concerned that only a Fijian-dominated Alliance government would protect their heritage and rights. A government headed by high chiefs had been in power since independence, and for many Fijians this was only natural and just and they wanted it to continue. Some scholars argued that the Fijian élite would accept the paraphernalia of electoral politics only to the extent that it served their interest, and that any deviation from the established path would not be tolerated.

Events following the general elections of 1982 gave credence to the view that the Fijian attitude to sharing power with others was hardening. The 1982 general election was a closely contested affair which the Alliance won with a four seat majority and a plurality of 2,000 out of 1,003,000 votes (Lal 1983a). Soon afterwards, irate Fijian landowners in western Viti Levu threatened to evict their Indian tenants for not 'fulfilling their pledges to vote for the Alliance' (Lal 1983b). The paramount chief of Sabeto said of the Indian tenants that as they 'are the ones who opposed us, I will have them no more'. In the Senate, several Fijian Senators came dangerously close to speaking in a manner popularised by the nationalist leader Sakiasi Butadroka, declaring that 'blood will flow' if Indians did not 'cling' to Fijians. Some even argued for the deportation of opposition leaders who were alleged to have insulted Fijian political chiefs.

The vehemence of the remarks was matched by the silence they received in response by the Fijian community. In parliament calls were made to revise the constitution to provide for Fijian parliamentary dominance. The most significant support for this view came from the Great Council of Chiefs. At its 1982 meeting on the chiefly island of

Bau, opened for the first time since cession by a reigning British monarch, the council castigated the opposition for allegedly criticising Fijian chiefs during the election, and took the unprecedented step of passing a resolution calling for the reservation of two-thirds of the House of Representatives as well as the positions of governor general and prime minister for indigenous Fijians. This view found an astounding amount of sympathy, mainly among literate urban Fijians. A survey by the Suva-based Market Research Bureau showed 70 per cent of urban Fijians were in favour of reserving the offices of prime minister and governor general for indigenous Fijians, while 64 per cent supported the reservation of seats in parliament. In contrast, only 55 per cent expressed no objection to the election of an Indian as prime minister.

Ratu Sir Penaia Ganilau, then president of the Great Council of Chiefs, expressed deep sorrow at the apparent loss of chiefly influence and urged Fijians to preserve their unity under chiefly guidance. The Bau resolution was seen by the NFP as being anti-Indian, though in truth, as one Fijian observer, Savenaca Nacanaitaba, commented, it was directed as much against commoner dissenting Fijians as it was at non-Fijians (*Fiji Times*, 29 July 1982). The chiefs, he suggested, were attempting to impose a 'culture of silence' upon their people. Significantly, 40 members present at the meeting, including Prime Minister Mara and some of his cabinet members abstained from voting on the motion, although Mara did speak against it. He subsequently defended himself by calling the resolution a 'waste of time' (Lal 1983b).

His critics argued that if, as the leader of a multiracial society, and as a committed multiracialist, he had spoken against what was primarily a racially discriminatory motion, much of the anxiety that the resolution caused among non-Fijians would have been avoided. But abstention made political sense in the circumstances. It enabled Mara to extricate himself from a difficult situation while allowing room for leverage in the future. In 1974, assured of wide support across the political spectrum, Mara took decisive action against Butadroka's motion to deport Indo-Fijians and put Fijians in political control. But the political climate had changed since then. In 1982, an Alliance victory was possible only because of the solid support of the Fijian community. Now to repudiate the wishes of the community's leaders for political supremacy would have

27

meant jeopardising his party's base. Thus, by abstaining, Mara did not overtly alienate his own constituency, while reminding the Indo-Fijian community of his moderate stand amidst extremism. Underlying the ire of the Fijian landlords against politically unreliable Indo-Fijian tenants, and the call for the revision of the constitution by the Great Council of Chiefs, lay a resurgent Fijian ethnonationalism. It was asserting its voice and seeking practical realisation of the concept of Fijian paramountcy. In effect, it represented a concerted challenge to the notion of political coexistence. Five years later, things would come to a head.

## Land

A more emotive issue than the distribution of political power was land and its use by different communities. Enveloped in prejudice and misunderstanding, the question of land always aroused great communal passion in Fiji. Land ownership was not at issue—that question was permanently solved by the constitution (and common sense)—access to it and security of tenure were. The bulk of the Indo-Fijian population lived in the sugar cane belt of Fiji, constituted over 80 per cent of the sugar cane farmers in the 1980s, and produced 90 per cent of the country's sugar, most of it on leased native land of limited tenure. The Indo-Fijian tenant community wanted more secure tenure, extending beyond 30 years. Fijian landowners, apprehensive of losing control over a vital resource and some themselves wanting to enter commercial agriculture, resisted. The ensuing stalemate generated bitterness, further fuelling ethnic tensions.

The land problem had become more acute, and certainly more politicised, in the last two decades since independence. However, its roots lay in the 1920s when, after the end of indenture, an expanding and rapidly diversifying Indo-Fijian community began to make increasing demands regarding the land. By the 1930s land had already emerged as a contentious issue in Fijian–Indian relations. The Indo-Fijian tenants were complaining of the difficulty of obtaining land and of the vexation and expense involved in negotiating terms with individual Fijian landowners. Ken Gillion (1977) describes the reasons for the Fijian apprehension.

> In the 1930s, they [indigenous Fijians] were becoming more aware of their economic weakness. Their numbers were on the rise just as were the Indians', the land was

28

needed for their children, and they wanted to grow more cash crops. In some cases when they could not afford to pay compensation for improvements, they were refusing to renew leases when they came up for renewal. Sometimes the land was then used for their own cultivation, but often it reverted to bush (Gillion 1977:90).

In 1936, in response to a CSR-inspired crackdown on recalcitrant landlords, the Council of Chiefs, encouraged by Ratu Sukuna, agreed to have the government assume control of 'all native land not required for immediate use and to administer such land in best interests of the Fijians' (Gillion 1977:191). This resolution led, four years later, to the passage of the Native Land Ordinance. Under it, an independent body, the Native Land Trust Board, was set up to manage and administer all native lands; its establishment brought a semblance of stability to land transactions between Fijian landowners and Indo-Fijian tenants. The length of leases was standardised to 10 years with the expectation, but not guarantee, of renewal.

The Native Land Ordinance also provided for a native reserve policy to demarcate gradually and set aside in perpetuity certain native lands 'for the use and maintenance of proprietary units'. How many native leases were put into reserve is not known, but the policy was a major source of friction between the tenants and the landlords. Driven off the reserved land and forced to fend for himself and his family without the communal or kinship support available to the Fijians, the Indo-Fijian tenant complained of harassment and hardship. His former farm went largely uncultivated and frequently reverted to bush; even when farmed, it operated far below its full economic potential. The Fijian landowner viewed the reserve policy differently, as a protection against the unquenchable thirst for ever more land by Indo-Fijian tenants. He saw reserved land and shorter leases to Indo-Fijians as incentives for him to enter the world of commercial cultivation and compete effectively with his Indo-Fijian counterparts.

The Native Land Ordinance of 1940 established the pattern of land tenure for the next two decades. In 1966, the Agricultural Landlord and Tenant Ordinance once again attempted to settle the problems of lease renewals, following continual complaints of unfair treatment from both the landowners and tenants (Legislative Council of Fiji 1966). The primary purpose of the legislation was to give tenants greater security than before.

It provided that a first or second ten-year extension would be granted to the tenants if the landlords could not plead enough hardship to justify terminating the lease. The new legislation left both parties dissatisfied. The Indo-Fijian tenant continued to complain about the insecurity of tenure while the Fijian landowner felt that the Agricultural Tribunal, which adjudicated the disputes, usually favoured the tenant because he was not able to plead hardship to the extent that the tenant could. Consequently, a working committee to review the ordinance was set up. It presented its report to parliament in 1975. The essence of its recommendation to amend Agricultural Landlord and Tenant Ordinance (ALTO) was the establishment of 30 years as the minimum period of tenure, with provision for renewal. The new bill provoked two distinct responses from the Indo-Fijian tenant community. One section accepted it as the best terms they could obtain in the circumstances; the other saw it simply as an extension of the existing uncertainties. The NFP, representing the Indo-Fijian tenant community, split on the issue. Opposition leader Koya, also President of the Federation of Cane Growers, opposed the bill, while K.C. Ramrakha and Irene Jai Narayan along with eight others crossed the floor to support it. The NFP rift, long in existence, was now in the open and would adversely affect the party's fortunes in the 1977 elections.

Land was again at the centre of a major controversy in Fiji in 1979, driving a wedge between the prime minister and the opposition leader, and effectively killed talks on a government of national unity, which was being tentatively mooted. At the NFP convention in Ba in 1980, the Leader of the Opposition Jai Ram Reddy criticised the Alliance government's policy, approved as early as 1975, of reserving large areas of Crown land, including Provisional Crown Schedule A land. Reddy asserted that reservation would affect 62,240 acres of Crown land, at least 192 existing leases and some five government projects. He questioned the need to reserve Crown land.

> Given Fijian strength in this area and the Indian vulnerability is it necessary to take over what little Crown land there is and convert it into Native land? You may have the power to do it, but the power to do what is right and good is also the power to do what is wrong. I would have thought that a reasonable government would preserve as much Crown land as possible consistent with the principles of fairness to all in order to settle future evictees from Native lands now waiting to be resettled (Reddy 1980).

For Reddy, the reservation of Crown land was a further attempt to weaken the Indian tenant community and compound its already considerable vulnerability.

Ratu Mara's response to Reddy's criticism typified Fijian attitudes on the subject of land. First, he described Fijian magnanimity in granting leases and lamented the lack of Indo-Fijian appreciation.

> Much of the capital for their [Indians'] successful ventures for the education of Indian professionals, came from cane money from leases on Indian land. Without resorting to the Bhumiputra type of xenophobic legislation used in Southeast Asia, the Alliance government supports the policy of free economy, even though it may follow Darwin's tenets of the survival of the fittest.

Indo-Fijians already controlled business and industry, and the Fijian people had not asked for a share in these, despite Indo-Fijians' demand for secure land leases, said Mara

> [i]f [Reddy's] contention is to be accepted, then all Indian tenancies, which cover much of the good land in Fiji, must be held by them in perpetuity. All the most valuable properties in urban areas must be their preserve and of course commerce, industry, transport and other professions must be completely controlled by them.

Instead of constructive dialogue on a vital national problem, racial stereotyping, distrust and misunderstanding once again won the day, as they have so often in Fiji's colonial and independent history. The vital question of why Crown land was being reserved, and whether the full implications of that action had been adequately discussed with representatives of the Indian Alliance, let alone the NFP, was left unaddressed.

The Fijian attitude on land had become much more politicised in the 1970s and the 1980s. As Brian Farrell and Peter Murphy (1978) correctly emphasised, the simple fact of possession gave Fijians 'power' that others did not enjoy; 'it is an effective cultural buffer to inroads made by Indians and Europeans' (1978:2). Threats of violence and upheaval were never too far from the discourse on land—'blood will flow in this country if Indians do not understand the deep emotional feelings Fijians have for their land', Ratu Mara said (*Fiji Times*, 3 March 1978). These sentiments were repeated by others in the following years. The leases under the Agricultural Landlord and Tenant Act (ALTA) began expiring in the late

1990s and many have not been renewed, to the detriment of the economy. The government wants native lands leased under a new act, the Native Agricultural Landlord and Tenant Act, which gives landowners greater leverage than under the ALTA, which is what the tenants want. But given the sensitivities and the political stakes involved, the land problem will not be resolved anytime soon.

## Education

It was often said that what land was to the Fijians, education was to the Indo-Fijians, although, of course, both the communities needed both land and education. The Indo-Fijians' success in the educational field, the Fijians' lack of it especially at the higher levels, and the government's sometimes desperate strategies to cope with the gap, constituted the core of the problem. Ironically enough, the Indians' success was caused in large measure by the nagging insecurity of land tenure. Education was seen early on as an important instrument for social advancement, upward mobility and economic security. The Indo-Fijians' push for education began early. As Gillion observes, the Indo-Fijians started with nothing 'except the keenness of the Indian parents and their willingness to sacrifice for their children' (1977:119). Private committee schools, often with little or no assistance from the colonial government, produced a steady stream of educated school leavers who filled the civil service and the teaching profession. When the University of the South Pacific opened in 1968, the majority of the students were Indo-Fijians, as they are today.

The Fijian experience was less successful, despite the early effort of the colonial government and the Christian missions. The reasons for this are complex. The 1969 Education Commission, appointed to draw up an agenda on the future direction of education in Fiji, noted among other reasons that the geography of Fiji, the isolation of rural Fijian teachers from any intellectual stimulus, the shortage of qualified Fijian primary school teachers, rural poverty and social distractions contributed to the problem of Fijian education (Government of Fiji 1969). To grapple with the widening gap, the commission recommended that 50 per cent of Fiji government university scholarship funds be reserved for Fijians on a 'parallel block' basis; that is, in the event of the quota being unfulfilled, the unallocated balance should be devoted to other specifically Fijian educational needs, such as repeats for university students. These provisions were to extend for a period of nine years, with a preliminary review at the end of six. Increasing competition for a restricted number of places at the University of the South Pacific's Foundation program brought the issue to a head in the 1977 elections.

Using the parallel block principle, the government awarded university scholarships to Fijian students with the university entrance pass mark of 216, while Indo-Fijian students needed a mark of 261 to qualify. Education became a highly emotive issue when cold statistics and abstract principles impinged on individual lives of Indo-Fijian students and parents. The NFP, which had tacitly accepted the principle of preferential treatment outlined in Development Plan VII, took up the issue, eager for political mileage. Koya denounced the policy in ringing terms. 'It is bound to produce recriminations, frustrations, bitterness, the destruction of the image and reputation of the university and indeed the government of the day in the eyes of the world' (*Fiji Times*, 18 March 1977). The Alliance reminded him and his party of Fijian concessions on land. Mara defended his government's policies as being necessary for lagging Fijians to 'catch up' with others. Koya linked Fijian demand for parity in education to the Indo-Fijian call for greater representation in the military, whose almost exclusively Fijian composition was a source of anxiety among Indo-Fijians. Failure to accept parity in both these areas was an 'example of a political party indulging in hypocrisy', said Koya (*Fiji Times*, 18 March 1977).

In the immediate aftermath of the 1982 general elections education was once again at the forefront. Frustrated by the continuing poor performance of Fijian students at senior high school and university level, the Fijian Teachers Association, an umbrella organisation of ethnic Fijian teachers, asked for the reservation of 70 per cent of government scholarships for university studies for Fijians. The new Minister of Education, Ahmed Ali, rejected the idea, but did make strenuous efforts to upgrade facilities in Fijian schools and to staff them with better trained teachers. In addition, he closed down the Nasinu Teachers College and turned it into a dormitory for University of the South Pacific's Foundation (mostly Fijian) students to provide them with more tutorial help and an environment more conducive to studying. In the 1990s, the government moved further ahead with legislating support for Fijian education through special schemes. The Qarase government explicitly endorsed a race-based program for Fijian education through its 'blueprint'. It waived fees for form seven Fijian students, and provided state assistance to Fijian-run schools, but not to Indo-Fijian schools even though, in many cases, these schools had high numbers of Fijian students.

The policy of discrimination—or affirmative action—that governed the Alliance government's educational efforts was alleged by its critics to exist in other spheres of national life as well, especially the civil service. Theoretically, all civil service appointments were made by the Public Service Commission. Promotions and opportunities for advanced training were in principle based on merit and qualification. In practice, it was alleged that the situation was far different. Jai Ram Reddy, in his address to the NFP convention in Ba in 1980, aired the feelings of many in his party and community when he asserted that 'Fiji is implementing a policy designed to ensure that all strategic levels of government are staffed by loyal personnel which in effect means that Fijians are placed in positions of command in order to deliberately create an "out group", namely the Indians'. The bitterness and distrust that this produced 'conflict alone may resolve', he said, using Mara's words (Reddy 1980).

In 1980, the deputy leader of the opposition, Irene Jai Narayan, put forward a motion in parliament expressing concern at the racial imbalance in the civil service. She urged that in addition to racial balance, there be parity at all levels in the civil service. Ratu Sir Penaia Ganilau, then acting prime minister, replied that the principle of parity applied only at the point of entry, and that promotions and other opportunities for advancement depended entirely on merit. He called Mrs Narayan's charges 'cheap political propaganda of the worst kind' (*Pacific Islands Monthly* 1980, cited in Nation 1982). To be fair to the government, there had been few cases of systematic discrimination on the basis of race and political affiliation, especially when compared to what happened in the post-coup years when nepotism and political patronage ran rampant. But, as John Nation pointed out in 1981 at a seminar held at the Australian National University, by the 1980s the feeling within the Indian community is that power over the civil service is in Fijian hands.

The direction of the Alliance government's development program and its utilisation of foreign aid were controversial both among Fijians as well as Indo-Fijians. Western United Front and the Fijian Nationalist Party argued, as we shall see shortly, that western as well as underprivileged Fijians had been neglected, and the Indo-Fijians alleged racial discrimination against their community. They pointed to the major development projects of the previous decade, and the crowning achievements of the Alliance government, the pine industry, cattle schemes, cane expansion at Seaqaqa, and fisheries development, all of which had been directed towards the development of the Fijian community. The major exception was the negotiations of the Lomé Convention, where a bipartisan approach to the vital sugar industry resulted in better prices for the largely Indo-Fijian sugar farming community. The Alliance government was clearly caught in a no-win situation. Many Fijians continued to complain about backwardness and neglect, seeking preferential treatment in selected areas of national life. The Indo-Fijians accused the government of being blatantly pro-Fijian. It was out of dissatisfaction with prevailing currents of politics that the Fiji Labour Party emerged in 1985.

## Political parties

In the 1980s, the Alliance and the National Federation Party were the dominant political parties, but they shared the national stage with two splinter Fijian parties, the Fijian Nationalist Party (FNP) and the Western United Front (WUF). The Alliance had won consistently at the polls since 1966, except for its first and only temporary defeat at the April 1977 elections. The experience of government, uninterrupted leadership, and the crucial support of the Indo-Fijian and European business sector gave it an edge over its rivals. Ratu Sir Kamisese Mara had been at the helm of party's leadership since its inception, and though there was overt criticism of his autocratic style, his tantrums and his banyan tree like effect on all around him, his position was not seriously challenged. Indeed, at critical times, such as in the 1982 elections, it was his stature that ensured the Alliance's success. In the 1980s, although he still walked tall, the aura of invincibility that surrounded him in the immediate aftermath of independence had weakened. The corrosive effects of ethnic politics and persistent criticism of his policies and style, from both Fijians and Indo-Fijians, had tarnished his earlier lustre.

The basic, communally-federated structure of the party remained intact. The Alliance was marginally more multiracial than its rivals, though since independence its claim on Indian votes had declined significantly. The Fijian Association was the backbone of the party, and Fijian solidarity behind it had been the most important factor in its electoral victories. The loyal support of the general electors, despite their sometimes bitter disagreements over candidate selection at election time, helped to consolidate the party's dominance at the polls.

The weakest spoke in the Alliance wheel was the Indian Alliance. Its credibility was seriously damaged by its consistent failure to attract significant numbers of Indo-Fijian voters to its ranks and by the departure from the party of its founding members. Sir Vijay Singh, a former Alliance attorney general, left the party in 1979, after being dismissed from the cabinet following weeks of controversy and speculation about the extent of his involvement in the now-infamous 'flour mills of Fiji' court case. He joined the NFP in 1982. M.T. Khan, another former Alliance cabinet minister, was not reinstated in the cabinet after he was unsuccessfully tried for corruption. He too joined the NFP and was a candidate until his death just before the election in 1982. The climax of Indian desertions from the Alliance came with the resignation in 1982 of James Shankar Singh, president of the Indian Alliance, on the grounds of 'irreconcilable differences' with Mara (*Fiji Times*, 11 January 1982). Failure to win the party ticket, personality clashes and a feeling of relative insignificance in the internal affairs of the party were all reasons for the desertions. Most of them also argued that the Alliance had abandoned its genuinely multiracial philosophy of the early 1970s and had taken a distinctly pro-Fijian stance.

The departure of the Indian Alliance old guard on the eve of the 1982 general elections was to some extent compensated for by two new sources of support in the Indo-Fijian community. The Indo-Fijian business community, primarily Gujaratis, allied itself more closely with the Alliance and the Fijian elite through joint commercial ventures. The Alliance promised 'business as usual'—the Indo-Fijian businessmen could not ask for better. The other major source of support came from the Muslims. The leadership of the Fiji Muslim League, the national umbrella organisation of the religious minority, had long been a supporter of the Alliance. In 1982, many of its ordinary members switched parties, alienated from the NFP as a result of the bitter 1977 elections. Perhaps more significant than the disenchantment with the NFP was the burgeoning sense of a distinct Muslim identity within the Indian community. The demand for Muslim separatism has a long history, but in the 1980s, it reached new heights. In a survey carried out in late 1979, two-thirds of the Muslim population indicated a desire for separate political representation in parliament. On the question of linguistic preference, 62 per cent gave Urdu as their first choice, 27 per cent Arabic, 8 per cent Fijian and a paltry 3 per cent desired Hindustani, the Indian lingua franca (Ali 1980:150). They therefore distanced themselves from the NFP, perceived as a Hindu party, and created stronger ties with the Alliance, encouraged by its cordial and accommodating attitude. But these changes did not seriously alter the basic party structure; the communally-federated structure remained. The dominance of high chiefs at the top gave the Alliance an aura of legitimacy as well as stability, enabling the use of traditional avenues to reconcile and resolve internal differences.

In contrast, the NFP was plagued by a continuous history of internecine struggle for leadership that seriously damaged its credibility as an alternative government. One difficultly for the party was its own ethnic constituency, the Indo-Fijian community, which was deeply divided along religious, cultural and regional lines. The roots of the division and factionalism go back to the immediate post-indenture period of the 1920s. An equally important factor was the party's problematic leaders, who invariably came from the legal community. Personality clashes rather than informed policy differences were the main cause of the interminable infighting.

Siddiq Koya, a leading criminal lawyer from the big, boisterous sugar province of Ba, took over the leadership of the party after A.D. Patel's death in 1969, and remained as the leader until 1977 when Jai Ram Reddy succeeded him. But Koya returned to party leadership again in 1984, after Reddy resigned from parliament over a dispute with the

Speaker of the House. The mantle of leadership never rested comfortably on Koya's shoulders. Party Secretary Karam Ramrakha, for example, resigned in 1972 over Koya's alleged unconsultative style. Koya's own, surprisingly cordial, relations with Mara immediately after independence, which soured after 1975, provided ample ammunition to his opponents within the party. Simmering tensions among the different factions came to a head during the 1976 ALTO debate in parliament.

Two senior party members, Ramrakha and Irene Jai Narayan, and eight others defied Koya and voted with the Alliance to get the bill passed. The differences were expeditiously patched up for the April 1977 elections, which the NFP won with the carefully crafted, though publicly disavowed, support of the Fijian Nationalist Party officially committed to the deportation of the Indo-Fijian community. Stunned by its narrow victory (26 seats out of 52), and unable to reconcile its internal differences about leadership, the NFP fumbled for a solution for four days, at the end of which the governor general, Ratu George Cakobau, 'exercising his deliberate judgement', appointed Ratu Mara prime minister. Certain members of the NFP were accused of betraying their leader by telling the governor general that they would not support Koya for prime minister. Karam Ramrakha, who was suspected by some of talking to Cakobau—an allegation he denied on oath, wrote, 'The brute and undeniable fact is that when Mr Koya went to the governor general to become prime minister, the governor general, and the governor general alone, refused to make him prime minister' (*Fiji Sun*, 24 January 1987). Ramrakha's contention is valid—it was Cakobau who breached the Westminster convention which requires the parliament to resolve the question and not have the governor general decide in advance what the outcome of the parliament's vote of confidence should be.

The April 1977 elections and the events which followed split the NFP into two bitterly opposed groups, which later crystallised into the 'Dove' faction led by Koya, and the 'Flower' faction led by Ramrakha and Narayan. At the September elections, with few policy differences to go on, the two factions turned upon each other with unprecedented bitterness in a campaign remembered in the Indo-Fijian community for the cynical manipulation of cultural and religious symbols and affinities of the voter. Fielding parallel candidates in several constituencies, the NFP handed the election to the Alliance on a platter. The Alliance won

the election with an unprecedented 36 seats. The Flower faction won 13
seats (58.2 per cent of Indian communal votes) and the Dove 3 (41.8
per cent). Koya lost his Lautoka seat and his position as the leader of
the opposition to Jai Ram Reddy.

Reddy was the leader of the opposition from 1977 to 1984. In many
respects, his experience in office paralleled Koya's. There was a short
period of fruitful cooperation with Mara and his government (1977–
79), followed by a period of bitter relations (1980–84) that resulted in
an almost total breakdown of communication between the two. The
latter's rise in national and NFP politics was meteoric. A New Zealand
trained lawyer, he was appointed to the Senate by Koya in 1974. He first
stood for election in April 1977 and became NFP leader just five months
later. His first major achievement was to bring about reconciliation
between the two warring factions of the party. Although tensions between
him and Koya remained, Reddy was able to bring about a semblance of
party unity that had seemed virtually impossible in 1977. But unity was
achieved on Reddy's terms; many former Doves were, or complained of
being, excluded from party affairs and in the selection of candidates for
the 1982 election in which his own supporters gained the majority. The
unsuccessful Doves crossed over to the Alliance and became a painful
thorn in the NFP's side by keeping alive lingering doubts about the
genuineness of party unity.

Under Reddy's leadership, the platform of the party was broadened
to increase its appeal to non-Indian voters as well as to enable former
Indian Alliance members to join the party without losing face. The old
ideological foundations of the party, its commitment to common roll,
for instance, were relegated into the background or silently discarded as
more emphasis was placed on sectarian social and economic issues. Reddy
explained his political philosophy in an interview with the *Fiji Times* in
these terms 'I am not a great believer in any "isms". Our political creeds
have to be relevant to our needs. We have a community already divided
on racial lines. We do not want to add to this by introducing yet another
division, a class warfare. I do favour a pragmatic, middle of the road
approach to our problems' (*Fiji Times*, 14 August 1981).

Consistent with this approach, Reddy advanced a new economic
platform that seemed to be at variance with the NFP's earlier

proclamations. Under Koya, the NFP had embraced a populist posture though with what seriousness it is difficult to tell. Thus in 1972, Koya spoke of nationalising vital industries, creating a welfare state, providing compulsory and free education, among other things. Although by 1977, some of the earlier rhetorical excesses had been discarded, Koya still advocated nationalisation when necessary, and promised to 'legislate against monopolies and cartels and other organisations which indulge in unfair practices'.

Reddy took a different path. In its manifesto for the 1982 general elections, the NFP proclaimed 'the NFP1-WUF Coalition subscribes to the economic philosophy of competitive free enterprise' because the 'allocation of resources based on private initiative and effort produce the best economic results'. Under its administration, the NFP promised, 'the role of government will be restricted to public administration, provision of social services, maintenance of law and order and the construction of the necessary infrastructure to assist the private sector investment'. And foreign investors would be 'assured of their right to the repatriation of their capital and profits'. The manifesto laid to rest whatever fears the Fiji business community had about the NFP being a 'left of the centre' party. In an effort to win a larger constituency, Reddy cut the NFP's ties with its past.

A final hurdle for Reddy was the dismal support for the NFP among the Fijians. The party had made various attempts in the past to get more Fijians into its fold, but with little success. The first experiment had been the merger of the Fijian National Democratic Party with the then Federation Party, leading to the creation of the National Federation Party. In 1970, the NFP embarked on the ill-fated 'operation *taukei*' though, as we have already seen, it was only able to attract a mere 2.4 per cent of Fijian communal votes in the 1972 election, a figure which subsequently— and unbelievably—declined even further. Aware of the need to attract more Fijians to increase the NFP's appeal as an alternative government, Reddy had told his party as early as 1974 that, without a multiracial base, the NFP was doomed to remain a 'permanent opposition'. His softening of the NFP's earlier confrontationist posture was, in part, a device to that end. Not surprisingly, therefore, he formed an electoral coalition with a splinter Fijian party, the Western United Front, in 1982. But for reasons mentioned above even the coalition failed to realise the goal of broadening the party's ethnic base. The net, perhaps unintended, result of Reddy's pragmatic endeavours was to cut the NFP loose from its traditional ideological moorings and to fashion it in the image of the Alliance.

Party politics dominated by the Alliance and the NFP, and dedicated publicly to the promotion of multiracialism and political coexistence, was challenged in the April 1977 general elections by the Fijian Nationalist Party (see Premdas 1980). Embracing emerging Fijian nationalism, the party rejected both multiracialism and equal political coexistence and instead espoused the cause of 'Fiji for Fijians'. Such a platform was not proposed for the first time in 1977. In 1972, Villiame Savu's Fijian Independent Party had espoused similar causes, wanting the Fijians 'alone to decide the destiny of their land'. The founder of the Fijian Nationalist Party, former Alliance Assistant Minister Sakiasi Butadroka, first came to national prominence in October 1975, when he moved a motion in parliament demanding the repatriation of Indo-Fijians to India, a sentiment that seemingly reflected the feelings of large sections of the Fijian community. At the same time, he also cut loose at the eastern chiefly establishment, especially Ratu Mara, accusing him of promoting the 'dictatorship' of Lau at the expense of other provinces, an allegation vehemently denied by Mara. Butadroka launched the platform of his party in December 1976, demanding Fijian paramountcy.

The interests of the Fijians must be paramount at all times.

The Fijians must always hold the positions of governor general, prime minister, as well as the ministries of Fijian affairs and rural development, lands, education, agriculture, home affairs, commerce and industry and cooperatives.

More opportunities should be given to Fijians to enter business and commerce.

The Fijian administration should be strengthened with government financial backing and support.

A Fijian Institute should be established to teach Fijians business. Indians should be repatriated to India after Fiji gained full independence.

More government development projects should be concentrated in rural areas.

All lands illegally sold should be returned to Fijians (*Fiji Times*, 20 December 1976).

41

Butadroka's message, delivered in emotional, accusatory tones, attracted mostly rural, illiterate and underprivileged urban Fijian voters. The Alliance's apathy helped the Nationalists to make deep inroads into the traditional Alliance constituency. In the April 1977 elections, Butadroka won the fiercely contested Serua-Namosi seat, obtaining 4,640 (52.1 per cent) of the total Fijian communal votes. Altogether, the FNP took away 20,819 (24.4 per cent) of the Fijian communal votes from the Alliance, causing it to lose six marginal national constituencies to the National Federation Party. Low Fijian voter turnout compounded the Alliance's fate at the polls. Butadroka had made his point: the victory of the NFP showed that the constitution did not protect the paramountcy of Fijian rights, an ideal cherished by many Fijians of all political persuasions. Enraged by the NFP's success and delighted with his own 'victory', Butadroka resorted to making inflammatory racial statements which contravened the Public Order Act and landed him in gaol. His absence from the campaign for the September elections, and the Alliance's concerted attempts to win back Fijian voters chastened by its unexpected loss, led to the Nationalists' defeat and to an overwhelming victory for the Alliance. Butadroka lost his seat, and the overall electoral support for his party declined from 24 per cent to 11 per cent.

Out of parliament from 1977 to 1982, the Nationalists maintained a low profile. The party also shifted its extremist stance somewhat. While keeping its Fiji-for-Fijians stance, the party adopted a less racially slanted position on the eve of the 1982 elections. Instead, the Nationalists now paid more attention to the preservation and enhancement of Fijian interest. The Nationalists now advocated that the constitution of Fiji should be amended to allow Fijians to occupy 90 per cent of the House of Representatives seats; that all Freehold and Crown Schedules A & B lands as well as traditional fishing rights be returned to Fijians; and that Fijian schoolchildren should be provided with free and compulsory education.

These policies, which should have been music to the ears of frustrated, extremist Fijians, elicited little electoral support in the 1982 elections. The FNP obtained only 7.7 per cent of total Fijian communal votes, although Butadroka himself made a strong showing, winning 30 per cent of the votes in Serua-Namosi. The rout of the Nationalists was not surprising. Its own rudimentary organisation was no competition for its more sophisticated and better-funded rivals. Many of its platforms were regarded correctly as being unrealistic and constitutionally unimplementable. The events surrounding the April 1977 elections, when the FNP helped to bring about NFP victory, cast a long and terrifying cloud over the thinking of those Fijians unprepared for a NFP government. The Alliance's own assiduous attempts to court the Fijian voter of the extremist persuasion cut the ground from under Butadroka's feet. The fact that soon after the elections the Alliance endorsed a former Nationalist candidate for the Suva municipal elections effectively demonstrated the extent to which the party was prepared to suppress its multiracialism to win back its constituency. The 1982 elections showed that the Nationalist platform was widely shared in the Fijian community. Just how widely would become clear five years later.

The Nationalists were joined by another splinter Fijian party, the Western United Front. The WUF, too, was founded on a grievance. Its main aim was to promote the particular interests of western Fijians who were alleged to have been neglected by the Alliance government. Western Fijians had long complained of regional discrimination and step-brotherly treatment. In the 1960s and early 1970s, several attempts were made to re-assert a distinct western identity, but the separatists were contained through traditional reconciliation ceremonies. The WUF was the latest and probably the most ambitious attempt to articulate western grievances in some coherent political fashion. The guiding force behind the formation of the WUF was Ratu Osea Gavidi, who had won his Nadroga-Navosa Fijian communal seat twice in 1977. Although a high chief with Western education, his popularity rested more on his defiant stand on the issue of contracts for pine harvesting. In fact, it was the pine issue which galvanised the western Fijians and led to the formation of the Western United Front.

Pine planting began in Fiji in the late 1950s and early 1960s, and by 1979, 28,000 hectares were under pine, mostly in western Viti Levu (see Gregor 1980). To govern the entire pine operation, the government created the Fiji Pine Commission (FPC) in 1976 to 'facilitate and develop an industry based on the growing, harvesting, processing and marketing of pine and other species of trees grown in Fiji' (Fiji Pine Commission Act no 5 of 1976). The pine industry was not the exclusive domain of

43

the Fiji Pine Commission, however. The other major partner was the land-owning *mataqali*, assisted by the Fiji Forestry Department. The Commission invited proposals from interested companies to harvest mature pine. Four proposals were received: from the M.K. Hunt Foundation, Shell/New Zealand Forest Products, British Petroleum (BP) Southwest Pacific Limited, and the United Marketing Company owned by a convicted US businessman, Paul Sandblom (see Martin 1981). The Commission accepted BP's initial proposals, because they appeared more flexible and promised a rational management of the industry. The landowners, led by Gavidi, leaned to the UMC proposal because it apparently recognised legitimate landowner rights, offered them a greater share of the profits, and allowed participation at all levels of the industry. The Fiji Pine Commission remained unconvinced, and the government declared Sandblom a prohibited immigrant.

The simmering conflict between Ratu Osea Gavidi and the Fiji Pine Commission, and through it the government, erupted in the open as landowners boycotted several of the Commission's pine planting programs. To the western landowners, the Alliance government's action was seen as another unacceptable interference in their right to utilise their resources as they saw fit. The Western landowners preferred, as the NFP-WUP Manifesto spelled out, 'the establishment of a decentralised, socially compatible, technologically appropriate and economically viable processing system for both native and exotic forests and [assisting] direct participation by forested lands in the exploitation of such forest resources'. The government, on the other hand, preferred more centralised control of a resource that has the potential to become a major revenue earner for Fiji.

The pine dispute unearthed subterranean private resentment among western Fijians at the perceived iniquitous treatment at the hands of the eastern chiefly establishment. It served to highlight other grievances such as the paucity of western Fijians in the civil service and other statutory bodies, disparities particularly glaring in view of the overall western contribution to the national economy. The issues were brought into sharper relief during a House debate on the allocation of $435,868 for the renovation of certain historic sites on the chiefly island of Bau. Tui Nadi, Ratu Napolioni Dawai, attacked the proposal as unjustified, and pointed to the more pressing needs of western Fijians: water supply, roads, dormitories for school children from outlying islands. Dawai resigned from the Alliance and joined the WUF.

The new party was launched in traditional Fijian style on 17 July 1981 in the presence of 20 ranking western chiefs. Ratu Osea, elected president, outlined the party's goals

- to protect and encourage the unity of western Fijians
- to protect the interests of landowners and defend their rights to develop their resources according to their aspirations
- to seek changes in the Ministry of Fijian Affairs and Rural Development to improve the lives of western Fijians
- to improve educational facilities of western Fijians and provide them opportunities in commercial and industrial enterprises.

Clearly, the WUF had a specific regional focus and a distinct regional constituency. To become effective nationally, it needed to be more broadly based. Cooperation with the Alliance was obviously out; Mara had castigated the party a day after its launch as a 'disruptive' force which preached 'ridiculous political ideologies' (*Fiji Times*, 18 July 1981). An attempt was made to form a progressive front with the FNP but this was abandoned after an irate Butadroka reportedly assaulted Solomone Momoivalu, an Alliance Minister of State, for accusing him of practising voodoism to attract Fijian voters. Gavidi then turned to the NFP in early 1981 because it was 'the most prominent political party opposed to the Alliance'. A NFP–WUF Coalition materialised on 11 January 1982. The exact terms of the arrangement were never publicly stated, but Reddy explained its significant aspects in the short-lived *Coalition Bulletin*.

> In this arrangement, each party is to maintain its independent identity and objectives. In other words, there is no submergence of one party into another. It must be remembered that the two parties are totally independent, with interests that each would like to protect. I don't envisage that where parties are independent and are being led by strong leadership with principles that they themselves espouse there is any real danger of anyone becoming subservient. It is a partnership of equals (*Coalition Bulletin* 1982).

The independent interests included such vital and sensitive issues as land and common roll, both of which were shelved. The coalition of an exclusively Fijian splinter party with a predominantly Indo-Fijian party was widely seen as a milestone in Fijian politics. To its supporters, it heralded a new era in multiracial politics; to its opponents, it represented an expedient political coalition with the sole purpose of dislodging the Alliance from from its political perch. There is little doubt that the NFP-WUF coalition was a politically convenient arrangement. WUF and Gavidi needed the extensive political machinery of the NFP to launch themselves on the national scene. The fact that Gavidi had broached cooperation with the FNP before he had approached the NFP was a clear enough indication that he did not necessarily share the NFP's views. Reddy and the NFP appeared to gain from the coalition an apparently swelling pool of dependable Fijian support that had eluded the party since its inception. Yet the coalition also entailed risks for both leaders. For Reddy, coalescing with a regionalist party detracted from his carefully-nurtured though potentially volatile national image as incipient prime minister. For Gavidi, cooperation with the NFP was equally risky, given the extent of ethnic polarisation endemic in Fiji's electoral system, especially during elections. But the risks appeared worth taking in view of the more than even chance of victory at the polls.

The results of the 1982 elections demonstrated the electoral failure both of the WUF as well as the coalition. Gavidi narrowly lost his seat (47.9 per cent of the votes) to the Alliance (50.5 per cent). The other WUF candidate to make a decent showing was Ratu Napolioni Dawai who got 22.8 per cent of the communal votes in the Ba-Nadi constituency. Overall, the WUF received a mere 7 per cent of the total Fijian communal votes. Three factors were responsible for the WUF's poor performance. One was Gavidi's poor campaign strategy that frequently took him away from his constituency, giving the impression that he took his own supporters for granted. Second, coalition with a predominantly Indian-based party produced harmful results in an atmosphere of tense ethnic polarisation. The third factor was the Alliance's concerted attempts to win back the vital Nadroga-Navosa Fijian communal seat. The coalition ended for all practical purposes with the campaign—unsurprisingly, given that it had failed to articulate an alternative vision of Fiji's future that went beyond seeking narrow political advantages over its rival.

The 1982 election was a typical affair, consistent with past trends. In one respect, however, it differed from the past—the allegation of foreign involvement in Fiji's electoral process. This was the major issue in the last half of the campaign. It set into motion a train of events which led to ethnic tensions not seen in Fiji since the by-elections of 1968. The first disclosures of foreign involvement in the Fiji elections were made by the Australian Broadcasting Commission's *Four Corners* program which highlighted the role of Australian multinationals in Fiji and probed allegations of misuse of Australian aid for political purposes by the ruling Alliance party. In particular, it dwelt on the contents of a privately-commissioned report (by Motibhai and Company) titled 'Report of Consultants to the Prime Minister of Fiji on the Economic and Political Outlook and Options and Strategy and Political Organization', prepared by Australian consultant Alan Carroll and his associates. The Carroll Report recommended strategies for winning the election that included, among others, utilising the existing cultural and religious divisions in the Indian community, buying off the FNP leader Butadroka, and accelerating pending prosecutions against WUF leader Gavidi to take him out of the running. The coalition accused the Alliance of implementing the recommendations as well as using Australian aid money to promote its political fortunes. The Alliance denied the allegations. An angry Mara dubbed the television program as 'an act of sabotage against a sovereign nation' and vowed not to forgive or forget its producers nor those officials of the coalition who were alleged to have colluded with the Australians. But the Alliance's masterstroke was to seize upon and twist the opening lines of the Four Corners programme that Fiji's present political leaders were descendants of chiefs 'who clubbed and ate their way to power' and to publicise this 'cannibal quote' and the entire television programme 'as a gross insult to Fijian chiefs and tradition', while expediently shelving the critical questions that were raised.

As the appointment of a Royal Commission to investigate the various allegations was under way, Mara made a sensational allegation of his own. In an interview with Australian journalist Stuart Inder, 12 days after the Fiji elections, he charged the coalition with colluding with the Soviet Union and receiving from it a sum of one million dollars to unseat him from power because he was the major impediment to Soviet expansion in the South Pacific. Further, Mrs Soonu Kochar, Fiji's Indian High Commissioner, was accused of meddling in Fijian politics, and her retired husband was linked as the go-between for the Soviets. Subsequently, in a letter Mara released to the Fiji media, he identified Siddiq Koya as the coalition member responsible for making the deal with the Soviets. The two sets of allegations were investigated by the Royal Commission of Inquiry headed by retired New Zealand judge, Sir John White (Government of Fiji 1983). The investigation of Mara's Soviet allegation was frustrated by the Alliance's successful withholding of the crucial evidence on grounds of national security.

The overwhelming feeling within Fiji was (and remained) that the initial allegation of Soviet involvement was baseless and that the Alliance, in fact, had no proof. Some saw it as a ruse to divert attention from the other issues before the Commission. At the end of the protracted hearings, Sir John White produced an inocuous document that absolved all parties to the dispute of any deliberate malpractices. Rosemary Gillespie, the Carroll team member who leaked the Carroll Report and other documents to the ABC and a star witness at the hearings, not inappropriately dubbed the final outcome a 'whitewash', an exercise in futility.

An unfortunate consequence of the Royal Commission hearings was the rekindling of the embers of ethnic tension generated in the campaign, and the hardening of attitudes on both sides of the House. A cycle was complete: the politics of old had once again returned to the fore, poisoning race relations and undermining the possibilities of national dialogue on a host of problems facing Fiji. Five years later, Fiji would discover to its enormous cost just how frayed political relations had become.

# 3
# Things fall apart

On 7 April 1987, Fiji held its fifth general election since attaining independence. After a long three-month campaign and a week's polling, the newly formed Fiji Labour Party-National Federation Party Coalition won a convincing and historic victory over the long-reigning Alliance party, capturing 28 of the 52 seats in the Fiji parliament. Dr Timoci Bavadra, the new prime minister, assumed power with quiet dignity but unmistakable firmness, and quickly set in motion a government intent on delivering early on its various election pledges. Bitterly disappointed with the unexpected results of the election, Ratu Sir Kamisese Mara, the Alliance leader, conceded defeat in a terse statement and urged his party to accept the verdict of the ballot box. This surprisingly smooth, textbook transfer of power led Sir Leonard Usher, the doyen of local journalists, to write, 'It had been a long—too long—campaign, and at times some unpleasant elements of bitterness had crept in. These were now set aside. Democracy, clearly, was well and alive in Fiji' (Usher 1986:146). As it turned out, this optimism was premature.

The 1987 election results both affirmed the dominant trends in Fiji's ethnically based electoral politics and heralded the faint beginnings of a new era that promised to break away from it. In the circumstances, it was the promise—as well as the fear—of further divergence from the established patterns of political behaviour that received the most attention. For the first time in Fiji, it was not one of the small but extremely powerful coterie of paramount maritime chiefs but a western Fijian of middling chiefly rank who was at the helm of national leadership. For the first time, too, the Fijians of Indian descent were able to achieve a significant measure of national political power. The new cabinet, whose members were young, exceptionally well educated and nominally left-leaning, inspired hope of a break from the communally divisive politics of the last 17 years. The promise of change threatened those intent on maintaining the *status quo*; among them were some members of the former Mara administration and the Alliance party. The malcontents formed a militant indigenous force, the 'Taukei Movement', which embarked a carefully orchestrated campaign to break the newly elected government. Within a week of the election, Fiji was rocked by a violent and terrifying campaign of arson, sabotage, roadblocks and protest marches, climaxing with the military-led overthrow of the Bavadra government on 14 May. The coup leaders attempted to reinstall the defeated Mara government, but were thwarted by determined but peaceful internal resistance and considerable external pressure. Frustrated by their inability to achieve their immediate goal, and ostracised and rebuffed by the international community, they then struck with a second coup on 25 September, severing Fiji's links to the British Crown.

The traumatic sequence of events that followed the election contrasted with the long and uninspiring campaign that preceded—and precipitated—it. The 1987 election provided both the text, as well as the pretext, for the coup of 14 May. In this chapter, I focus on certain important aspects of the campaign in order to understand its character as well as the causes of the historic outcome. In particular, I look at the political parties that contested the election, the important campaign issues and strategies, and, finally, the voting patterns that led to the Coalition's victory. Towards the end, I provide a brief account of the coup and its aftermath, eschewing the task of a more comprehensive coverage because the subject has received extensive treatment in scholarly literature.

## Political parties

The 1987 election was contested by four political parties or coalitions, two of which were born on the eve of the campaign. The Alliance party, led by Ratu Sir Kamisese Mara, had been continuously in power in Fiji from 1966 to 1987, except for a brief four days in April 1977. Its long reign in office was the result of many factors, including, strong leadership, effective use of political power and patronage, solid support by its traditional constituency, the indigenous Fijians, and, not least, the absence of a credible alternative among the frequently warring opposition parties. In 1987 the Alliance appeared to be the political party best placed financially to last the distance in a long campaign. To further improve its prospects, the Alliance fielded a safe team, dropping four cabinet members and seven backbenchers who were considered to be liabilities and thus potential targets for political point-scoring. Some of the discarded members formed their own parties or contested the election as independents.

The Fijian Association constituted the backbone of the party, consistently capturing over 80 per cent of the Fijian communal votes. Chastised by the temporary loss of power in April 1977, brought about by a split in the Fijian communal vote, the Fijian Association began to expand and consolidate its base and, turning a blind eye to the party's public proclamations on multiracialism, welcomed to its ranks members of nationalist Fijian parties. Thus in 1987, the Alliance gave a blue-ribbon Fijian communal seat to Taniela Veitata, a Fijian Nationalist Party candidate in 1977, while another former FNP strategist was recruited to help diffuse the impact of Fijian splinter parties in marginal national constituencies. Fijian unity above all else, and the promotion of ethnic Fijian interests, became the over-riding goal of the Fijian Association and the Alliance party in the 1987 campaign.

The General Electors Association (GEA), composed of Europeans, part-Europeans, Chinese, and others of mixed descent, was the smallest, though financially perhaps the strongest, of the three Alliance branches. Ever since the advent of party politics in Fiji in the early 1960s, the GEA had thrown its weight solidly behind the Alliance. History, race, economic interest and a keen sense of power all helped to forge this politically expedient bond of trust. But in 1987, for the first time, a rift appeared in the GEA ranks, with the younger as well as the working class members of the part-European community joining the Labour party. Others deserted the Alliance complaining of stepchild-like treatment. The shift was small but significant, and it helped the Coalition in crucial marginal constituencies, such as Suva.

Of the Alliance's three constituent bodies, the Indian Alliance was the weakest spoke in the wheel. Its credibility in the Indo-Fijian community, always low, was seriously compromised by the defection of many of its disillusioned former leaders to the rival NFP. Unhappy with its performance and prestige, Ratu Mara ignored the Indian Alliance establishment altogether and recruited Indo-Fijian professionals and political opportunists personally loyal to and dependent on him to boost the party's prospects in that community. In 1987, he bagged what he thought was the prize catch of Irene Jai Narayan, who was not only a skillful politician—she had held her Suva Indian communal seat continuously since 1966—but was also a former president of the rival National Federation Party and the deputy leader of the opposition. Ousted from the NFP after an internal power struggle in 1985, she had briefly flirted with Labour, then joined the Alliance in November 1986. Political survival rather than a genuine conversion to Alliance philosophy appeared to be the main reason for her switch, as Mrs Narayan justified her action thus, 'Let's face it, whether one likes it or not, the Alliance will remain in power for a long time. It is difficult for an independent member to do much' (*Fiji Times*, 8 November 1986).

Mara selected Mrs Narayan for the crucial Suva national seat. This was a critical tactical mistake which was to cost the Alliance dearly, as the Alliance leader had badly underestimated the Indo-Fijian electorate's unwillingness to forgive Narayan's defection to a party that she had so vehemently criticised all her political life. And Narayan's own unexpectedly virulent attack on her former party and her erstwhile colleagues, mounted with the fanaticism of the twice converted, damaged her prospects further. As one voter told me, 'If Mrs Narayan had fallen from a mountain top, I would have caught her in my lap. But what do you do when she has fallen in your esteem?' The response of the Indian Alliance leadership, or what was left of it, to being ignored and bypassed was a quiet withdrawal of its support for the party and a silent move to the Coalition camp. In the end, the Alliance was left banking on the charisma of a single candidate for a crucial seat, while the Coalition remorselessly exploited Narayan's formerly vitriolic attacks against the Alliance to great effect. But these were errors that surfaced only at a later stage in the campaign. For much of the time the Alliance was confident of a victory and dismissive of its opponents.

Unlike the Alliance party, the Coalition was launched on the eve of the election. It was a coalition of two parties drawn together into an expedient, and initially reluctant, political union for the larger purpose of defeating the Alliance. The older partner in the Coalition was the mainly Indo-Fijian-supported National Federation party. We have already discussed its fluctuating fortunes in the previous chapter. On the eve of the 1987 elections, the National Federation Party's unity was fragile, and its public esteem low. Several of its sitting parliamentarians had switched to the FLP, as had many longtime party loyalists, disheartened by years of damaging, internecine fights at the top. Coalition with another party was the only alternative to avoid almost certain political demise.

That prospect was provided by the emergence of the Fiji Labour Party, whose rhetorically non-ethnic platform, multiethnic composition and vehement opposition to the ruling Alliance made it an attractive partner. The trade union-backed Labour party was launched in July 1985, primarily in response to the questionable tactics used by the government to address the economic problems that plagued Fiji. One such tactic was the wage freeze imposed in 1984, to boost an economy severely damaged by hurricanes, droughts, rising foreign debts and burgeoning civil service salary bills. The government wanted to use savings from the wage freeze—to the tune of F$36 million—to expand the primary sector and assist the employment-generating business sector (see Narsey 1985). The unions criticised the freeze as unnecessary and oppressive, especially to lower income groups, and, moreover, as a breach of the spirit of the Tripartite Forum.[1]

Anger about the government's economic strategies was further fuelled by the bitter and prolonged conflict between the Ministry of Education and the teachers' unions. The Volunteer Service Scheme, devised by the government to give fresh graduate teachers employment on a cost-share basis, incurred the wrath of graduating teachers, who accused the government—rightly as the courts subsequently agreed—of reneging on the earlier promise of regular employment. The government's policy of large-scale arbitrary transfer of teachers, part of a wider policy to integrate Fiji's communally oriented schools, smacked of an arrogant and confrontational attitude. The Education Minister, Dr Ahmed Ali, was accused by both Indo-Fijian and Fijian teachers of 'adopting an anti-teacher stance designed to undermine the professional status of teachers in the country'. Indeed, Ali's policies unwittingly provided the foundation for a common front between the Indian-based Fiji Teachers' Union and the exclusively *taukei* (indigenous) Fijian Teachers' Association, both of which protested against the government's educational policies (*Fiji Times*, 8 November 1986).

Coming at a difficult economic time, and carried out in stark contrast to the Mara administration's earlier record of consultation and dialogue, these actions politicised the traditionally apolitical trade union movement, which in turn led to the launching of the Fiji Labour party in July 1985. New on the scene, brimming with enthusiasm and armed with progressive social and economic policies contained under the general rubric of 'democratic socialism', the FLP promised, among other things, public ownership of vital industries, minimum wage legislation for the manufacturing sector, and increased local participation in such vital industries as tourism.[2] Not surprisingly, the party attracted significant local attention. Just four months after being launched, Labour won the Suva City municipal elections and made a strong showing in the North Central Indian national constituency by-elections. But for all the euphoria and early unexpected success, the FLP remained primarily an urban-based party, led by white-collar trade unionists. To become a national force strong enough to contend for government, the party had to broaden its base.

Initially, however, the FLP scorned the idea of a coalition. As party secretary Krishna Datt claimed in July 1986, '[bo]th the Alliance and the NFP work within the framework of capitalism and the FLP cannot share their ideologies' (*Fiji Times*, 20 July 1986). Yet a few months later, chastened by the hard realities of Fiji politics and realising the folly of confronting the Alliance alone, the FLP changed its tune and initiated discussions with the NFP, which it had recently criticised as being a party of 'a handful of businessmen and lawyers'. By October the two parties had held seven private meetings, and by December a coalition had been arranged. The terms of the arrangement were never made public, though several features later became clear. One was a seat-sharing formula, according to which the NFP agreed to give the FLP six of its 12 blue-ribbon Indian communal seats as well as half of the winnable Indian and Fijian national seats.

This formula enabled the Labour to project itself into the hitherto inaccessible rural areas, while the NFP was spared the almost certain humiliation of losing its traditional iron-clad grip on the communal seats to Labour's Indo-Fijian candidates. Another notable feature was the acceptance by the predominantly Indo-Fijian-based NFP of an ethnic Fijian, from another party, as the leader of the coalition. This was both a tacit acknowledgement of weakness by the NFP as well as a concession to the non-ethnic philosophy of the Coalition. It also represented a significant shift in Indo-Fijian political opinion, which only a decade earlier had rejected a Fijian leader for the party (Ratu Julian Toganivalu). But the reality of ethnic politics in Fiji was that an Indo-Fijian prime minister would not be acceptable to the majority of the *taukei*, and, for the NFP to achieve any measure of political power, a coalition with another party with a Fijian leader, and a political philosophy broadly compatible to its own, was the only route to victory.

The third outcome of the coalition arrangement was the formulation of a compromise manifesto that whittled down some of the FLP's radical-sounding economic policies, such as encouraging worker participation in the management of industry and the nationalisation of selected industries, and that removed from the electoral arena such perennially contentious issues as land tenure and education. Finally, both parties agreed to present a combined, fresh slate of candidates. A start was made by endorsing only five of the 22 sitting Opposition parliamentarians.

The Labour Coalition, however, was not the only coalition to contest the 1987 elections. There was another, consisting of a faction of the NFP and the Western United Front, the NFP's 1982 election partner. The NFP-WUF coalition was the handiwork of Shardha Nand, the deposed secretary of the NFP, and other politicians discarded by the Labour Coalition's candidate selection committee, including Siddiq Koya. They massaged their personal grievances into a political cause, presenting themselves as champions of Indo-Fijian rights placed in danger by having a Fijian (Dr Bavadra) as the leader of the mainly Indo-Fijian-supported opposition party. Taking the logic of ethnic politics to its extreme conclusion, they argued that only an Indo-Fijian could be trusted to lead the Indo-Fijian community. Among other things, this faction of the NFP demanded a separate Ministry for Indian Affairs along the lines of its Fijian counterpart, 99-year leases on Crown lands, and the allocation of jobs in the public sector according to the percentage of seats occupied by each ethnic group in Fiji's parliament, that is, 42 per cent each for the Fijians and the Indians and the remaining 16 per cent for general electors.[3]

The Western United Front was a reluctant and silent partner in the coalition. Its leader, Ratu Osea Gavidi, the charismatic campaigner of 1982, was quiet and generally inaccessible, spending more time battling his irate creditors in court than fighting political opponents in elections. Since 1982 the WUF itself had become somewhat of a spent force. The policies for harvesting pine, the dispute about which had led to the formation of the party, was now a non-issue, and many western Fijians outside of the Nadroga/Navosa region had been enticed back into the Alliance fold. Further, the WUF had lost credibility with many NFP leaders because of its withdrawal from the royal commission investigating allegations suggesting that Soviet money was used by the original NFP–WUF coalition in the bid to defeat the Alliance in the 1982 election. The NFP–WUF coalition campaign began promisingly, but its prospects vanished when Koya and other candidates withdrew, ostensibly to avoid being tainted with the spoiler's role. In the end, most of the Indo-Fijian members of the coalition, widely perceived as grasping opportunists, suffered defeat, losing their deposits by getting less than 10 per cent of the total votes cast in their constituency. Gavidi lost (42 per cent of the votes) to his old Alliance rival, Apenisa Kuruisaqila (53.5 per cent).

Of all the political parties, the Fijian Nationalist Party maintained the lowest profile in the 1987 campaign. The party maintained its stridently anti-Indian stance while at the same time advocating a platform designed to promote Fijian interests. It proposed the 'thinning out' of Fiji Indians through an active policy encouraging emigration, to be funded by the British government which had introduced Indians into Fiji in the first place. The FNP made an issue of the paucity of Fijians in commercial and industrial sectors, which it saw as a direct result of a conspiracy by the Indo-Fijian and European business classes. It drew attention to the disparity between the numbers of Fijians and Indo-Fijians employed in the public sector, blamed the Alliance for the problem, and demanded that this disparity be redressed. Finally, and unsurprisingly, it demanded an exclusively *taukei* parliament through revision of the 1970 Constitution; absolute Fijian control of the political process was seen as a precondition for Fijian economic and social progress. In the end, however, while there was personal support and sympathy for Butadroka, who won 37.9 per cent of the votes— an increase of 7.3 per cent over the 1982 figure—the FNP failed to recapture old ground, though its candidates drew sufficient Fijian support in marginal national seats to help the Coalition defeat the Alliance.

## The campaign

The campaign for the general election began early in the year, partly in anticipation of a February poll. It was long and unremarkable, lacking, for instance, the dramatic tension of the last stages of the 1982 campaign when the contents of the so-called Carroll Report were revealed in an Australian television program, or the intense and ultimately self-destructive struggle between the competing factions of the NFP in the September 1977 elections. But the campaign had its own unique features that helped to define its character. Learning from past experience, both the Alliance and the Coalition dispensed with the problematic public spectacle of touring the country to select candidates from a list prepared by constituency committees. Instead, each party appointed a small committee that made the selection, and whose decision was final and irrevocable. This swift, if somewhat heavy-handed, action gave them more time to focus on each other instead of having to contend with internal selection squabbles. It also produced an avalanche of defections as the frustrated aspirants switched parties. In the end, however, most of the defectors suffered ignominious defeat at the polls.

Another significant difference between the 1987 election and previous ones was that, for the first time since the advent of elections in Fiji, the leaders of both the ruling and leading opposition parties were ethnic Fijians. This fact diluted—though never completely eliminated—the exploitation of racial fear during the campaign. However, the divisive race issue was supplanted by other emotional distinctions, such as regionalism and class. Many Fijians saw in the election a contest between commoner Fijians from the west led by Dr Bavadra, and the traditional chiefly élite and eastern Fijians led by Ratu Mara.

As the campaign progressed, the strategies of the two rival parties revealed themselves. Confident of victory, the Alliance adopted a dismissive attitude toward the opposition. Ratu Mara set the tone in November 1986 when, referring to the Labour politicians, he asked: 'What have the Johnnys-come-lately done in the promotion of national unity?' (*Fiji Times*, 28 November 1986). He returned to this theme time and again throughout the campaign. Dr Bavadra became the target of a sneering newspaper campaign. In a typical advertisement the Alliance said: 'Bavadra has never been in parliament. He has no EXPERIENCE. He has no INFLUENCE. The Council of Chiefs do [sic] NOT listen to him. The international scene where we sell our sugar has NEVER heard of him. He cannot get renewal of leases for farmers' (*Fiji Times*, 15 March 1987). In the opening Alliance campaign address over Radio Fiji, Mosese Qionibaravi, the deputy prime minister, called Bavadra an 'unqualified unknown'. The Coalition was often portrayed as weak, vacillating and not to be trusted. One typical campaign advertisement ran: 'The opposition factions are fragmented and quarrelling among themselves. Their policies are confused and shift constantly as one group or would-be leader gains ascendency. Principles are proclaimed as fundamental and are then dropped when pressures are applied by vested interests, or for political expediency'. The Alliance on the other hand presented itself as the very model of stability: 'united in purpose, strong and fully accepted leadership, clear and consistent policies, and a political philosophy with values that have been proved by experience'.[4]

Other important features of the Alliance campaign strategy were to appeal for Fijian ethnic solidarity and to instill fear among the *taukei* about the consequences of a Coalition victory. The unmistakable Alliance message was that only an Alliance government headed by paramount chiefs could guarantee the security of Fijian interests. Once again, Ratu Mara led the Alliance charge. 'Fijians have the political leadership despite being outnumbered in this country', he said, and 'if they failed to unite that leadership would slip away from them' (*Fiji Times*, 24 September 1986). And Mara accused the Coalition of trying to undermine Fijian leadership by taking up Fijian causes with the intention of discrediting the Alliance, such as the Nasomo land dispute in Vatukauloa, the plight of the cocoa growers in Vanua Levu, and competing claims of ownership of Yanuca island in which his own wife was involved. Mara's racial appeal became so blatant that he was taken to task in a *Fiji Sun* editorial, the only political leader to be criticised in this way throughout the entire campaign.

> In past elections, Ratu Sir Kamisese Mara called for political parties not to indulge in politics of fear, and not to fight the election on racial lines. But now the Prime Minister himself has begun a racially oriented campaign. His call for the Fijians to unite to retain political leadership is unwarranted. If every individual race began campaigning on these lines, the country would be in trouble (*Fiji Sun*, 24 September 1986).

Fear was an important aspect of the Alliance campaign strategy, fear not only of the *taukeis* losing control over their land but also of being forced to embrace an alien ideology. The Alliance warned the Fijian electorate, particularly those residing in rural areas outside the purview of modern influences, about the evils of democratic socialism—the Coalition's creed borrowed from the Anglo-Australasian tradition. It was a system, the Alliance claimed, 'in which LAND, FACTORIES, MINES, SHOPS, etc. are ALL OWNED by the STATE and the COMMUNITY. This is opposed to the present system in Fiji where ownership of Fijian land rests exclusively with Fijian *mataqali*, and businesses belong to individuals or shareholders in a public company'. The fact that some of the trade union leaders had visited Moscow (as indeed had some government ministers) was presented as indisputable proof of the Coalition's sinister designs.

In contrast to the Alliance, the Coalition entered the campaign as the distinct underdog. It was new and inexperienced, underfunded and comparatively disorganised, unable to match its rival in the media war. Its candidates, therefore, ran their largely self-financed campaigns in pocket meetings in their own constituencies. But the Coalition message was clear: it charged the Mara administration with abuse of power and reminded the electorate of the mounting economic difficulties for lower-income families. Bavadra, in his concluding campaign speech, said, 'Wage and salary earners remember the wage and job freeze; farmers remember their extreme hardships and insecurities; rural dwellers remember the high prices; parents remember the increased bus fares; squatters remember physical removal and neglect; teachers remember Dr Ahmed Ali's reign of terror in the Ministry of Education; students remember the pain of their hunger strike; the *taukei* remember that most of Fijian development money goes to a few provinces'.[5] The Coalition, for its part, promised a new direction and a clean and compassionate government. Its election theme, 'time for a change', caught the mood of the electorate as the campaign concluded. It was, by all accounts, a remarkable transformation, brought about as much by the Coalition's own effort as by the voters' deepening disenchantment with the Alliance's negative campaigning.

## Leadership

Leadership was an important issue in the campaign. The Alliance projected an image of unity, purpose and experience. The Coalition, on the other hand, was portrayed as a bunch of professional critics whose view of the real world was 'so flawed that it would not pass as seconds'. Ratu Mara was once again the party's trump card, and he vowed to fight to the end: 'I have not yet finished the job I started and until I can ensure that unshakeable foundations have been firmly laid and cornerstones are set in place, I will not yield to the vaulting ambitions of a power crazy gang of amateurs, none of whom has run anything, not even a bingo party'.[6] He assured the nation that 'as long as the people of this blessed land need me, I will answer their call. I will keep the faith. Fear not, Ratu Mara will stay' (Final election broadcast). The future of Fiji and the Alliance party were inextricably linked, it was suggested; one could not exist without the other. Without his and his party's leadership, Mara said, Fiji would go down the path of 'rack and ruin'; it would become another of those countries 'torn apart by racial strife and drowning in debt, where basic freedoms are curtailed, universities closed down, the media throttled and dissenters put into jail and camps'.

Ratu Mara's long incumbency presented a real challenge for Dr Bavadra; unlike Mara, Bavadra was a newcomer to national politics, and virtually unknown outside Fiji. By profession a medical doctor, Bavadra had held a number of senior positions in the civil service before retiring in 1985 to head the newly formed Fiji Labour Party. Bavadra came from a chiefly background, though he was not himself a paramount chief. He was a sportsman, and had attended the Queen Victoria School, but his credentials with the Fijian establishment were tenuous and suspect.[7] His cause was not helped by the Alliance's concerted effort to paint him as a tool of Indo-Fijian politicians and therefore an untrustworthy guardian of Fijian interests. Thus Bavadra was forced frequently to defend his own 'Fijian-ness' as well as his party's platform.

By the end of the campaign, however, Bavadra had managed to turn public opinion in his favour. His unassuming character and his common touch, accessibility and openness, contrasted with Ratu Mara's characteristic aloofness, and projected an image of a compassionate man who could be trusted. His style of leadership received praise from his colleagues. Commenting on Bavadra's 'first among equals' approach to leadership, Satendra Nandan wrote: 'It is a type of leadership which a democracy requires in the modern world, by the command of the people rather than by an accident of birth. It is a leadership which encourages growth in a team, rather than the banyan tree leadership under which everything else dies for lack of light. It is the leadership by a man who is known nationally as a leader, not identified with one particular province of a country; by a man chosen by a genuinely multiracial party, a leader who is easily approachable, not held in awe but in affection; a leadership which sincerely believes in collective responsibility for collective decision for the collective good' (*Fiji Times*, 24 March 1987). Never before in Fiji had the contrast between two competing styles of leadership been presented so starkly to the public.

## Conduct of government

The Alliance campaigned on its record of experience and stability, while the Coalition drew support by launching a concerted attack against it. 'We have all become accustomed to the arrogance of power, abuse of and insolence of office', said Dr Bavadra (*Fiji Times*, 24 February 1987). The Alliance had 'reneged on the fundamental principles of democratic responsibility and accountability. It pretends to be democratic but in fact puts all decisions in the hands of a very few. This brand of democracy aids a few at the expense of the vast majority'. This theme was pursued throughout the campaign. The Coalition accused the Alliance of practising the politics of racial separation, similar in effect if not in name to the apartheid regime of South Africa. The difference between the two was 'one of degree, not one of substance'. In rebuttal, the Alliance affirmed its commitment to opposing 'any suggestion of constitutional change that would weaken or destroy the principle of guaranteed on of Fiji's major racial groups in the House of Representatives' (Alliance Party Manifesto 1987:2).

To check what it saw as abuse of power, the Coalition proposed an anti-corruption bill, a code of conduct for parliamentarians, and the abolition of legislation that allowed secrecy in government, specifically the Official Secrets Act. For the most part, The Alliance chose to dismiss the issues raised by the Coalition. As Mara declared, 'Allow me simply to say that there is no country in the world today in which similar concerns do not emblazon the headlines. The fact is that these problems are a by-product of modernisation. Fiji neither has a monopoly on these problems nor are they extensive and corrosive here' (Alliance Party Political Broadcast). His point was valid, of course, but the Alliance's acceptance of these issues as political reality contrasted sharply with the Coalition's promise to tackle these problems with vigour. The above attitude seemed to symbolise the Alliance's apathy to many in the electorate and certainly hurt the Alliance in the urban and peri-urban areas where violence and crime had increased dramatically in the previous five years.

## The economy

The economy was another important campaign issue. Predictably, the Alliance trumpeted its record: inflation remained around 2 per cent, the balance of payment figures were sound, with foreign reserves at record levels, and the country was assured of guaranteed prices for its basic export item, sugar, through long-term international agreements. The Alliance reaffirmed its commitment to the promotion of individual enterprise within a capitalist framework. In short, the Alliance promised 'business as usual' along an assured and well-trodden path.

But the Alliance's optimism about the state of the economy was based on shaky foundations. A number of experts pointed out that the Fijian economy was in serious trouble from over-planning and over-reliance on the public sector to generate employment and investment. The Coalition criticised the Alliance's management of the economy, but in general its economic strategy and philosophy didn't differ substantially from their opponent's. The Coalition went to great lengths to assure the business community that it was not anti-business. Its election manifesto stated that 'employment creation through an expanding private sector will form a major thrust of our economic policies'. To generate private-sector growth, the Coalition promised to facilitate 'easy access to long-term loan finances at low interest rates'. And in his closing campaign address, Bavadra left no doubt of his support for the private sector: 'I reaffirm the Coalition's recognition and acceptance of the vital role of the private sector in the development of the nation. There is no threat. The private sector must remain. It will remain'.[8] This was a politically sensible stance that prevented the otherwise almost certain large-scale defection of the Indian business community to the Alliance fold. Their support in the marginal Suva seat proved crucial for the Coalition.

While the two parties agreed on broad issues of economic philosophy, they differed on both the performance as well as the management of the economy. The Coalition made an issue of unequal regional development in Fiji, pointing out that certain areas had been developed at the expense of others. A campaign attack alleged that Lau, Ratu Mara's own province, had received a disproportionate share of development aid, scholarships and hurricane relief money (*Fiji Sun*, 30 March 1987). Mara denied the charge of favouring Lau, but statistics confirmed the Coalition allegations. For example, between 1984 and 1986, Lau, one of the smallest of the Fijian provinces, received F$528,099.05 in scholarships, 21 per cent of all the money allocated for Fijian scholarships. On the other hand, much larger provinces received far less: Ba, F$156,085.25 (6.2 per cent); Tailevu, F$364,244.44 (14.5 per cent); and Rewa, F$221,638.93 (8.3 per cent).[9] At the First Annual Convention of the Fiji Labour Party, Bavadra said 'it is important to remind ourselves that the government resources poured into Lakeba are derived from wealth produced by others elsewhere in the country. It is time that the government stopped viewing the rest of Fiji as serving the interest of a few centres in the east. The people of Lakeba are entitled to a share in the national interest, but just a share. It is time we had a government that is more truly national in outlook' (Bavadra 1986:n.p.).

The Coalition also highlighted the plight of the disadvantaged sectors of Fiji society that had missed out on the Alliance's 'economic parade'— the grossly underpaid garment factory workers, squatters and other poor families. Indeed, the Coalition alleged collusion between big business and the Alliance government in keeping wages down, and made the still unrefuted charge that Indian garment manufacturers had contributed about F$51,000 to the Alliance campaign fund to prevent the legislation of a minimum-wage policy for the industry. Pointing to the Alliance's record of high foreign reserves, Bavadra asked, 'But what use is that when there is so much unemployment? What use is that if people can't afford bus fares? What use is that if business confidence is lacking?' (Bavadra 1986). Bavadra's logic appealed to those who felt marginalised and left out of the economic picture portrayed by the Alliance.

Another difference between the Alliance's and the Coalition's economic policies was the latter's emphasis on the need to promote greater local participation in Fiji's economic development. This was in direct response to the increasing feeling that the Mara government had become less concerned over the years to the plight of local entrepreneurs and to local sensitivities. The difference between the two parties was aptly captured in their respective approaches to the promotion of the tourist industry. Both parties supported the promotion of tourism in Fiji, but the Coalition went further. It proposed to develop hotel-linked farms owned by neighbouring villages, to facilitate greater equity in the participation of local people in the hotel and allied transport industries, and to provide special incentive allowances to those reinvesting tourist dollars in Fiji. The Coalition presented itself as a friend to local business and local entrepreneurs, helping it to allay their fears and win their much-needed financial support. The Alliance, in contrast, appeared to be a part of and for big business.

## *Taukei* affairs and national development

The Alliance and the Coalition differed sharply in their policies and visions for the nation and for the *taukei*. Both parties accepted the provisions of the constitution that entrenched certain vested ethnic political interests. Not surprisingly, however, while the Alliance championed its long-held view that 'race is a fact of life' and pledged not to disturb the *status quo*, the Coalition was committed to non-racialism. It pressed for a common, unifying national name and identity to forge a genuine multiracial nation out of its component ethnic parts. The Alliance, on the other hand, rejected the notion of a common designation for all Fiji citizens, arguing that it would pose a serious threat to specific *taukei* rights, particularly land. The Alliance similarly rejected out of hand the Coalition's proposal to reform the Native Land Trust Board (NLTB) to make it more efficient and responsive to both landowners' needs and tenants' concerns. As Bavadra noted in July 1986, 'my concern is that the NLTB has become too much the tool of certain vested interests in this country and that all too often steps taken by the NLTB are not in the best interests of the majority of the landowners themselves'.[10] To improve the situation, the Coalition proposed to establish a National Lands and Resources Council, composed of tenants' and landowners' representatives, that would oversee the NLTB and work to provide a fair return to the owners as well as ensure greater security of tenure to the tenant community. But the Coalition made it clear that it would not 'attempt to change the existing land laws without the full consultation and approval of the Great Council of Chiefs' (Bavadra 'Closing election address'). The Alliance opposed any reform to the NLTB whatsoever, and Mara called the FLP's thinking on the subject extremely dangerous: 'Fijians should be wary of it because it could lead to the slipping away of native land' (*Fiji Times*, 17 August 1986). Precisely how that was possible when Fijian land rights were deeply entrenched in the Constitution the Alliance party left unexplained, but the effect of the Alliance's strong public opposition was to plant fears in *taukei* minds about the possible loss of their cherished rights under a Bavadra government.

On Fijian leadership and politics, the Alliance position differed markedly to the Coalition's. The Alliance preached the need to maintain Fijian ethnic unity under chiefly leadership. 'The chiefs represent the people, the land and the custom. Without a chief there is no Fijian society', said Senator Inoke Tabua, a close Mara associate (*Fiji Times*, 17 August 1986). But in recent years, both the role of the chiefs, as well as the formerly cohesive nature of traditional Fijian society, were being threatened by modern influences—education, urbanisation and mass media. To stem the tide, and to reinforce chiefly authority, the Mara administration attempted to reintroduce selected aspects of the old Fijian Administration. A specially commissioned report, prepared by Pacific Islands Development Program of the Honolulu-based EastWest Center, under the leadership of ex-Fiji colonial official Rodney Cole, provided the blueprint for reforms in the system (Cole et al. 1984).[11] Among its specific recommendations were the retention of many hitherto discarded customary laws and the official recognition of village leaders. These recommendations, formally implemented in March 1987, would, so the administration hoped, buttress chiefly authority and protect the traditional structure of Fijian society by insulating it from the corrosive influences in the larger society. Withdrawal into the shell of communal isolation rather than the initiation of a national dialogue was the Alliance's response to a host of serious social and economic problems facing the *taukei*. This approach received wide support across many rural areas and in the islands where the *taukei* were practicing subsistence agriculture and had minimal contact with other ethnic groups, but it had little relevance and meaning in urban areas where individual struggle for existence took precedence over communal solidarity.

The Coalition's markedly different line on Fijian leadership drew a clear line between modern political and traditional roles for Fijian chiefs. The Coalition promised to educate the *taukei* on their constitutional rights as opposed to their traditional and customary obligations. As Bavadra said, 'so long as the Fiji constitution specifically guarantees individual political freedoms and associations, no individual irrespective of his colour, creed or sex is obligated to be subservient to a master, whether it be a chief or a political party, other than what his conscience dictates'.[12]

Neither did the FLP support further insulation of Fijian society from the mainstream of Fiji society, as the Alliance promised to do. Bavadra told a meeting in Suva, 'by restricting the Fijian people to their communal lifestyle in the face of a rapidly developing cash economy, the average Fijian has become more and more economically backward. This is particularly invidious when the leaders themselves have amassed huge personal wealth by making use of their traditional and political powers' (*Fiji Times*, 17 November 1986). Needless to say, this attitude presented a direct and unprecedented threat to the chiefs who had acquired wealth and influence by juxtaposing their modern political and traditional roles. They naturally reacted with unremarkable indignation, and predicted a dire future for the *taukei* under a Coalition government.

# Foreign policy

Foreign policy was not a significant campaign issue in Fiji but received considerable attention externally. A large part of the reason for outside concern was the widely, if inaccurately, held view that the Coalition consisted of leftist radicals bent on wrecking Fiji's traditionally pro-Western policies. In fact, the Coalition's foreign policies were almost identical to those of the NFP–WUF coalition's 1982 platform. In 1982, the NFP–WUF had promised to 'maintain an active policy of nonalignment'; to 'keep the Pacific region free of big power rivalries, and in cooperation with countries in the region, oppose all forms of nuclear testing or nuclear waste disposal in the Pacific'; and to 'support, by all peaceful means, the struggle of peoples of remaining colonies in the Pacific for independence and self government'. The Coalition promised to pursue these same policies, with one curious exception. Whereas the 1982 coalition had sought to 'establish and strengthen Fiji's relationship with all nations without prejudice to their political ideologies', the 1987 Coalition said it would not allow the Soviet Union to open an embassy in Fiji. The 1982 coalition, it appears, was even more 'left-leaning' than its 1987 counterpart, though, of course, its views had not received as much scrutiny or publicity.

For its part, the Alliance, too, committed itself to a nonaligned policy for Fiji, a nuclear-free Pacific and independence for New Caledonia. But it added, significantly, that it would pursue its policies 'bearing in mind that it [Fiji] is a small nation and needs friends for its security'. One friend that the government courted assiduously, and with promising result, was the United States, which had begun to view Fiji as the key player in regional politics. Fiji's strategic importance to the United States was enhanced by New Zealand's firm antinuclear stance, and the consequent problems with the ANZUS alliance. In the final analysis, however, as on many other issues, the difference between the Coalition and the Alliance on important matters of foreign policy was more one of degree than of substance. Once in government, the Coalition was intent on pursuing a prudent and moderate foreign policy course, seeing the need to consolidate its power within Fiji as its most important challenge.[13]

As the campaign ended, the two parties painted contrasting visions of Fiji under their respective rules. Dr Bavadra's Fiji would be committed to

67

social justice and economic equality. The Alliance promised to keep Fiji on its accustomed path, firmly ensconced within a capitalist framework; without the Alliance, the electorate was told, Fiji had no democratic future. In his last election message to the nation Mara said, 'I firmly believe that these elections will be crucial to the future of our homeland. Let there be no doubt in your mind: Fiji is not so much at a turning point, as it is at the crossroads. If we take the wrong direction, we will finish up in blind alleys, from which there is no return and no way out'.

# Voting

Given the communal electoral system, it is not surprising that voting follows an ethnic pattern. As Table 3.1 shows, Fijians always voted overwhelmingly for the Fijian-dominated Alliance and the Indians have rallied behind the NFP. The general electors were consistent in their support for the Alliance, 90 per cent in 1982 and 85 per cent in 1987. Political success in Fiji was thus contingent on maintaining solidarity in one's own ethnic community while actively promoting disunity among the opposition's. The Alliance played the game with much skill, preserving Fijian unity while capitalising on dormant factionalism and disunity in the Indian community. The NFP, as the figures show, has not encountered much success in splitting the Fijian communal vote in its favour.

The 1987 election confirmed the historic trend of predominantly ethnic patterns of voting, but the figures also belie the emergence of some new trends. Although Indo-Fijian support for the Alliance remained constant around 15 per cent, that support was not as broadly based as it had been in the past. In recent years, the Indo-Fijian business class and a significant section of the Muslim community constituted the base of the Indian Alliance; the party's support among the South Indian community, or among the reformist Arya Samaj religious group, important in the past, declined significantly in 1987. And while it remained true that the majority of Fijians supported the Alliance, it was also significant that 21.8 per cent voted for other parties and independents, thus indicating that among many Fijians the Alliance was not regarded as the sole representative voice of the Fijian community. On the other hand, the Coalition was able to make significant inroads into the Fijian constituency, enough to cause the Alliance's defeat in marginal seats.

An important feature of the 1987 election was a record-low voter turnout, the lowest since independence. Indo-Fijian turnout declined from 85 per cent in 1982 to 69 per cent in 1987, while in the same period the Fijian turnout dropped from 85 per cent to 70 per cent. This decline affected the outcome in the marginal constituencies. The reasons for the drop are not clear, though several plausible explanations exist. One, undoubtedly, was the confusion caused by the omission of names from the hastily prepared and improperly checked electoral rolls; names of voters were inadvertently transferred from one polling station to another, thereby causing unsuspecting voters to miss the deadline for casting their votes at a specified time and place. Another reason could have been the widespread feeling that the election was a foregone conclusion in the Alliance's favour, thus causing some supporters to stay away. Among some Fijians, especially in urban areas, absence from the polling booth was a protest against the Alliance. The Alliance suffered from a decline in Fijian voter turnout in all except four of its twelve communal constituencies, the largest decline being in areas where it was already particularly vulnerable. In Lomaiviti/Muanikau the Fijian turnout dropped by 23 per cent, in Rewa/Serua/Namosi by 17 per cent, in

**Table 3.1    Voting patterns in Fiji, 1972–87** (per cent)

| Party | 1972 (April) | 1977 (September) | 1977 | 1982 | 1987 |
|---|---|---|---|---|---|
| Fijian communal vote | | | | | |
| Alliance (per cent) | 83.1 | 64.7 | 80.5 | 83.7 | 76.6 |
| NFP (per cent) | 2.4 | – | 0.1 | 0.8 | 9.6 |
| FNP (per cent) | – | 24.4 | 11.6 | 7.7 | 5.4 |
| WUF (per cent) | – | – | – | 7.0 | 3.4 |
| Total no. of votes cast | 76,462 | 82,651 | 94,038 | 121,366 | 120,701 |
| Indian communal vote | | | | | |
| Alliance (per cent) | 24.1 | 15.6 | 14.4 | 15.3 | 15.1 |
| NFP Labour Coalition (per cent) | 74.3 | 73.2 | 84.9 | 84.1 | 82.9 |
| Total no. of votes cast | 84,753 | 103,644 | 103,537 | 110,830 | 122,906 |

Source: *Fiji Gazette*, various years.

Kadavu/Tamavua by 16 per cent, and in Ra/Samabula by 13.4 per cent. Tamavua, Samabula and Muanikau are all a part of the greater Suva area and within the Suva Fijian national constituency where a voter turnout drop and a swing to the Coalition caused the Alliance's defeat. This was a constituency that the Alliance had always won with the slightest of margins, and, in the 1987 elections, it was widely viewed as the seat most likely to tip the balance of the election. It had a total of 41,179 voters (16,962 Fijians, 20,778 Indians and 3,439 general electors).

The Alliance's candidates were Ratu David Toganivalu, the deputy prime minister, and Mrs Irene Jai Narayan. Pitted against these two seasoned politicians were the Coalition newcomers, Dr Tupeni Baba, a Fijian academic at the University of the South Pacific, and Navin Maharaj, former Suva (and Alliance) mayor and businessman. The Alliance counted on the experience and popularity of its candidates to carry the constituency. But that was not to be. Maharaj, a veteran of municipal politics, mounted an effective door-to-door campaign, and Baba developed with the campaign to become an articulate and accomplished spokesman for his party, connecting especially with the city's younger voters, both Indo-Fijian and Fijian. Business community support for Toganivalu was neutralised among the powerful Gujarati community by Harilal Patel, who contested the Suva Indian communal seat. And Mrs Narayan, instead of being an asset, became a liability. Her previous record of solid opposition to the Alliance was used against her; many of her former supporters refused to overlook her defection from the NFP to the Alliance; and the Indian Alliance, feeling discarded and discredited, refused to campaign for the party. Making matters worse for themselves, leading Alliance party functionaries, including Mara, devoted an inordinate amount of time in western Viti Levu hoping, at long last, to win an Indian communal seat.

Another marginal seat was the southeastern national (Naitasiri/ Nasinu area), which the Alliance also lost to the Coalition. Here, there were 22,228 Fijian registered voters, 19,974 Indians and 761 general electors. Several factors helped to defeat the Alliance. But perhaps more important was the effect of the Fijian Nationalist Party, which collected 8.5 per cent of the Fijian communal votes that otherwise, it can reasonably be supposed, would have gone to the Alliance. The Coalition candidate, Joeli Kalou, a teacher and a trade unionist, was an accomplished campaigner, while his Alliance rival, Ratu George Tu'uakitau Cokanauto, youngest son of the late Ratu Sir Edward Cakobau, remained uncomfortable on the hustings, relying more on traditional political connections than on active campaigning. For its Indian candidate, the Coalition astutely chose a Muslim, Fida Hussein, for an area with a large Muslim population. His presence on the ticket helped to blunt the effect of the Alliance's assiduous courting of Muslim voters. The Alliance's downfall in this constituency, as elsewhere, came about through shrewd Coalition strategy, as well as through the Alliance's own complacency and ineffectiveness.

At his first news conference after being sworn into office on 12 April, Dr Bavadra briefly reflected on the momentous events of the previous week. He viewed the 'the peaceful and honorable change of government' as the reaffirmation of the 'deep democratic roots of our society and the profound unity of our people' *(Fiji Times*, 13 April 1987). He saw in his triumph the dawn of a new era, full of new potential and opportunity. 'Together', he said, 'let us write a new chapter, which, God willing, will be one which we and our children will be proud of' *(Fiji Times*, 13 April 1987). Unfortunately for him and his supporters, neither the gods nor his opponents were willing or prepared for change.

## The 14 May coup

While the new government set about its work, its opponents—defeated after almost two decades of untrammelled rule—organised to oppose and eventually overthrow it, climaxing with the military-led and Alliance-condoned coup of 14 May 1987. The Fiji coup is probably the most written about event in modern Fijian and Pacific islands history. The story is too well known to need retelling here.[14] I shall therefore refer only to major events and developments to complete the picture. The immediate interpretation of the May coup was that it was essentially an ethnic conflict, with the Fijians asserting their power against a government that they themselves did not control. The ethnic factor was certainly mobilised, by the Taukei Movement among others, to support the destabilisation campaign. But the coup was not simply an ethnic conflict.

A whole variety of individuals and groups felt threatened by the Coalition's victory. Some former cabinet ministers feared that the new government would investigate allegations of abuse and mismanagement. Politicians at risk of losing their jobs—some had no other career to fall back on—contributed to inflaming opposition to the new government. Prominent leaders supported the usurpers by joining the new post-coup administration rather than taking a stand for the democratic ideals that they had previously championed. The election of a middle-ranking chief as prime minister unsettled some Fijians used to being governed by paramount chiefs. Bavadra's championing of democratic values, his plea to observe distinctions between modern and traditional roles did not sit well with some. For others, Bavadra's ascension from western Viti Levu to the office of the prime minister threatened the traditional structure and distribution of power in Fijian society. For a whole variety of reasons, then, the Labour government had to go.

The full truth of the complex motivations of the principal players will never be known, though they all have advanced self-exculpatory reasons for their behaviour. Ratu Mara justified his participation in the first coup administration on the grounds that his house was on fire and he had therefore no choice but to get involved to save his life's work, which led someone to quip that he should have in that case joined the firefighters and not the arsonists. No direct evidence has linked him to the pre-coup machinations, although Rabuka remembers mentioning to the former prime minister the scenario he had in mind during a game of golf.[15] The overwhelming impression in Fiji is that Ratu Mara was not directly involved, but that it is inconceivable that a politician of his experience and contacts did not know what was in the offing. There is also a deep sense of disappointment on all sides that Mara did not do more to save the fledgling democracy at the moment of its greatest crisis. Other observers implicate Ratu Sir Penaia Ganilau, Rabuka's paramount chief, of being aware of what was about to take place. There is little doubt that Ganilau had emotional sympathy with the purported aims of the coup,[16] but whether he sanctioned it is impossible to determine. For his part, Rabuka has never implicated Ganilau.

Rabuka himself, in 1987 a lieutenant colonel and the third ranking officer in the Fiji military, captured the limelight and provided a host of self-serving reasons as to why he had executed the coup. Above all, he claimed it was the interest of law and order and in the national interest of Fiji. He portrayed himself as the humble servant of the Fijian cause. He talked at length in his first authorised biography (see Dean and Ritova 1988) about his loyalty and devotion to chiefs but then showed no hesitation in usurping their authority when they stood in his way. He executed the second coup in September, undermining the Deuba Accord that the Coalition and the Alliance had signed to lead Fiji back to democracy. He continued to talk about his love for the army but then refused to retreat to the barracks. He assured the Indo-Fijians that he would look after their welfare but suggested they might be better off converting to Christianity. The saga of confusion and contradiction went on. Rabuka sought, to some degree convincingly, to portray himself as the champion of Fijian rights, but few believed—or believe—that he had carried out the coup all on his own, without the prior knowledge of important sections of the Fijian society.

Two weeks after the coup, Ratu Penaia Ganilau appointed a council of advisors to assist him to restore normalcy to Fiji. Fourteen of the 18 members of the Council were personally endorsed by Rabuka; only two its members were from the coalition—Timoci Bavadra and Harish Sharma. Critics accused Ganilau of putting in place a process designed to 'realise the aims of the coup' through legal means. In July, Ganilau appointed a constitution review committee to conduct public hearings throughout the country to gauge public opinion on how best to achieve the goal of strengthening 'the political rights of the indigenous Fijians'. Despite deep reservations, the Coalition agreed to participate in the committee.

The views expressed to the committee were predictable. Most in the Indo-Fijian community opposed any change to the 1970 constitution without full national debate. The only exception was the Fiji Muslim League, which generally supported the Fijian position on constitutional matters. The Coalition argued that the incumbent political system was

…just, fair and equitable. The system has withstood the test of time and has become accepted by the majority of the citizens of this country. It protects the special interests of the indigenous Fijians through special provisions of power of veto by the nominees of the GCC [Great Council of Chiefs]. To devise changes to the existing constitution on the basis of the preponderance of any particular race must in the end be harmful to race relations as it would enhance polarisation of our communities along racial lines. It will also disturb the power in the current constitution. This could lead to loss of confidence in the long-term stability of the country to what has been evidenced since the coup.[17]

Views varied among indigenous Fijians, but on the whole there was enthusiastic support for the coup and for the recognition of nationalist Fijian aspirations. Most Fijian individuals and groups who appeared before the committee wanted Fijians to be in control. The various strands of Fijian thinking were encapsulated in the submission of the Great Council of Chiefs. Its constitutional review committee, headed by Ratu Mara and Rabuka, demanded that Fiji be made a Christian state, departing from the sectarian principles of the 1970 constitution. The constitution, the Great Council of Chiefs argued, should expressly incorporate provisions for preferential treatment and affirmative action for Fijians in public offices, statutory bodies and even private companies. It suggested the abolition of the Senate and the creation of a 71-member House of Representatives with 40 Fijians (28 of whom were to be nominated by the Provincial Councils, 8 nominated by the Great Council of Chiefs and 4 nominated by the prime minister; 22 Indo-Fijians, 8 general electors and one Rotuman nominated by the Council of Rotuma. Four of the 22 Indo-Fijian seats were to be reserved for Muslims. Apart from demanding Fijian numerical dominance in parliament, the Great Council of Chiefs also wanted certain positions reserved for Fijians, including the offices of prime minister, and ministries of Fijian affairs, agriculture, home affairs, finance and industry. The commander of the Fiji military forces would always be a Fijian, as would be the Commissioner of Police, the chairman of the Public Service Commission and secretary to cabinet.

With the Great Council of Chiefs and the Coalition espousing diametrically opposed views about the best constitutional arrangements for Fiji, it was a foregone conclusion that the constitution review committee's report would be a divided one. And it was. With his plans to return Fiji to normalcy in disarray, Ganilau set in motion a fresh proposal to move the country forward. He appointed a politically balanced council of advisors to help him usher in an interim administration under his control, among whose tasks would be to lay the ground work for a new constitution. His proposal, which came to be known as the 'Deuba Accord'—after the location where it was formally negotiated—was about to be enacted into legislation when Rabuka executed the second coup on 25 September.

Rabuka was not party to the negotiations. His exclusion from the talks was an error of judgement on the part of Coalition politicians. It is tantalising to ask what sort of future of Fiji might have had had he been present. Rabuka might not have accepted the inclusion of Indo-Fijian Coalition members in the caretaker administration. But seeing Bavadra, Mara and Ganilau on the same side might have dissuaded him from the route he subsequently took on 7 October when he unilaterally declared Fiji a republic. On 9 October, Rabuka swore in a Military Administration consisting of Fijian nationalists and members of the Taukei Movement.

The Military Administration was in power from October to December. It was a period of wanton disregard for human rights and rampant racial extremism. Coalition leaders were harassed and some were put in prison. A series of decrees curtailed the freedom of speech and movement. All political activity was banned, and a strict observance of the Sabbath enforced. Civil servants could be dismissed on the grounds of 'public interest'. Making matters worse for the administration was a rapidly deteriorating economy. The rising cost of living, the increasing inflation, a compulsory 25 per cent salary cut for all public servants at a time when the Fijian dollar had already been devalued by 35 per cent compounded the misery. Projects soon to be started were put on hold, and foreign and local investors eyed their prospects warily. International condemnation was unsparing. Ratu Mara correctly surmised that unless the economy were revived, Fiji would face bankruptcy by the end of the year.

With the military administration in disarray, Rabuka was persuaded to hand power back to his chiefs. He did so but not before a number of his prior conditions were met. No Coalition member was to be included into the new cabinet, and military representation in the new administration had to be guaranteed. Mara and Ganilau accepted the preconditions. With details out of the way, Rabuka formally approached Ganilau to accept the presidency of the new Republic of Fiji, which he did on 5 December. The following day, Ganilau told the nation that 'the future protection of the indigenous Fijian interests is in safe hands'.

Mara accepted his appointment as prime minister with 'honour and pride', telling his people that they had nothing to fear from his administration. With Ganilau and Mara back in office, one chapter in Fiji's recent past had closed, and another was about to open.

## Notes

1   The Tripartite Forum—composed of the Fiji Trade Union Congress, Fiji Employees Consultative Association, and the government—was formed in 1976 to reach 'common understanding [on issues] which affect national interest such as industrial relations, job creation, greater flow of investment and general social and economic development of the country'.

2   The full manifesto is reprinted in Lal 1986.

3   The manifesto was largely the handiwork of Shardha Nand.

4   A typescript of the address is in the author's possession.

5   Quote from a typescript of the concluding address in the author's possession.

6   Quote from the opening campaign address, a copy is in the author's possession.

7   For an introduction to Bavadra's life, see Bain and Baba 1990.

8   From his closing campaign address.

9   These figures are derived from a report prepared by the Fijian Affairs Board and presented to the Great Council of Chiefs at their 1986 Somosomo meeting.

10   Bavadra's speech, First Annual Convention of the Fiji Labour Party, Lautoka, 19 July 1986. Similar sentiments about the NLTB were expressed throughout the campaign.

11   For a discussion of the problems of Fijian Administration in the 1960s, see Lasaqa 1984.

12   Bavadra's speech, First Annual Convention of the Fiji Labour Party, Lautoka, 19 July 1986.

13   Coalition Foreign Minister Krishna Datt told General Vernon Walters that his government was re-examining its stance on the nuclear issue.

14   For an early literature review, see Lal and Peacock 1990.

15   For Rabuka's version, see his authorised biography (Sharpham 2000).

16   Though less politically ambitious than Ratu Mara, Ratu Penaia Ganilau was nonetheless a staunch Fijian nationalist, as seen from his speeches and statements in the 1960s.

17   The quote is from a transcript of the Coalition's submission to the Constitution Review Committee, as cited in Lal 1988.

# 4

# Back from the abyss
# 1992

Fiji's 1992 election was an important and welcome development, marking Fiji's first tentative steps toward restoring parliamentary democracy and international respectability, and replacing rule by decree with rule by constitutional law. The elections were held under a constitution rejected by half the population and severely criticised by the international community for its racially discriminatory, anti-democratic provisions. Indigenous political solidarity, assiduously promoted since the coups, disintegrated in the face of election-related tensions. A chief-sponsored political party won 30 of the 37 Fijian seats in the 70-seat House of Representatives, and was able to form a government only in coalition with other parties. Sitiveni Rabuka, the self-confessed reluctant politician, became prime minister after gaining the support of the Fiji Labour Party—which he had overthrown in 1987—and despite the opposition of his predecessor and paramount chief of Lau, Ratu Sir Kamisese Mara. In a further irony, a constitutional system intended to entrench the interests of Fijian chiefs placed a commoner at the national helm. On the other side of the political divide, the triumphant 1987 coalition of the National Federation Party and Fiji Labour Party disintegrated in the weeks before the elections, split over the best strategy to restore Fiji to genuine parliamentary democracy.

Fiji had been run by an interim administration since Rabuka relinquished power to his paramount chief and former governor general, Ratu Sir Penaia Ganilau, who in turn invited Ratu Sir Kamisese Mara to form an interim government that ruled Fiji from December 1987 to May 1992. The Mara administration was confronted by an array of problems, two of which required immediate attention. One was resuscitating an economy shattered by reduced investor confidence, the haemorrhaging of skilled personnel from the public sector, the flight of capital, the interruptions in the sugarcane harvest, and the severe downturn in the tourist industry. The other was the restoration of the country to at least a semblance of civilian rule through the promulgation of a constitution that realised the publicly stated aims of the coups while maintaining the symbolic paraphernalia of parliamentary democracy. To those tasks, Mara and his ministers dedicated most of their efforts.

On the economic front, the interim administration initiated policies that promised to chart a radically different path for Fiji's economic future (Elek and Hill 1991; Stratton and McGregor 1991). Led by Finance Minister Josefata Kamikamica, it attempted to develop commercial links with ASEAN countries, in part to lessen traditional dependence on trade with Australia and New Zealand, whose criticism of the coups had angered the Fijian leaders (Sutherland 1989). This effort bore some fruit as Japanese, Korean, Malaysian and Taiwanese companies invested in tourism, agriculture and other primary production.

The government also began deregulating the economy and eliminating Fiji's import-substitution policies. It started a tax-free zone under which companies exporting 90 per cent or more of their products would be granted tax holidays for up to 13 years and would be exempt from customs duties on imported equipment and production materials. By 1991, more than 300 companies had invested a total of F$102 million, and another 100 were approved.[1] The tax-free base was extended beyond the garment industry, where it had received its initial and greatest success, to include timber processing for furniture and fittings and manufacturing of light technical equipment (*Pacific Report*, 25 July 1991). Critics complained about the unequal distribution of income generated by the new industries and about sweatshop conditions (Barr 1990), but the scheme had improved Fiji's balance of payments and provided much-needed local employment.

These new economic programs required strict regulation of the labour market and a corresponding reduction in the power of trade unions, which were prohibited in the tax-free zones. The trade union movement was the backbone of the Fiji Labour Party and a continuing source of irritation to the government (Slatter 1989). In May 1991, the government enacted a series of repressive labour laws intended to control the trade unions, but officially justified in the name of improving the country's international competitiveness and internal economic flexibility. The new decrees enabled the prosecution of trade unions for damages arising from 'unlawful' trade disputes; introduced company-based unions; amended the Trades Disputes Act to include other forms of industrial action such as go-slow, work-to-rule, and the withdrawal of goodwill; provided for the use of postal or workplace ballots for the election of union officials; and abolished minimum-wage councils. In retaliation, the Fiji Trades Union Congress, with 25 trade unions and 45 per cent of Fiji's full-time workers among its members, threatened a massive strike. This was averted when the government retracted the decrees (*Islands Business*, June 1991).

The scene was also set for confrontation in the sugar industry. Dispute there centred on two issues. One was the farmers' demand for a full forecast price of cane of F$43.70 per tonne, and not the F$34.96 offered by the Fiji Sugar Corporation—a reduction it justified in the name of falling international prices, bad weather, increased costs of production and harvest delays (*Pacific Report*, 30 May 1991). The other was the farmers' demand for prompt elections, postponed since 1987, for the Sugar Cane Growers' Council. When their demands were refused, the farmers threatened a strike, whereupon the government passed decrees declaring the sugar industry an essential service and proposed 14-year jail sentences and fines up to F$14,000 for anyone interrupting the running of the industry. Once again the government backed down when faced with further industrial action. Nonetheless, the imminent confrontation between the government and the farmers sowed the seeds of bitterness and distrust that resurfaced later in the political arena.

One beneficiary of the disputes in the sugar industry was the National Farmers' Union, formed in the 1980s—the brainchild of the trade unionist Mahendra Chaudhry, finance minister in the Bavadra government. The Union's success helped to undermine the influence of its much older rivals, the Kisan Sangh and the Federation of Cane Growers. When elections were held for the Sugar Cane Growers' Council early in 1992, the National

Farmers' Union won a majority of the seats. It became, in effect, the Fiji Labour Party's rural arm and the main reason for Labour's electoral victory in the cane belts in the 1992 elections. Chaudhry, too, gained in stature (or notoriety). The National Farmers' Union had enabled him to extend his power base beyond his urban trade union base, and he used his new connections to great political advantage (*Islands Business*, June 1991).

Another unexpected winner from the post-coup industrial tremors was Sitiveni Rabuka, who distanced himself from the interim administration's policies to create a niche for himself as a moderate consensus builder. In the nurses' strike and the long-festering Vatukoula gold mine strike, for example, he sympathised with the strikers. He went further. In June 1991, he said that Mara's administration 'had got their industrial policies wrong, and ought to resign...This government is a reactionary government', said Rabuka, 'made up of overpaid people who sit on their laurels and wait for something to happen before they react'. He even threatened to 'repossess' the power he had vested in the president (*Fiji Times*, 8 June 1991). A few days later he apologised to the government for this blistering criticism, and for 'insulting' his paramount chiefs. Even more incredibly, he joined Mara's cabinet as deputy prime minister. One interpretation of this development was that he had been co-opted, and thus marginalised, by Mara. Nonetheless, Rabuka had signalled his independence. This, together with the government's confrontational industrial policies, was an important reason why, after the 1992 elections, he was able to get Labour's support in his bid to become prime minister.

## Constitution

Several attempts soon after the 1987 coups to produce a broadly acceptable constitution had failed. Then, in October 1988, the interim administration appointed the Constitution Inquiry and Advisory Committee to produce a constitution 'having regard in particular to the failure of the 1970 Constitution to provide adequate and full protection of the rights, interests and concerns of the indigenous Fijian people, and having regard to the all the circumstances prevailing in Fiji' (Fiji Constitution Inquiry and Advisory Committee 1998). The loaded terms of reference—how was it determined that the 1970 constitution had failed and by whom?—needed little comment. The coup leaders were described by the committee as 'members of the security forces who assisted in the change of government in 1987'. The committee presented its report early in 1990, and a new constitution was promulgated by the president in July of that year.

The new constitution provided for an executive presidency and a bicameral legislature consisting of an appointed Upper House, the Senate, and an elected Lower House, the House of Representatives. The president, always to be a Fijian chief, was to be appointed by the *Bose Levu Vakaturaga* or Great Council of Chiefs and responsible to that body alone in the exercise of the powers of office. These were considerable, including appointing the prime minister (again, always to be a Fijian) and members of the president's advisory council, and presiding over other important functions of the state.

The Senate consisted of 34 appointed members, 24 nominated by the Council of Chiefs and the remaining 10 by the president. The council's senators retained the power of veto over all legislation that impinged on Fijian interests, including land and traditional customs. Given their strength in the Senate, they could, if they wished, frustrate the legislative efforts of any government, even one dominated by Fijians. In effect, the chiefs and their nominees in the Senate enjoyed untrammelled powers to control the legislative agenda.

The elected House of Representatives consisted of 70 members, of whom 37 were indigenous Fijians, 27 Indo-Fijians, and 10 'others'. Here, the new constitution differed from the old one, which had established parity between the two major ethnic groups, then roughly equal in numbers. In another major change, all the members were to be elected on purely racial rolls, with Fijians voting only for Fijians, Indo-Fijians only for Indo-Fijians, and others (Chinese, Europeans and part-Europeans, Pacific Islanders) voting only for their ethnic candidates (the 1970 constitution provided for half the parliamentary seats to be elected from multiracial constituencies). The racially based rolls left little opportunity or incentive for multiracial politics, and they discouraged the adoption of more broadly based political platforms that transcended racial and parochial concerns. There was no practical advantage in a multiracial philosophy, as was painfully evident in the 1992 elections.

Of the 37 Fijian seats, 32 were to be elected from the rural constituencies and the remaining 5 from urban ones. The allocation of seats became an issue. Why, argued many, should the province of Ba, for instance, with more than 55,000 ethnic Fijians, have the same number of seats, three, as Lau, with a population of 14,000? Why should Rewa, with 48,000 Fijians, get two seats while Cakaudrove, with 29,000, got three? Why indeed? And why should urban Fijians, who made up more than one-third of the Fijian population, have only five seats? The main reason for this gross malapportionment was to reduce the voting strength of the urban Fijians whose support, however small, for the Labour Party had contributed to its 1987 victory. It was also part of the larger effort to preserve the Fijian *status quo*.

The constitution thus became a major issue before and during the elections. Most Fijians appeared to support it and to welcome the dominant voice it gave them, although many from western Viti Levu questioned their electoral under-representation and the rejection of their claim for a separate confederacy, the *Yasayasa Vaka Ra*, to complement the existing three (the Tovata, the Burebasaga and the Kubuna) and give them a national voice commensurate with their numbers and contribution to the national economy. In a submission to the Constitution Inquiry and Advisory Committee, a twelve-member delegation of western Fijians criticised the constitution for discriminating 'against the progressively productive, better educated, forward-thinking Fiji citizens of all races in favour of that minority segment of the community that represents (and seeks to reserve for itself) the aristocratic, undemocratic, privileged pattern of colonial life' (cited in Sutherland 1992:190). Their protests went unheard, but were voiced again in the elections. The Coalition (of the National Federation Party and the Fiji Labour Party) rejected the constitution too, denouncing it as racist, feudalistic, undemocratic and authoritarian, and promised an international campaign to overturn it. The difference of opinion within the Coalition on how best to achieve this goal led to its collapse.

## Conflict in the Fijian camp

With the constitution formally promulgated in July 1990, the Council of Chiefs launched a new political party that it hoped would unite the people under one umbrella, in the manner of the Fijian Administration of colonial days. Thus united, the chiefs hoped, the Soqosoqo ni Vakavulewa ni Taukei (SVT, or Fijian Political Party) would lead the Fijian people to electoral victory and fulfil the aims of the coup. The reality turned out to be different. Even as the party was being launched, some Fijian leaders questioned the wisdom of the Council of Chiefs, as a formal non-political body, sponsoring a political party. One critic was Apisai Tora, who wanted the chiefs to remain above the fray of ordinary politicking. What would happen to the dignity of the council if it failed to capture all the Fijian seats? 'Our firm view', he said, 'remains that the *Bose Levu Vakaturaga* should be at the pinnacle of Fijian society, totally removed from the taint of ordinary politicking' (*Fiji Times*, 10 October 1991).

Such views went unheeded, paving the way for further problems. The first of these emerged over the election of the president of the Fijian Political Party. Many Fijians wanted a non-political chief, chosen through consensus, to lead the party and provide it with a semblance of impartial traditional authority. Once again, the reality turned out to be different. There were three contenders for the presidency: Ratu William Toganivalu, a high chief of Bau; Lady Lala Mara, the paramount chief of Burebasaga and Ratu Mara's wife; and Sitiveni Rabuka. To the surprise of many and the consternation of others, Rabuka defeated the chiefs, winning 9 of the 19 ballots of the Management Committee of the Fijian Political Party, while Lala Mara got 6 votes and Toganivalu 4. This stunning result intrigued many Fijians, including the Fijian Nationalist Party leader Sakiasi Butadroka, who remarked: 'if the SVT delegates can put a commoner before a chief, then I don't understand why the Great Council of Chiefs is backing the SVT…I don't know why a chiefs-backed party can do such a thing', he said, 'putting a chief—in this case the highest ranking chief, Ro Lady Lala—before a selection panel' (*Fiji Times*, 4 November 1991).

Rabuka's ascendancy troubled many Fijians, including some of his former (but now disenchanted) supporters, who had expected him to fade away after the coup. Among the reasons for their disenchantment were his mercurial character and bursts of sharp criticism of Mara's administration. His aggressive pursuit of political power disturbed them, as Rabuka made no secret of his ambition to become prime minister. He demanded complete loyalty from his colleagues and saw his election to the presidency of the Fijian Political Party as bringing him a step closer to the top job (*Fiji Times*, 1 November 1991). Other aspirants disagreed, citing the constitutional provision that the appointment of prime minister was the prerogative of the president, to be exercised in independent deliberate judgment.

As he manoeuvred for the prime ministership, Rabuka began to develop ideological justifications for his ambitions. Although still proclaiming himself a loyal commoner, he wondered whether it was appropriate for chiefs to involve themselves in the cut and thrust of electoral politics. Their proper role was at the local village level, because 'when it comes to politics, the chiefs do not have the mandate of the people' (*The Age*, 17 August 1991). To underscore his point, he stressed that 'there are a lot of capable commoners who can play a very, very important role in the Fiji of the next decade' (*Islands Business*, July 1991). Implicitly, he counted himself among them. He also noted that 'the dominance of customary chiefs in government is coming to an end' and soon 'aristocracy' would be replaced by 'meritocracy' (*Fiji Times*, 29 August 1991). None too subtly, he was invoking the 'Melanesian' model of achieved leadership against the 'Polynesian' model of ascribed leadership. He compared his paramount chiefs—he had Mara in mind—to the towering banyan tree 'where you don't see anything growing', and suggested that they should step aside (*Pacific Islands Monthly*, August 1991). No one was indispensable, he said, and 'those defeated in elections should take it in their political stride, accept defeat and move out gracefully' (*Fiji Times*, 1 November 1991).

Ratu Mara, the intended target of Rabuka's barb, was among those disturbed by Rabuka's strident ascendancy. He thought Rabuka an 'angry young man', a naive soldier, erratic, 'speaking off the cuff in any instigation', and implicitly unworthy to be his successor (*Matangi Tonga*, November 1991). The Fijian Political Party under Rabuka's leadership was a 'debacle', 'an organisation in disarray', Mara reportedly told his political intimates (*Washington Pacific Report*, 5 March 1991). Rabuka retaliated, calling Mara a 'ruthless politician who has been allowed to get away with a lot. Maybe it's because of the Fijian culture that he is a big chief and because he was groomed well by the colonial government' (*Daily Post*, 11 December 1991). Early in 1992, Mara encouraged the formation of an informal 'Diners' Club' in which he shared his experiences with a select number of prominent and aspiring Fijian leaders. Rabuka was not among them. Mara went further and backed Josefata Kamikamica as his preferred successor. The rupture between Mara and Rabuka was complete; yet they were more alike in autocratic temperament and in their fatalistic approach to their public roles than they care to acknowledge.

Tensions within the Fijian Political Party erupted openly when candidates were selected for the 1992 elections. In province after province aspiring candidates questioned the selection procedures, threatened to stand as independents, and sometimes formed their own parties even as they pledged their loyalty to the chiefs. In Macuata, the situation had so deteriorated that it required Rabuka's personal intervention. Here, first ballot choices had to be discarded to accommodate rebellious would-be independents. One of the stranger ironies of the selection process was that some of the most ardent supporters of the coup missed out altogether. Many of them became bitter critics of Rabuka. Rabuka also had to contend with new Fijian political parties that challenged the authority and legitimacy of the Fijian Political Party. There was Sakiasi Butadroka's Fijian Nationalist Party, revamped and renamed the Fijian Christian Nationalist Party in 1991. Characteristically anti-Indian, Butadroka called for more balanced development in the Fiji provinces; decentralisation of the Ministry of Fijian Affairs; reversion of all fee-simple and Crown lands to their native owners; complete Fijian ownership of all rents from the exploitation of mineral and natural resources; reactivation of traditional, rural administrative structures; support for a fourth confederacy and the rotation of the presidency among all of them; and an all-Fijian parliament within 10 years, in recognition of the Fijian people's 'full authority and absolute power'. [2] In April 1992, Butadroka joined forces with Ratu Osea Gavidi's newly formed, Nadroga-based, Soqosoqo ni Taukei ni Vanua (STV, Party of the People of the Land), which was essentially a revival of the long-dormant Western United Front.

This coalition's rival for support among Fijians outside the Fijian Political Party generally (and in western Viti Levu in particular), was Apisai Tora's All Nationals Congress, launched on 22 June 1991. Tora, the cigar-chomping, self-styled Fidel Castro of the Pacific, militant trade unionist of the 1960s turned ethnic chauvinist of the 1980s, was the quintessential survivor of Fiji politics. Once a member of the Indian-based National Federation Party, he joined the Alliance Party in the late 1970s and was rewarded with a cabinet portfolio. After the Labour Coalition's victory in 1987, he helped found the Taukei Movement, and was a member of the various post-coup cabinets until forced out by Mara when he, Tora, founded the All Nationals Congress.

This party presented itself as a moderate, multiracial successor to the defunct Alliance Party, which had ruled Fiji for nearly two decades. It committed itself to rethinking the interim administration's social, economic and industrial policies, promoting regional development to favour economically depressed provinces, reviewing such statutory organisations as the Native Land Trust Board and, most importantly, the constitution. The anti-eastern Fijian sentiment was there, too, as Tora made 'no secret of his desire to end the political dominance of eastern Fijians, as represented by Ratu Mara and Ganilau' (*Islands Business*, October 1991). Tora remained a steadfast advocate of the fourth confederacy, and presented himself as a progressive—an agent of change (*Pacific Islands Monthly*, July 1991). Tora, Butadroka and leaders of a few ephemeral parties that disappeared just as soon as they were launched came from different ideological backgrounds and had diverse political agendas. What they all shared was an unmistakable hostility toward the hegemony of eastern Fijians and toward the Fijian Political Party, which they saw as Mara's instrument.

On the eve of the election the Fijians seemed less united than ever before. Rabuka's leadership of the Fijian Political Party and his prime ministerial aspirations were contested. Triumphant post-coup Fijian nationalism was in danger of derailment. The removal of the perceived threat of Indian dominance that had distorted political discourse in Fiji for so long had allowed further discussion of internal Fijian issues that had long remained hidden from the non-Fijian public. As one *Fiji Times* editorial put it, 'the Fijians are now facing so many issues that challenge the very fabric of traditional and customary life. Things they thought were sacred have become political topics, publicly debated, scrutinised and ridiculed'. 'Now', the editorial continued, 'the threat is coming from within their own communities where the politics of numbers are changing loyalties and alliances. For the first time in modern history, the Fijian community is in danger of fragmentation; democracy is taking its toll. The chiefs are losing their mana and politicians enjoy increasing influence' (*Fiji Times*, 21 March 1991).

## Coalition in disarray

Fortunately for Rabuka and others in the Fijian camp, things were little better on the Coalition side, where internal divisions and differences over strategy proved even more irreconcilable and destructive. The coalition between the National Federation Party and the Fiji Labour Party had fallen on hard times. It had become a moribund marriage of convenience marooned in the shallows. Its unity, evident following the coups, had been subsumed by personal leadership ambitions, following the death of Timoci Bavadra in 1989, and shattered by deep differences over strategy. The Coalition had denounced the new constitution vehemently, but the partners disagreed over how best to work for its repeal. Should they participate in the elections and initiate a dialogue with the new government in parliament, or should they boycott the elections and rely on international pressure to effect the necessary changes?

The National Federation Party, led by its former parliamentary leader Jai Ram Reddy, decided in late July 1991 against the boycott option, choosing to participate in the elections under protest. Several considerations informed this decision. The party leaders realised that international pressure, by which the Fiji Labour Party placed much store, would be to no avail, and that in the end the Indo-Fijian leaders would have to deal with the elected representatives of the Fijian people. Only if the Fijian leaders rejected dialogue and refused to consider issues of concern to them would the National Federation Party use the boycott weapon. Participation in the election did not mean acceptance of the constitution. 'If you get elected and do nothing, then you are accepting it', said Reddy. 'If at every single opportunity, you raise your voice, and if need be, walk out of the House: that is not accepting the constitution' (*Fiji Times*, 28 August 1991).

The NFP leaders also realised that a boycott would be doomed to fail as many Indo-Fijians would stand for election anyway, and present themselves as leaders of their people. Indeed, small anti-Coalition, pro-

87

election Indo-Fijian political parties had already begun to emerge, among them the Fiji Indian Congress and the Fiji Indian Liberal Party. Participation under protest was consistent with the National Federation Party's past history. In 1965, for instance, it had been unhappy with the outcome of the London constitutional conference, which favoured Europeans and Fijians, but had worked under the new constitution for two years before staging a boycott in 1967 and precipitating a by-election a year later. The NFP leaders also heeded the advice of leaders overseas that the boycott option should be the last resort (*Daily Post*, 19 May 1992). As for the FLP leaders, Reddy said: 'they are by nature negative and their language is boycott, strike, disrupt, destroy and wreck. They want to destroy everything in sight' (*Daily Post*, 11 May 1992).

The Fiji Labour Party disagreed. How could it participate in an election under a constitution it had roundly condemned as racist, authoritarian, undemocratic and feudalistic? To do so would accord legitimacy to that flawed document and undermine the party's credibility internationally. The Fiji Labour Party told visiting Australian Foreign Minister Gareth Evans in February 1992: 'we do not wish to be a party to an election that will not return Fiji to genuine democracy but instead entrench an authoritarian racist government similar to that of South Africa' (Fiji Labour Party Press Release, 4 February 1992). International pressure, the party believed, would force the government into a dialogue on the constitution. Said Navin Maharaj, its secretary general, 'nothing can be done by going into parliament and success can only come through international pressure, and that is what we intend to do' (*Daily Post*, 27 April 1992). 'Rabuka has explicitly told us that the Constitution cannot be changed and likewise the Soqosoqo ni Vakavulewa ni Taukei has not given any assurance of any change', said Mahendra Chaudhry. 'Do you think the coup-plotters carried out so much atrocities for the last five years just to change the constitution?' (*Daily Post*, 11 May 1992).

That was the Fiji Labour Party's public stance. In private, however, it was characteristically pursuing other options. While it would formally maintain its boycott stance, the party encouraged its indigenous Fijian members to forge a broad coalition with parties outside the Fijian Political Party, including the Fijian Nationalist Party and the All Nationals Congress, and even to contest election as independents. Such a move was, in fact, made in October 1991, and a 38-point joint platform was prepared. Among other items, it included the promotion of indigenous Fijian aspirations in accordance with international conventions; the creation of a fourth Fijian confederacy; the introduction of a national leadership code of conduct; the preservation 'of the dignity and integrity and independence of the *Bose Levu Vakaturaga* so that it is not manipulated to support the type of politics that diminishes people's respect for the chiefs'; condemnation of the anti-urban bias of the constitution; and an urgent review of the constitution to make it 'consistent with democratic principles, United Nations human rights conventions and Commonwealth statements of principles and thus enable Fiji to apply for membership of the commonwealth as soon as possible'.[3]

At first the prospects looked promising, but they fell apart when Butadroka had second thoughts about what the proposals would do to his own credibility. 'If there is any work done with the FLP, our image as a deeply-rooted Fijian party will be tarnished', he said. 'Either you come in as independent candidates on our party ticket or we stand as adversaries in the election'. Koresi Matatolu, the All Nationals Congress general secretary, laid down other preconditions. His party would join, he said, if Butadroka retracted his call to deport Indians from Fiji and if the Fiji Labour Party recognised the constitution. Talk of solidarity remained just talk.

The FLP leaders had also been seeking to merge the Fiji Labour Party and the National Federation Party into a single party (*Fiji Times*, 18 August 1991). Labour reminded the National Federation Party of its apparent commitment to a merger in the late 1980s, which the party disavowed. It rejected the merger option, too, in the interest of political survival. The coalition arrangement had worked well, said Reddy, and should continue. 'We can speak out without treading on each other's toes. In a merged party, I would be very unhappy if the party agreed to nationalisation. Then, we would project an image of division'. He went further: 'I am more and more intrigued, as time progresses, about the real motive behind this move. Is it unity or is it because the NFP has become too much of a nuisance for the Labour Party?' (*Fiji Times*, 21 August 1991).

Reddy and other NFP leaders were not the only ones opposed to the merger. Vocal opposition came also from some leading Fijian members of the Fiji Labour Party, among them Simione Durutalo, its founding vice president. He called the merger proposal a strategic mistake that would 'lock everybody back into pre-1987 voting patterns with people voting on racial lines rather than for parties', by once again raising the spectre of Indo-Fijian domination (*Fiji Times*, 16 August 1991). He went on that it would be far better for the Fiji Labour Party to prepare its groundwork and position itself for victory in the 1996 elections than attempt to win through a merger in 1992: 'then, if the military comes in, we will have the people's support'. The only way forward in Fiji politics, he said, was to 'democratise Fijian society'. 'The Fiji Labour Party is the only political party able to create an interethnic alliance that can simultaneously champion the Indo-Fijian interests for long-term political security as well as indigenous Fijian commoners' interests and aspirations for long-term economic security' (*Fiji Times*, 16 August 1991). Durutalo and others became disenchanted with the Fiji Labour Party when its leaders ignored their advice and refused to reconsider the party's boycott strategy. On the eve of the elections, some of them left the party or began to forge links with other Fijian parties.

In a last, almost desperate, attempt to maintain a facade of unity and to prevent a splitting of the Indo-Fijian community, the Fiji Labour Party offered not to disrupt the National Federation Party's election plans if it obtained the government's assurance that it would immediately address all issues of concern to the Coalition (foremost among them a review of the constitution). Without such assurance, the National Federation Party would boycott parliament. But if the government agreed to its demands, it would enter parliament and participate in deliberations 'only to the extent of giving effect to redressing those grievances'. Furthermore, the National Federation Party would 'consult with and obtain the agreement of FLP at all stages of the negotiation' (Fiji Labour Party Press Release, 30 April 1992).

It was a fantastic demand, which the National Federation Party could not accept 'without sacrificing for all time NFP's reputation and integrity'. One NFP leader likened the ultimatum to the extortionate demands of a tyrannical landlord. Perhaps the Fiji Labour Party did not really expect the National Federation Party to accept its conditions. Perhaps it wanted to use rejection as an excuse to participate in the elections, for by early

1992 the boycott option had become untenable and was being severely criticised throughout Fiji. Even its respected international advisers were of that mind. Among them was Professor Yash Ghai, who wrote

>...[i]t is possible to attack a Constitution and yet take part in the elections. But it is absolutely essential that the terms on which it [the party] takes part is made clear so that it [taking part] is not interpreted as an endorsement of the constitution. A party may wish to take part in the elections with a view to changing the constitution, or making the political system under it difficult to operate, or not letting its rivals dominate parliament and government. So while there may be a strong moral case for a boycott, it may occasionally make sense to take part in elections while simultaneously attacking the constitution. The really important question was not to boycott, but whether to endorse the constitution (*Fiji Times*, 7 May 1992).

Unable to coerce the National Federation Party into acquiescence, with its own house in disarray, public opinion heavily in favour of participating in the elections, and facing marginalisation because of the NFP's election decision, the Fiji Labour Party acknowledged the inevitable and late in April announced its decision to participate. By any measure, this was a stunning *volte face*. How did the Fiji Labour Party explain its new position? Said Navin Maharaj: 'it was only a change in strategy: from boycott of the election to boycott of parliament'. Why? 'The change came about because the NFP has no clear picture' (*Daily Post*, 11 May 1992). Its flip-flop left its supporters dismayed and uncertain. Amid acrimony and vacillation, the Coalition had collapsed.

The one major political party that was not as consumed by bitter internal divisions was the General Voters Party (GVP). It was in some ways a resurrection of the pre-coup General Electors' Association, which was a small but influential spoke in the Alliance Party wheel. The only difference now was that the general electorate had been widened to include not only part-Europeans, Chinese and people of mixed ancestry, but also other Fiji citizens of Pacific islands ancestry who, before the coup, were registered on the Fijian roll. Like the other ethnically based parties, the General Voters Party's concerns were parochial, focusing on the interests and aspirations of its own community. It proclaimed itself in favour of 'a system of democracy which incorporates the principle of guaranteed representation of major ethnic groups' in parliament, and opposed to 'any attempt to weaken or remove a legally established right to the existing ownership of land, whether native or freehold' (General

Voters Party manifesto). Large portions of freehold land in Fiji were owned by Europeans, and the five General Voters Party seats in parliament were grossly out of proportion to their numbers.

## The campaign

The campaign itself was much more subdued than in previous years. The interim administration's decree making libel a criminal offence punishable by up to two years imprisonment and a F$1,300 fine, together with the memory of the harassment of journalists since the coups, deterred the media from heavily scrutinising the election platforms and personalities. The racially segregated electoral system encouraged candidates to confine themselves to issues of particular concern to their ethnic communities, or, in the case of the Fijians, their provinces and regions. National, non-racial issues were present in the election platforms and in the campaign rhetoric, but were not given serious consideration.

Reddy, for example, talked of a government of national unity 'based on a formula of power-sharing which would ensure that every community is represented at the decision-making level' (*Daily Post*, 9 May 1992), but his proposal was ridiculed by the Labour Party, which said that such an arrangement would 'both implicitly and explicitly give credence and legitimacy to the decreed constitution', and reduce the National Federation Party to a 'subservient position...depending on the mercy of the Fijian side in parliament' (Fiji Labour Party Press Release, 11 May 1992). Ratu Mara and Ratu William Toganivalu attempted to distance themselves from the constitution they had generated, much to the annoyance of Rabuka and his allies. But for the most part such issues remained in the background. Instead, internal fighting in both camps dominated the news.

In the Fijian Political Party, the main question centred on who would be prime minister, Sitiveni Rabuka or Josevata Kamikamica. Sometimes the campaigns on behalf of the two men became unpleasant, even vicious. As was his wont, Rabuka changed his tune often, depending on his audience. To the fundamentalist members of the Methodist Church, he renewed his call to declare Fiji a Christian state and reimpose the Sabbath decree; from his militant nationalist supporters, he demanded complete loyalty and promised action, if needed, 'in order to complete what they started'; to the media and to his opponents, he was the very essence of good sense and moderation, talking of national reconciliation and dialogue ('what happened to the Pacific way?' he asked—without irony, so far as one could tell (*The Review*, May 1992)). For his part, Kamikamica, who was outwardly confident of his chances, highlighted his administrative experience, distanced himself from the extreme rhetoric of his more nationalist-minded compatriots, and promised to work toward genuine multiracialism.

In the former Coalition camp, the exchanges were equally pointed and unpleasant. Leaders exhumed each others' records of public service since the coups, ridiculed their personal commitments to Fiji—many of them had visas for permanent residence overseas—and traded insults, accusing each other of opportunism, arrogance and treachery. The vehemence of the attacks was especially surprising in view of the virtually identical platforms of the two political parties. The republic's first election campaign produced more heat than light, as the confused electorate pondered their limited choices.

Polling lasted a week. In the Fijian constituencies, the SVT won 30 of the 37 Fijian seats, the Fijian Nationalist Party 3, the Soqosoqo ni Taukei ni Vanua 2, and independents 2. The Fijian voter turnout averaged 78 per cent. A further breakdown of these figures reveals noteworthy trends. The SVT achieved its greatest triumph in the small eastern constituencies of the Koro Sea, getting 89.1 per cent of all votes cast (27,658). Accounting for its spectacular success was a well-organised campaign, and the undivided support of the provincial councils. In the urban constituencies, too, the party did relatively well, capturing 74.7 per cent of all the votes. Again a more effective campaign organisation and an attractive slate of candidates helped this party.

In the rural constituencies generally, however, the SVT did less well, winning only 63.3 per cent of all the rural votes (80,195). In rural Viti Levu, it won only 49.7 per cent of the total Fijian votes (52,538); the main reason for its modest showing there being the challenge of the other Fijian parties, especially the Fijian Nationalist Party and the Sogosoqo ni Taukei ni Vanua, which together won 26.5 per cent of all the Fijian votes. Butadroka, the Fijian Nationalist Party leader, was a well-known personality and a charismatic campaigner. His grassroots style of campaigning, and his uncomplicated political message laced with earthy humour, won him support, as it had done in previous elections. His running mate, Ratu Mosese Tuisawau, was a high chief of the Rewa province, appealed powerfully to the Rewans' sense of pride by demanding a greater Rewan voice in national Fijian affairs. One of the Fijian Nationalist Party's proposals was the rotation of the presidency among the four confederacies, with Rewa next in line. Ratu Osea Gavidi and his running mate, Mosese Tuisawau, campaigning under the banner of the Fijian Nationalist Party and the Soqosoqo ni Taukei ni Vanua, won the 2 Nadroga/Navosa seats, again by focusing on local issues.

The other major party that had threatened to erode support for the Fijian Political Party in Viti Levu was the All Nationals Congress. It did not win any seats, but only narrowly missed out in Ba where it managed to capture 5,775 votes; it gained 8,384 votes in rural Viti Levu as a whole (10.5 per cent of the Fijian votes cast). Why did the All Nationals Congress fail? Tora's own chequered political career was a factor, as was the fear among many Fijians that anything short of a clear victory for the Fijian Political Party could see Fiji facing more political upheaval (as Rabuka seemed to hint in his speeches).

Labour's dismal performance in the Fijian constituencies was not surprising. It was underfunded, underprepared and was late to enter the fray. Labour put up disenchanted candidates, who were merely expected to keep the party flag flying, in only a handful of constituencies. Disunity among its leaders did not help matters, nor did public criticism of the party's election strategy by some of its leading Fijian members, such as Simione Durutalo. Many Fijians who had joined the party in 1987 had left, including such luminaries as Joeli Kalou and Jo Nacola, both ministers in the Bavadra government—the former contesting the election on the SVT ticket and the latter as an independent. On the eve of the election, Labour had come to be regarded among many Fijians as an Indo-Fijian party.

Among the Indo-Fijians, where the voter turnout was 76.7 per cent, the results confounded all predictions. The National Federation Party, which had been widely expected to win nearly all the 27 Indo-Fijian seats, won only 14, the remaining 13 going to the Fiji Labour Party. Minor Indo-Fijian parties failed to make any mark. The National Federation Party won 50 per cent of the total Indo-Fijian votes cast

(114,005) and the Fiji Labour Party 47.6 per cent. A breakdown of the figures shows important trends. Labour won most of the seats in the cane belts of Fiji, whereas the National Federation Party, founded as a cane farmers' party in the early 1960s, achieved its greatest success in the urban areas, which should have been Labour's domain.

Labour's victory in the cane belt benefited from the success in the Sugar Cane Growers' Council of the National Farmers' Union, whose real leader, Mahendra Chaudhry, also led the Fiji Labour Party. In the countryside, Labour and the Farmers' Union were seen as one and the same. The National Federation Party had let the Fiji Labour Party claim public credit for the Coalition's role in resolving the dispute in the sugar industry, which Labour was now portraying as its own, rather than a joint, achievement. The National Federation Party was not helped by being portrayed as a party of the Indo-Fijian bourgeoisie. In urban areas, it was better funded, fielded better candidates and was able to benefit from bitter divisions within the ranks of the trade unions. Some of Chaudhry's harshest critics, such as trade union leader James Raman, were NFP candidates. Labour's victory was as unexpected as it was sweet. Its sharper message, better organisation, and strong support among Indo-Fijian voters for whom the National Federation Party's earlier anti-colonial struggles were a vague memory, had worked to Labour's advantage, ensuring its important role in the Indo-Fijian community for some time to come. The National Federation Party, on the other hand, is, and sees itself as, essentially a communal party, but the interests of Indo-Fijians are not as homogeneous as they once appeared to be. Its message was blurred, and its viability as a credible force is unclear.

## The race for prime minister

The race for prime minister started even before results were known, as leading candidates Rabuka and Kamikamica began to campaign for support among the opposition parties. The exact details and sequence of events in the hectic few days following the elections will probably never be fully revealed, but the basic outline is clear. As soon as the final results were announced, the parliamentary board of the Fijian Political Party met, on 31 May, to elect its leader, who would be its candidate for prime minister. At this meeting, Rabuka repeatedly won 18 votes, Kamikamica 2, Filipe Bole 4, and Ratu William Toganivalu 3. With his party's mandate, and with the Fijian Political Party lacking an outright majority to form a government, Rabuka began to explore a coalition with the General Voters Party (which had won all the five general seats), the Fijian Nationalist Party, the Soqosoqo ni Taukei ni Vanua, and the two independents. Again the details are unclear, though we do know from press statements that the General Voters Party opposed any coalition that included the Fijian Nationalist Party, whose extremist platforms it had denounced during the campaign. The General Voters Party preferred Kamikamica for the top job.

When Rabuka went to Government House on 1 June to be sworn in, claiming the support of 42 members of the House, President Ganilau told him to produce the signatures of all those who supported him before 10am the next day. The president, thought to be leaning in Kamikamica's direction, was aware of the split in the Fijian Political Party over the leadership and was mindful of Mara's preference. Equally, he was mindful of the constitutional requirement to appoint as prime minister the Fijian best able to command the majority support of all members in the House of Representatives, including the twenty-seven Indo-Fijian members.

Obtaining the signatures was not as easy as Rabuka might have supposed; by the time he returned from Government House, new tensions had arisen. Some Fijian members who had supported him initially opposed any formal association with the Fijian Nationalist Party and threatened to support his opponent. The situation was also complicated by the National Federation Party's public support for Kamikamica. Reddy had told Rabuka's emissaries that he could not support the major general, whom he did not and could not trust. He considered Kamikamica a safer bet as he had verbally assured the National Federation Party of his willingness to initiate immediate debate on the constitution. By late the same evening, Rabuka's fortunes were uncertain; by then, according to some sources, Kamikamica had secured the support of 30 parliamentarians (10 Fijian Political Party members, 1 Rotuman, 5 of the General Voters Party, and 14 from the National Federation Party), while Rabuka was supported by 29 from the Fijian Political Party, 5 Nationalists, and 2 Independent. Faced with this crisis, Rabuka's emissaries contacted the Fiji Labour Party in the early

hours of 2 June. Soon afterward that party wrote to Rabuka. Their historic
letter is reproduced here.

2 June 1992 (CONFIDENTIAL)
Major General Sitiveni Rabuka (Hand Delivered)
Dear Major General Sitiveni Rabuka
The Fiji Labour Party has agreed to lend support to you for the position of
Prime Minister on the basis that our party would be given firm assurance on the
following issues in writing:
A. CONSTITUTION
The new government would immediately initiate a process of review and change
of the 1990 Constitution by a jointly appointed team that would take into
regard the objections that have been expressed by the Fiji Labour Party on behalf
of the Indian community, urban Fijians and Western Fijians, and take
immediate measures to address such objections.
Such a process to be initiated as soon as parliament convenes.
B. LABOUR REFORM DECREES
That the new government would urgently seek to have the labour decrees
revoked to take account of the objections by the trade union movement in Fiji.
C: VAT (value-added tax)
That the new government would urgently scrap VAT as a matter of priority.
D: LAND
That the new government would convene a machinery to facilitate discussions
on the issue of land, particularly relating to the extension of ALTA [Agricultural
Landlord and Tenant Act]
That as soon as the parliament convenes, such a machinery be deliberated upon.
The Fiji Labour Party is awaiting your urgent and serious consideration of our
request.
Yours Sincerely Jokapeci Koroi (Mrs) (President)

Rabuka replied immediately

Mrs Jokapeci Koroi President
Fiji Labour Party Suva.
Dear Mrs Koroi,
I acknowledge the proposals outlined in your letter (2 June 1992) delivered this
morning.
I have considered your proposals favourably and agree to take action on all the
issues, namely the constitution, VAT, labour reforms and land tenure on the
basis suggested in your letter.
I agree to hold discussions on the above issue in order to finalise the machinery
to progress the matter further.
Yours Faithfully
S. L. Rabuka (Major) General President.

Significantly, the Fiji Labour Party also obtained an undertaking from the Fijian Nationalist Party and the Soqosoqo ni Taukei ni Vanua, which, according to some sources, had been instrumental in initiating the dialogue between Rabuka and Labour. These two parties' five parliamentarians (Butadroka, Gavidi, Lepani Tonitonivanua, Ratu Mosese Varasikete Tuisawau and Mosese Tuisawau), and the nationalist-minded independent, Kolonio Qiqiwaqa, wrote to the Labour Party: 'We give our assurance that should the President accept his nomination we will support your conditions as set out by the new Prime Minister'.

This stunning development left many in Fiji and outside gasping and shaking their heads in confusion. Labour supporting Rabuka? And the Nationalists agreeing with Labour's demands, among them the review of the constitution? Rabuka's courting of Labour's (or anyone else's) support is simply explained: he desperately needed the numbers Labour could deliver. Mahendra Chaudhry suggested that Labour supported Rabuka probably more for reasons of public consumption than out of genuine conviction; Rabuka was 'a changed man', who had admitted being used 'by certain chiefs' for their own purposes (*Fiji Times*, 2 June 1992). Moreover, Rabuka had been an ally in the resolution of the industrial disputes, whereas Kamikamica's policies had precipitated them. Some Labour leaders saw Kamikamica as a Mara 'puppet', and nothing was less acceptable to them than Mara's continuing influence, however indirect or slight that influence might be. Politics played its part too. By supporting Rabuka, and hence the next government, the Labour strategists hoped to deal a deathblow to the National Federation Party.

Some Labour leaders thought themselves the real winners in the 1992 elections. The party that had been given little chance of electoral success had managed to insert itself centrally into the national political process. Labour, they thought, would be the tail wagging the dog, or, as one of them said to me, while they could not be kings, they would be king-makers. Such euphoric thinking was short-lived, for, once installed, Rabuka went back to his old ways, changing his mind or denying the substance of the deals he had made. He refused to review the value-added tax, as he had promised, and he dismissed any urgency to review the constitution. Three months after the election, he said he wanted a constitution 'that's totally Fijian-oriented', and expressed sympathy for the Fijian Nationalist Party's wish to repatriate the Indo-Fijians to India (*Canberra Times*, 1 October 1992). In December, he mooted the idea of a government of national unity, with what seriousness and commitment remained to be seen. With his own support base to safeguard, and his public support among ordinary nationalist Fijians high, Rabuka was in no hurry to keep his promises. Promises, his utterances implied, were made to be broken.

Rabuka was sitting on the horns of a dilemma. Nationalist-minded Fijians would remind him of his oft-repeated promise to fulfil his stated goals of the coup, while Labour and others would hold him accountable for his promises to them to lead Fiji toward a more just society. Then there were people within his own party, with different allegiances and with personal ambitions, who regarded him as an unwelcome intruder, an illegitimate usurper of their own power. Clearly, Rabuka was in an unenviable position. Leading the Fijian ship of state through turbulent, uncharted waters would require vision, skill, tact and patience.

Rabuka, however, was not the only one who faced a dilemma. The Fijian people themselves were caught between the competing demands of two worlds, neither of which they could easily hope to escape. On the one hand was the call to retreat from the modern world, seek succour in traditional custom, and entrust power 'to a few well-meaning and knowledgeable people' because 'majority rule can turn into the rule of prejudice and the power of the many to violate the rights of the few' (Ravuvu 1980:x). On the other hand was the call by the Fijian Political Party, sponsored by the chiefs, to promote 'a more rapid movement from subsistence activities to commercial enterprises and paid employment...to encourage greater economic freedom and competition and allow world market forces to determine prices and production for export and local markets through an efficient and private enterprise sector' (Soqosoqo ni Vakavulewa ni Taukei Manifesto). There was a contradiction here that the elections, caught in the politics of race and regionalism, failed to address; it could not be ignored, or ignored at the peril of the people of Fiji.

## Notes

1   In May 1992 F$1.00 was equal to US$1.47.

2   From his manifesto, a copy of which is in the author's possession.

3   A copy of this document is in the author's possession. The quotes following are from the same document.

# 5
# Rabuka's republic

In February 1994, only 18 months after the first post-coup elections of 1992, Fiji went to the polls again. The snap election was called after the defeat of the government's budget in November 1993. Sitiveni Rabuka's opponents on the government benches hoped to use the election to oust him from office. They had miscalculated. Rabuka and his party, the Soqosoqo ni Vakavulewa ni Taukei (SVT), returned to power with 32 of the 37 seats reserved for ethnic Fijians under the 1990 constitution. A coalition government was formed with the General Voters Party (GVP), which won four of the five seats allocated to that community. On the Indo-Fijian side, the National Federation Party (NFP) increased its representation from 14 to 20 seats, while the Fiji Labour Party won the remaining seven.

His mandate seemingly secure and his personal popularity high, Rabuka was unanimously re-elected head of his party and reclaimed the prime minister's office.

In the previous chapter, we saw why, not having an outright majority of seats in parliament, the SVT was forced to seek the support of other parties. It managed to secure the support of Labour after Rabuka agreed to undertake a review of the constitution, resolve the land problem posed by the imminent expiry of leases under the Agricultural Landlord and Tenant Act, and re-examine the anti-labour legislation and the value-added tax enacted by the interim administration that had governed Fiji from 1987 to 1992. However, once ensconced, Rabuka reneged on the spirit of the agreement. The Labour Party could not continue to support a leader who procrastinated on his promises to them, nor could it withdraw its support without appearing petulant. With its plea for dialogue ignored, Labour abandoned Rabuka in June 1993 and its members walked out of parliament. By then the party's fortunes were floundering; its milestone decision to back Rabuka had become a millstone.

At the other end of the spectrum, Rabuka had to contend with the demands of Fijian nationalists, who held five seats. The Fijian nationalists had also supported him against Kamikamica. They wanted the government to honour its campaign commitment to 'realise the aims of the coup'; that is, to achieve the ideal of Fijian paramountcy. On a number of occasions, fringe elements of the movement took to the streets and threatened Rabuka with political reprisals, scorning his efforts to promote multiracialism. The nationalists could not be ignored, since they commanded substantial support in Viti Levu.

In May 1993, a group led by Sakiasi Butadroka and Ratu Osea Gavidi of the Fijian Nationalist United Front launched the Viti Levu Council of Chiefs, demanding recognition of the fourth confederacy, the Yasayasa Vaka Ra, and the rotation of the presidency among all four. They also demanded that the all non-native land be converted to native titles and landowners' interests be given priority in the exploitation of resources on their land (*Fiji Times*, 22 May 1993). The formation of the Viti Levu Council was the latest of many vain efforts by western Fijians to gain a voice commensurate with their numbers and contribution to the national economy. Like many previous efforts this too died a quiet, unmourned death.

Labour and the Fijian nationalists were not Rabuka's only problems. He had powerful dissident elements within his own party and in the Fijian establishment generally, who had never accepted him as a legitimate leader. The circumstances that brought him to power weighed against him. He was not forgiven for defeating the paramount chief of the Burebasaga confederacy, Adi Lala Mara, for the presidency of the SVT. Nor, especially, was he forgiven for his startling public criticism of Ratu Mara, calling him a *baka* (banyan) tree under which nothing grew—'a ruthless politician who has been allowed to get away with a lot', a man who had the temerity to criticise a constitution that had made him vice-president (*Pacific Islands Monthly*, August 1990; *Daily Post*, 11 December 1990). Nor, again, was Rabuka's expressed preference for basing social status on achievement rather than birth well received among chiefly Fijians.

For his part, Mara ridiculed Rabuka as an angry, simpleminded colonel. Mara said that Rabuka's rival, Kamikamica, 'will make a good prime minister' (*The Weekender*, 23 July 1993). Mara was also critical of Rabuka's stewardship of the SVT, blaming him indirectly for poor relations with the Great Council of Chiefs (*Islands Business*, February 1994). The tension between the two men was not surprising; they were similar in temperament: authoritarian, autocratic, emotional and convinced of their role as saviours of their people. Mara was also conscious of his chiefly role and responsibilities and seemed inclined to regard Rabuka as an upstart commoner. The pro-Mara faction of the SVT not only refused to join Rabuka's cabinet but also became vocal critics. Among them were Mara's son, Finau, and Kamikamica, who had refused the offer of a position in Rabuka's cabinet several times. In the Senate, Adi Finau Tabakaucoro, a minister in Mara's interim administration, championed the anti-Rabuka cause.

Rabuka's own conduct did not help his image or performance. His itinerant thoughts on sensitive subjects, and his tendency to think aloud on important policy matters bewildered his colleagues and left him open to public ridicule. His inexperience was apparent. According to critics, Rabuka did not behave in a manner befitting the dignity of the country's highest elected official. One Fijian observer articulated a widely held view that

> Rabuka is sometimes unpredictable, tends to be highly emotionally inclined and apparently tries to please everyone. Despite his most valiant efforts, the result of this is more often than not he winds up contradicting himself or his cabinet (*Islands Business*, June 1993).

Rabuka came across as a simple man with a decent heart who was locked in a military mind-set of command and obedience, albeit qualified by impulsiveness, and, at times, capriciousness. His openness, accessibility and eagerness to please, as well as his inability to discipline dissidents, contributed to his parliamentary downfall as much as the machinations of his opponents.

On winning office in 1992, the government faced two immediate tasks. One was to consolidate its position among the *taukei*, particularly among its potentially explosive nationalist fringe. The other was to improve the country's coup-scarred image internationally. The latter was relatively easy. Rabuka made state visits to Australia and New Zealand and represented Fiji at the South Pacific Forum in Honiara. Everywhere he maintained the appropriately low profile befitting a new leader. The visits were successful in restoring full diplomatic and defence links with Australia and New Zealand, and in reassuring friends in the region. Fiji was still out of the Commonwealth, although rejoining was a long-term goal of the Great Council of Chiefs. Older Fijians also wished to re-establish direct links with the British monarchy, but that was unlikely in the absence of a widely acceptable constitution.

Locally, Rabuka's performance was not as smooth. His power base within the SVT caucus and in the provinces was insecure. To consolidate it, he tried to co-opt potential opponents who had lost in the elections. Many were rewarded with seats in the Senate, diplomatic jobs or positions with statutory bodies. In cabinet and other appointments, Rabuka worked on the principle of provincial balance. Each province had to be represented in the cabinet and in the higher echelons of government. Indeed, when some members were demoted or dismissed for poor performance, they attacked the prime minister. Viliame Saulekaleka, dismissed assistant minister from Lau, Mara's province, accused Rabuka of being anti-Lauan (*Daily Post*, 30 October 1993). Ilai Kuli, mercurial sacked minister of posts and telecommunications, treated his dismissal as a betrayal of the people of Naitasiri. Bua threatened to block the opening of the F$10 million Nabouwalu Hospital if its representative in the cabinet, Koresi Matatolu, was removed (*Fiji Times*, 28 May 1993). Rabuka may have had his mandate, but he had to work with a team whose political loyalties were divided—and who had their own mandates.

In his first few months in office, Rabuka promulgated a number of pro-Fijian policies. The government announced that it would continue to support the special Fijian Education Unit established in the Ministry of Education to monitor the progress of students. The ministry also created special educational media centres in Fijian schools to improve the teaching of science. On the economic front, while continuing its privatisation policies, the government proposed measures to propel more Fijians into the commercial sector, where they were conspicuous by their absence. These included a small business agency to advise and train Fijians, providing loans to provincial councils to increase their shares in Fijian Holdings Limited, giving that investment company priority in buying shares from privatised government enterprises, and proposing income-tax exemption for Fijian-owned businesses for up to twenty years (*Fiji Times*, 27 August 1993). The government also set aside a fund worth F$2 million to provide interest-free loans payable over thirty years to certain *mataqali* to buy back freehold land (*Fiji Times*, 25 February 1993). Late in 1993, it announced the transfer of the administration of all Crown Schedule A and B lands from the Department of Lands to the Native Land Trust Board. Eventually, these lands would revert to native title.

Many of the government's pro-Fijian initiatives were cautiously supported by Indo-Fijian members of parliament, though Labour leader Mahendra Chaudhry asked the government to examine the fundamental reasons why Fijians were not succeeding in certain fields. 'There must be something wrong within the system itself that with all these resources, the results are not forthcoming' (*Islands Business*, August 1993). At the same time, they pointed out the blatant discrimination against their community in the public sector. The principle of balance had been ignored, said Chaudhry. Of 9,597 civil servants in 1992, 5,897 or 61.4 per cent were ethnic Fijians and only 3,186 or 33.2 per cent Indo-Fijians. On the boards of statutory organisations, the paucity of Indo-Fijians was glaring. For instance, there was not a single Indo-Fijian on the board of the Reserve Bank of Fiji, the Fiji Broadcasting Commission, or, incredibly, the Fiji Sugar Corporation. Opposition leader Jai Ram Reddy pleaded with the government for fairness and equity, but the government had no political incentive to address concerns of the non-Fijians. Consequently, Indo-Fijian disenchantment grew. Rabuka was indifferent.

No one felt more betrayed than the Fiji Labour Party, whose support had made Rabuka prime minister. The conditions for that support were not observed by the government. The 10 per cent value-added tax on most goods and services was retained as part of the government's progressive tax-reform package. The labour-reform legislation, whose ultimate intention was to cripple trade unions, was unenforced though it remained on the agenda. And though there was some talk, there was no action on the pressing issues surrounding the renewal of leases after the expiry of the Agricultural Landlord and Tenant Act. On his promise to initiate a review of the constitution, Rabuka retorted

[t]o review means to look at what has been done. It does not mean that we have committed ourselves to making any changes or abolitions (*Pacific Report*, 28 June 1993).

In fact, the government had committed itself to a review within five years but did not regard it as a matter of any urgency. Then, suddenly in December 1992, Rabuka mooted the idea of a government of national unity. Rabuka's proposal caught the country by surprise. The idea had a long history. Some form of coalition government was mentioned in the negotiations leading to independence, but nothing came of it. In 1977, the Alliance Party mooted the idea, only to withdraw it when the NFP criticised it as the party's effort to bolster its sagging image as a multiracial organisation. Rabuka's concept was equally vague and emotional (*Fiji Times*, 5 December 1992). In May 1993, Rabuka elaborated

[w]hat I and those who support my idea envisage is a style of government that brings the communities together, that enables all ethnic groups to cooperate jointly in the affairs of government and the work of legislature. I want the leaders of Fijian, Indian and general voters to define the middle ground, the political centre, where they can pool their wisdom and their abilities in the national interest. I want to see them united in pursuit of defined national objectives-objectives that serve the interests and welfare of us all, Fijians, Indians and general voters. In my vision of what I consider to be the ultimate good of the country, I see very clearly that it is in all our interest to develop a social and political partnership that transcends suspicion and distrust, that elevates us as a nation and gives us a combined sense of common destiny and purpose (*The Weekender*, 21 May 1993).

This statement was hailed as a major declaration by the government, though, in truth, it was much the same as what Rabuka had stated in 1990.

I would like to have a government of national reconstruction. First we look at what Fiji needs first. You won your seats on these policies, we won our seats on these policies. You have extreme left views. We have extreme right wing views. Let's forget about these extremities where they sort of merge. That's where we run Fiji for the next five years (*Pacific Islands Monthly*, August 1990).

Rabuka's national unity government would have eighteen cabinet members, twelve from the ruling all-Fijian SVT, two each from NFP and

Labour, and one each from the Nationalists and the GVP. In this respect, Rabuka's offer differed little from the Alliance Party's offer in 1977.

Rabuka's proposal received a mixed response. The SVT caucus complained of not being consulted. The Fijian nationalists supported the concept, but only on condition that their program for Fijian supremacy 'will still be maintained through the government of national unity' (*Fiji Times*, 11 December 1990). A faction of the Taukei Movement urged all Fijian members of parliament to 'completely reject and throw out of the window with precipated [sic] haste the devilish concept of government of national unity' (*Fiji Times*, 22 December 1992). They postponed their protest marches only when Rabuka assured them that promoting national unity should never be misinterpreted or misconstrued by anyone to mean that he and his government were giving away the special position conferred on the Fijians and Rotumans, as the host communities in Fiji, under the 1990 constitution (*Fiji Times*, 19 February 1993).

Many in the opposition treated Rabuka's proposal cynically. Labour's Simione Durutalo argued that the unity proposal was nothing more than an attempt 'to repackage his 1987 image of an anti-Indian' (*Fiji Times*, 19 February 1993). NFP leader Reddy was sceptical but gave Rabuka the benefit of the doubt. Again, as in 1981, he raised probing questions. There had to be some consensus on the basic principles before the proposal could be discussed further. 'I am not going to nominate numbers', he said, but 'at the end of the day in a government of national unity, Indians should be fairly represented. We should have a figure that bears some resemblance to their numbers, contribution and work, and not just a token number' (*The Review*, March 1993).

In March 1993, the government did what it should have done in the first place: it presented a paper to the Great Council of Chiefs, adding that the proposal was not of 'paramount importance' (*Fiji Times*, 18 March 1993). In the Council many chiefs, including Mara, questioned the prospects for a government of national unity under the 1990 constitution. Mara's public doubts and his advice that the government 'should not overly make their intention known to others' (*The Weekender*, 28 May 1993) sealed the fate of the issue. The council decided on more grass-roots consultation and sent the proposal to the provincial councils. The chiefs' decision was puzzling. A *Fiji Times* editorial said,

[c]onsultation is a good thing. But somewhere along the line someone has got to be able to make the decision. In this case it is the Great Council of Chiefs. If it cannot deal with the issues that it has been entrusted to deal with, then it should reconsider its role. Why do the chiefs need to refer back to the people? The people have picked their representatives to the Council. The people should have discussed these things before the meeting (*Fiji Times*, 29 May 1993).

With these proposals languishing, Rabuka was forced to address the issue of constitutional review sooner than he had anticipated. As the first step, he set up a cabinet subcommittee to draft the terms of reference for an independent constitutional commission. Chaired by Deputy Prime Minister Filipe Bole, the committee was expanded to include four members of the opposition, including Jai Ram Reddy. After several meetings, the committee agreed on a broad set of guidelines. The review would take place before the 1997 general elections, which would be held under a new constitution. Moreover, the review would not be confined only to the electoral provisions of the 1990 constitution, 'but would be of a broad nature, covering the 1990 constitution as a whole', and it would also include a consideration of the system of government deemed most appropriate for Fiji. The aim would be to produce a autochthonous constitution that addressed the needs of the country. Finally, the constitution would reflect some basic principles 'that would serve as the foundation for the promotion and reinforcement of national unity in Fiji' (Reddy 1993).[1] The new constitution, Rabuka said,

...is to be an agreed statement of our national purpose, an agreed covenant binding all our different communities and citizens of Fiji to a solemn commitment to work for the peace, unity and progress of our country and to promote the welfare and interests of all its people.[2]

After intense private negotiations, the subcommittee prepared draft terms of reference. Bearing in mind the need to promote 'racial harmony and national unity and the economic and social advancement of all communities and bearing in mind internationally recognised principles and standards of individual and group rights', the commission would

...take into account that the Constitution shall guarantee full protection and promotion of the rights, interests and concerns of the indigenous Fijian and Rotuman people...Scrutinise and consider future constitutional needs of the people of Fiji, having full regard for the rights, interests and concerns of all ethnic groups of people in Fiji...Facilitate the widest possible debate throughout Fiji on the terms of the Constitution of Fiji and to inquire into and ascertain the variety of views and opinions that may exist in Fiji as to how the provisions of the Fiji Constitution can be improved upon in the context of Fiji's needs as a multi-ethnic and multi-cultural society [and]…report fully on all the above matters and, in particular, to recommend constitutional arrangements likely to achieve the objectives of the Constitutional Review as set out above.

These terms caused controversy. Labour thought them too restrictive and called in its campaign literature for specific reference to the 'internationally recognised principles and standards of civil, political, cultural, economic and social rights as enshrined in the United Nations Universal Declaration of Human Rights and related covenants'. The interests of indigenous Fijians and Rotumans should be protected 'without sacrificing the rights, interests and concerns of all other people in Fiji'. The 1970 and not the 1990 constitution should form the basis for future constitutional review. The commission, the Labour Party said, should report within 12 months. Labour also argued that the terms of reference should have been drafted by a parliamentary committee, not by a lopsided cabinet subcommittee.[3] The government had, in fact, changed the sequence of the review process and authorised the cabinet subcommittee to draft the terms of reference for and appoint the independent commission. Labour was being effectively marginalised in a process it had helped initiate. The procedures for the review and Reddy's participation in it became an issue in the campaign among the Indo-Fijians.

Unfortunately for the government, many of its initiatives were overshadowed by scandals conveying the impression of disarray and discord. There was the strike in Fiji Posts and Telecommunications department in 1992 over the sacking of the chief executive, which led to the relegation of Telecommunications Minister Ilai Kuli. Fijian Holdings Limited was facing allegations of insider trading by leading members of its management board. Similar allegations surrounded the awarding of a tender to upgrade the Nadi International Airport to a company, Minsons Limited, in which Rabuka had shares. The Ports Authority was rocked by a report detailing uncovered excess expenditure on overseas trips by its board members, irregularities in sales of equipment, personal insurance discrepancies and misappropriation of funds. Questions were asked about the purchase of the prime minister's new residence (owned by the Ganilau family's Qeleni Holdings) for F$650,000 when the government valuer had estimated its value at F$465,000.

These incidents epitomised the general culture of corruption in public life that seemed to have 'reached alarming proportions', made even worse by 'the lack of action taken by the authorities on some of the more serious misappropriation cases involving hundreds of thousands of dollars' (*Fiji Times*, 21 August 1993). Politicians and civil servants demanded bribes openly; greasing the palm was becoming an accepted fact of life in contemporary Fiji. Jai Ram Reddy raised some of these issues in his budget speech in November 1993

> [w]hen a quarter of a million dollars go missing from our police force; when exhibits seized by police from suspects go missing from police stations, when stolen goods exhibited in a court of law disappear; when frauds and dubious political hangers-on can get into key positions in important public sector organisations, then it is time for the people of this country to sit up and think about the rot and it is time for this House to do something for this state of affairs.[4]

But these allegations paled into insignificance beside the so-called Stephens affair. Anthony Stephens, adviser to the Fijian nationalists, a businessman with previous brushes with the law, was arrested in 1988 and detained for forty days in connection with the importation of pen pistols. Discharged, he sued the government for F$30 million in damages, but agreed to settle for F$10 million. Under the terms of a deed of settlement agreed on between him and the attorney general, Stephens was to be paid F$980,000 cash in an out-of-court settlement. For the remaining amount, the government would pay off two mortgages under Stephens's name with the Home Finance Company and the National Bank of Fiji, settle claims with the ANZ Bank for a guarantee to Stephens's company, Economic Enterprises, dismiss a bankruptcy action against him, transfer the Soqulu Plantation in Taveuni, under mortgage control of the National Bank of Fiji, to Stephens, and settle all matters relating to three land titles owned by Stephens's family. According to Stephens and his associates, money from the settlement would be used to arrange a F$200 million loan from a Kuwaiti source to further Fijian business interests.

Astonishingly, the attorney general signed the deed, which was exempt from income tax, land-sales tax and the value-added tax. As became clear later, Stephens's connections evidently reached the highest levels of government. But before the deed could be executed, it was exposed in parliament by Jai Ram Reddy. The deed was merely an attempt to defraud the government, said Reddy. A public uproar greeted the revelations, and people wondered who else, besides the attorney general (Aptaia Seru), was implicated. As a *Fiji Times* editorial said, 'the sorry mess suggests powerful forces, answerable to no one but themselves, are at work to undermine constituted authority...What remains to be seen now is government's commitment to honest and clean government. Will the Stephens's claims be properly investigated or swept under the carpet?' (*Fiji Times*, 26 October 1992). Faced with public pressure, the government agreed to a commission of review. Sir Ronald Kermode, retired Supreme Court justice, was appointed to head the inquiry.

In July 1993, Kermode presented a report that was damaging to anyone even tangentially involved (Parliamentary Paper 45/1993). Etuate Tavai, the nationalists' contact in the prime minister's office, 'was not a truthful witness' and had 'deliberately misled parliament'. Attorney General Seru was a weak man who had strayed from the path of rectitude under pressure. Most seriously, Kermode found Sitiveni Rabuka's conduct wanting. The prime minister had ignored advice from his legal officers and selectively opted for information that supported Stephens's claims; he had interfered in the attorney general's 'area of responsibility by sending him a minute which directed him to settle a claim that he must have known was outrageously high'; he 'had conspired with Stephens to obtain an overdraft from the National Bank of Fiji by false pretences or by fraud'; and he had deceived parliament. In a sentence that was widely quoted, Kermode wrote: 'in my opinion the prime minister's actions as regard the events leading up to the execution of the Deed were not only improper but *prima facie* illegal' (Parliamentary Paper 45/1993).

The opposition asked Rabuka to step aside until an independent inquiry cleared him of involvement. Rabuka refused to act at all on the grounds that Kermode had exceeded his terms of reference, but agreed reluctantly to a judicial review of the commission's findings when some of his backbenchers threatened rebellion. In fact, Ilai Kuli filed a no-confidence motion in Rabuka's government in September 1993, which he withdrew under pressure from the Methodist Church leader Manasa Lasaro. For its part, the Taukei Movement, or what was left of it, threatened to take to the streets in support of the beleaguered prime minister, only to be told that those who planned to take the law into their own hands should 'prepare themselves to face the consequences of their actions' (*Fiji Times*, 27 November 1993). The judicial review was nominally begun but nothing ever came of it.

The Stephens affair provided the opportunity to topple Rabuka during the November 1993 budget session, when his Fijian opponents voted with the opposition Indo-Fijians. The substance and direction of the budget was consistent with the government's broad philosophy of economic development, which included deregulation of the economy and structural market and labour adjustments to increase Fiji's international competitiveness. The government proposed to reduce duties on most imported goods to 20 per cent (from 50 per cent in 1989); remove licence control on basic food items such as fish, rice and powdered milk, with butter and panel wood targeted for zero tariff in the near future; increase duty on alcoholic beverages, tobacco and fuel; and extend tax concessions to companies exporting 30 per cent of their products. The defence force would be returned to its pre-1987 levels over two to three years and the public sector pay package kept to 3 per cent of GNP. Government expenditure was expected to be F$800 million and revenue to be about F$644 million, providing for a net deficit of F$105 million or 4.8 per cent of GDP. This was 'an unacceptable level' of government spending, Finance Minister Paul Manueli said. 'We must start to control the size of the deficit, early, before it starts to control us' (Budget speech 1994).

For Jai Ram Reddy, that was the heart of the problem. 'The government has been strong on rhetoric but weak on action. There is a yawning gap between what this government says and what it does, raising serious questions both about its competence and ability to manage the nation's economy'.[5] He and others criticised the high level of expenditure and deficit, misguided expenditure priorities, and socially regressive aspects such as higher fiscal duties on basic consumer items and transportation goods. The overall picture of economic management was disturbing. Government expenditure had increased from F$723.4 million in 1992 to F$829.9 in 1993 revised estimates and was projected to increase to F$847.2 million in 1994; the gross deficit had increased from F$120.9 million in 1992 to a F$184.5 million revised estimate in 1993 and was projected to

F$150.2 million in 1994; net deficit after loan repayment had increased from F$68.7 million in 1992 to F$105.3 million in 1993 and was projected optimistically for F$84.0 million in 1994. Government expenditure as a percentage of GDP had increased from 35.1 per cent in 1992 to 38 per cent in 1993 and was projected to increase to 36.9 per cent in 1994.

Reddy's criticism was not surprising; that of the government's own backbenchers was. Kamikamica led the charge. He did not question the broad direction of government economic policy, for he had, as interim finance minister, been author of many aspects of it. The government's direct involvement in economic activity should be steadily wound down. And he urged the government to do more to promote specifically Fijian projects in the educational and economic sectors (Parliament of Fiji, *Hansard*, 17 November 1993).The thrust of his criticism was that the government lacked financial discipline to implement correct policies. At least Kamikamica was consistent. Finau Mara acknowledged that the finance minister had 'very little choice in this budget', but he was instrumental in orchestrating the Fijian vote against it though he was away in Australia when the vote was taken. Cabinet minister Ratu Viliame Dreunimisimisi was 'not convinced that the budget should be abandoned' (Parliament of Fiji, *Hansard*, 29 November 1993), but six hours later he voted against it.

Emboldened by mild criticism, the government rejected the opposition's offer to help it revise the budget. Even the prime minister's confidential memorandum to his two deputy prime ministers and the minister of finance to decrease the deficit by F$35 to F$39 million, increase the police allocation by F$2 million, and reduce the duty on basic food items was ignored. The government's complacency was misplaced. Knowing that the 27 Indo-Fijian members of parliament were going to vote against it, Rabuka's opponents saw their chance. When the budget came up for the second reading on 29 November, it was unexpectedly put to the vote. To the government's consternation, six Fijian members and one GVP member (David Pickering) joined the 27 Indo-Fijians in voting against it. Miscalculation and misplaced trust had cost the government dearly. Rabuka accepted part of the blame. 'I think my military officer mentality came into focus and led me to believe that once a directive is given, everybody would toe the line, which they did not' (*Fiji Times*, 3 December 1993).

The manner of the defeat was surprising. In normal parliamentary practice, the second reading is regarded as procedural. It is followed by the committee stage (in this case 30 November to 3 December), when the whole house would constitute itself a committee and scrutinise the proposed legislation. At this time, members of parliament can propose changes and amendments or seek explanation of particular parts. The substantive vote on a bill then takes place. But in this case, the budget bill was defeated before it reached the committee stage. It seems certain that the Fijian dissidents had not planned to use the budget to bring down the Rabuka government. Their plans materialised only as the debate proceeded and only when the position of the Indo-Fijian parties became clear. They thus seized the second reading of the budget 'as their best politically credible opportunity to bring down the government' (*The Review*, December 1993).

Rabuka questioned the dissidents' motives in his address to the Great Council of Chiefs on 15 December. There were some members of his party who voted against the Bill while wanting the government to make changes before it came up for the substantive vote. This would have been consistent with the decision of the parliamentary caucus meeting of the SVT. The government had been deprived of the opportunity to consider amendments at the third reading (committee stage). Perhaps, Rabuka told the chiefs, 'there might have been other considerations that lay behind their determination to vote against their own government' (Rabuka, Statement to the Great Council of Chiefs 1993). Indeed there were. As some Fijian dissidents told Manueli, 'they were going to challenge the budget not because they were opposed to it, but because they wanted to change the leadership' (*The Review*, December 1993).

Before informing the SVT caucus, the dissident group had informed Mara of their intention so that 'he would have more time to prepare himself for the outcome of the voting' (*Fiji Times*, 8 December 1993). How the dissidents expected Mara to behave is unknown, but this is what the Fiji Labour Party wrote to Mara

> It is quite evident to us that the defeat of the 1994 budget had other quite compelling reasons than the unacceptability of the budget itself. Over a period of the last few months, the credibility of the Rabuka Government has been brought [in]to serious question. The government has been rocked by one scandal after another...However

Prime Minister Rabuka seems to have cared very little, if at all, about these matters and has carried on in the fashion of business as usual. These incidents have seriously eroded the confidence of the opposition members and a number of government members of parliament in Prime Minister Rabuka. We feel Prime Minister Rabuka no longer enjoys the confidence of a majority of members of parliament and should therefore be asked to tender his resignation, following which Your Excellency should appoint a new prime minister who has majority support. The new prime minister should then appoint his cabinet and carry on the task of governing Fiji. We, Sir, would urge you to explore the above suggestion should it be constitutionally possible for you to do so.

Whatever the Fijian dissidents and the Labour Party proposed, the constitution gave the prime minister three options. Within three days of a crisis, he could advise the president to dissolve parliament and call for fresh general elections. Second, he could tender his and his government's resignation and allow the president to choose another (Fijian) member of parliament. Only if the prime minister failed to act within the stipulated three days could the president pursue his own initiative.

Rabuka acted expeditiously. At 7:30pm on the night on which the budget was defeated, he advised Mara to prorogue the parliament from 19 January and call for a general election within 30 days. Reddy, himself a lawyer, endorsed Rabuka's decision, which led Mara to say somewhat opportunistically, 'Mr Reddy saved my day'. The Fiji Labour Party used this comment in the election campaign to hitch Reddy to Rabuka, insinuating that Mara would have replaced Rabuka had it not been for Reddy's contrary advice. In truth, it was not Reddy but the constitution that saved Mara's day, for any other decision would not only have been unconstitutional, but would have implicated him even deeper in the machinations of the anti-Rabuka faction. That said, it was in Reddy's interest to go to the polls to capitalise on his party's strong showing in public opinion polls.

Eight major political parties contested the election, four of them Fijian. These included the SVT, the Fijian and Rotuman Nationalist United Front, Soqosoqo ni Taukei ni Vanua (STV), and the Fijian Association Party. Non-Fijian parties were the General Voters Party and the All Nationals Congress, and, in the Indo-Fijian community, the National Federation Party and the Fiji Labour Party. We will look briefly at the platforms of the various parties, though it is hard to say whether manifestos mattered much in voters' minds.

The SVT was the main Fijian political party, sponsored by the Great Council of Chiefs. Sitiveni Rabuka was its president and parliamentary leader. But although sponsored by the chiefs and intended to be an umbrella organisation for Fijians, the SVT was not supported by all, as was evident in the 1992 elections when it got only 66 per cent of all the Fijian votes and a substantially lower figure in important regions of Viti Levu. Others disliked Rabuka's leadership of the party and had not forgiven him for his 'flagrant flouting of tradition and chiefly protocol' in defeating Mara's wife, herself a high chief, for the post of party president (*Fiji Times*, 4 December 1993). There were problems, too, in the party's organisation. Theoretically the management board ran the party's affairs, but what was the role and responsibility of the 14 provinces that subscribed to its coffers? Should not the Great Council of Chiefs have been consulted over major policy decisions before the government embarked upon them? These issues were raised in the campaign. The SVT fielded candidates in all 37 Fijian constituencies.

Soon after the defeat of the budget, the SVT attempted to forge a coalition with other Fijian parties. It proposed not to contest seats already held by the nationalists 'if the favour was reciprocated' (*Fiji Times*, 6 December 1993). Butadroka did not respond. Similar negotiations with the All Nationals Congress also collapsed when the SVT refused to reconsider the Sunday prohibitions and the idea of the fourth confederacy. The SVT then decided to contest the elections alone on a platform that stated, among other things, that cabinet members would be chosen on merit, not on provincial affiliation; there would be a minister of national planning to coordinate developmental activities; shipping to the outer islands would be improved; the value-added tax would be reviewed; deregulation would be balanced against the interests of local manufacturers; there would be more effective support for law and order; efficiency in the public sector would be improved; and an SVT government would give priority to the promotion of national unity. Where the SVT's fortunes looked uncertain, such as in Rewa, Rabuka contradicted himself by promising that province a seat in his cabinet (*The Review*, March 1994). Elsewhere, he hinted that the country could explode if his party were not returned to power.

Rabuka reminded the Fijian electorate of his many pro-Fijian initiatives. He admitted that he had still a lot to learn, and he asked for forgiveness. His opponents had criticised his leadership; Rabuka said, 'no leader could really be effective if from within the ranks of his or her team there were people who were not prepared to show their loyalty to the team leader and commitment to play their role as team members' (Sitiveni Rabuka, Statement to the Bose Levu Vakaturaga).[6] Could such people be trusted to safeguard the future of the Fijian people? He may have erred, Rabuka said, but 'what I have never been, and what I will never do, is to be disloyal to the Fijian and Rotuman communities, and to give away what I had personally sacrificed myself to achieve in 1987— and that is to secure and to safeguard the interests of the Fijian and Rotuman people' (Rabuka, Statement to the Great Council of Chiefs 1993). He was astounded at the disloyalty of his colleagues who 'almost handed over power of effective control of the national Government of Fiji to the other communities'. Fijian people were at the crossroads, and the only way forward for them was to remain united. Loyalty was a virtue that Rabuka emphasised over and over again. 'We must be unremitting in our loyalty to each other, to our chiefs, to this highest of all Fijian councils, the Bose Levu Vakaturaga'. And Rabuka, the uncompromising Fijian nationalist, was the people's saviour.

The SVT's chief rival for Fijian votes was the Fijian Association, the vehicle for the dissident, anti-Rabuka Fijians, headed by Josefata Kamikamica and quietly supported by Ratu Mara. The idea of reviving the old Fijian Association as an alternative to Rabuka's SVT had been mooted as early as January 1992, two years before the election, though nothing came of that initiative (*Daily Post*, 17 February 1992). The Association's founding principles were a mixture of the pre-coup Alliance platform and that of the Mara-led interim administration (1988–92) in which Kamikamica was a key figure. The party would respect multiracialism but in the context of promoting and safeguarding indigenous Fijian interests, it would seek re-entry into the Commonwealth, and, following World Bank initiatives, it would pursue privatisation and corporatisation of profitable enterprises. In truth, the Fijian Association's policies differed little from the SVT's.

On the campaign trail, the Association had only one issue: Rabuka
was an unworthy leader. Said Kamikamica, 'the SVT leader, over the
last 18 months, has followed a path full of broken promises,
contradictory statements, reversal of policy, and dishonourable behaviour.
Fijian and national unity cannot be achieved through cheap political
point scoring just for the sake of rallying together, or for any other selfish
vested interest' (*Fiji Times*, 21 January 1994). He pointed to Rabuka's
involvement in the Stephens affair, his close association with Butadroka's
brand of nationalism, and his administrative inexperience. 'Another five
years of this style of leadership and it will be very difficult for the country
because the network of interests that feed upon each other in a situation
like that will be very difficult to break' (*The Review*, February 1994). It
was thus in the national interest to stop Rabuka now. The Fijian
Association was not disobedient toward the Great Council of Chiefs, as
the SVT alleged. It pointed to a number of high chiefs among its party
leaders, including Ratu Apenisa Cakobau (son of the late Vunivalu of
Bau), Ratu Wili Maivalili of Cakaudrove, and Ratu Aca Silatolu from
Rewa. Moreover, it attempted to promote itself as the true servant of
the Great Council of Chiefs. If elected to government, the party would
work hard to reestablish the chiefs' links to the British monarch. Rabuka
appealed to another tradition in Fijian society. 'The sooner we realise we
are out and out, the better it will be for us rather than crying over spilt
milk. We are a proud race. We won't go crawling back to the British and
the Commonwealth' (*The Review*, February 1994). In this stance, Rabuka
echoed the sentiments of ordinary Fijians.

The third Fijian party in the election was Sakiasi Butadroka's newly
renamed Fijian and Rotuman Nationalist United Front. Butadroka's
fortunes had fallen on hard times. Once an Alliance Party assistant
minister dismissed for his anti-Indian remarks—that Fiji's Indian
population should be repatriated to India—Butadroka had launched his
Fijian Nationalist Party in 1975 and was elected to parliament on his
extremist platform on several occasions. He had formed a coalition, the
Fijian Nationalist United Front, with Ratu Osea Gavidi's Soqosoqo ni
Taukei ni Vanua (STV), but that coalition collapsed weeks before the
1994 election and contested the elections separately. Butadroka

championed his causes in his own inimitable style. He opposed any review of the constitution until non-Fijians unconditionally accepted the principle of Fijian political supremacy. Butadroka had been one of the founders of the Viti Levu Council of Chiefs, but his reputation for integrity had been tarnished by the Stephens affair and his base weakened by the desertion of his former coalition partner. Ratu Osea Gavidi had fallen on hard times, too, his STV a pale shadow of its 1980s counterpart, the Western United Front. Gavidi's platform was identical to Butadroka's, except for the higher frequency with which Gavidi invoked God's name. He was an advocate of western Fijian interests and co-founder of the Viti Levu Council of Chiefs.

Apisai Tora's All Nationals Congress, launched in 1992, was a Fijian-based party with a multiracial philosophy. A few key issues characterised the All Nationals Congress platform. One was its repeated view that the Great Council of Chiefs should not endorse any one Fijian party, but should stay above the electoral fray. Unless the disengagement was effected, said Tora, the traditional usefulness of the Great Council of Chiefs would be destroyed

> [t[heir reason for existence will be questioned in an increasingly hostile manner. Their survival will for the first time be a matter of serious conjecture. We foresee that their decline will gather such momentum that they will be unlikely to survive as an institution beyond the next ten years (*Fiji Times*, 11 January 1993).

Tora was also a strong, longtime advocate of greater restructuring of power within Fijian society to give western Fijians more voice in national affairs. He made 'no secret of his desire to end the political dominance of eastern Fijians' (*Islands Business*, October 1991). He was one of the principal architects of the fourth confederacy platform. Before the elections, Tora had explored cooperation with the SVT, but the talks collapsed when the SVT refused to accept his demand for, among other things, recognition of the fourth confederacy. His multiracial proclamations, coming from a founding member of the Taukei Movement, did not ring true.

These divisions caused much anguish among ordinary Fijians. They were puzzled. How could a constitution that entrenched their political supremacy have produced so much division and bitterness among their leaders? One answer was obvious. The removal of the threat of Indo-

Fijian dominance had opened up space to debate issues relating to the structure and processes of power within Fijian society that had remained hidden from the public arena. The absence of the once unifying leaders such as Ganilau, Cakobau and Mara encouraged democratic debate among Fijians. Rabuka was no Mara. He lacked Mara's *mana* and knowledge of the mantras of national politics. Moreover, he was a commoner.

Nonetheless, the extent and significance of the division and discordance should be kept in perspective. In the end, although the Fijian parties may have differed about the formula for the distribution of power and resources among the *taukei*, they agreed that Fijians must always retain political control. Kamikamica and Tora espoused multiracialism, but only on terms acceptable to the *taukei*. They advocated (token) Indo-Fijian participation in government; none wanted a full partnership.

The Fijians, however, were not the only ones who were politically divided. There was internal friction among the category of general electors, which included all non-Fijians and non-Indo-Fijians, though it was not publicly aired. The General Voters Party had done well as SVT's coalition partner, securing two senior cabinet positions. However, its parliamentary leader, David Pickering, a known Mara supporter and a Rabuka critic, had refused to join Rabuka's cabinet in 1992. He was a vocal critic of Rabuka's 'inconsistent statements and indeterminate stance' (*The Review*, August 1993). Not surprisingly, Pickering left the GVP to stand, and win, as an All Nationals Congress candidate in the 1994 elections, defeating his former party by 893 votes to 554. The real cause of friction seems to have been the extent of the party's support for Rabuka. Many general electors were pro-Fijian but not necessarily pro-Rabuka. A faction of the GVP wanted greater independence, while the party leaders, whatever their personal misgivings about Rabuka's character and consistency, supported him. In the end, despite internal differences, the GVP won four of the five general seats and returned once again as the SVT's coalition partner.

Among Indo-Fijians, the divisions were deeper and more public, with both the National Federation and the Fiji Labour parties running fierce campaigns to claim the leadership of a drifting, disillusioned Indo-Fijian community. Several issues divided the two parties. One was disagreement over participating in the 1992 elections. The NFP decided to fight the elections under protest, arguing that boycotting it would be futile. The Indo-Fijian community's future lay in dialogue and discussion with Fijian leaders, and parliament would provide the forum. Labour favoured boycott. How could it participate in an election under a constitution that it had roundly condemned as racist, authoritarian, undemocratic and feudalistic? To do so would accord legitimacy to that flawed document and undermine the party's credibility internationally. International pressure was the only way to change the constitution. However, a few weeks before the election, the party revoked its decision and took part in the elections.

Another issue was Labour's decision to support Sitiveni Rabuka in his bid to become prime minister; the NFP had backed his rival, Josefata Kamikamica. Labour explained its action as a strategic move. When Rabuka, once in power, disavowed the spirit of the agreement and disclaimed any urgency to address issues Labour had raised, Labour's credibility in the Indo-Fijian community was severely tested. To salvage its reputation, Labour walked out of parliament in June 1993 only to return in September, using the terms of reference for the review of the constitution as a pretext. The NFP exploited Labour's misfortunes. Chaudhry, it said, had committed the 'third coup' by supporting Rabuka in 1992, its agreement with him 'neither politically feasible nor legally enforceable' (*Fiji Times*, 15 December 1993). Labour had practised 'flip-flop' politics. Labour countered that the 'problem with the NFP [is that] it never struggled in its lifetime and buckles under pressure' (*The Weekender*, 4 February 1994). For the NFP, the main issue was credibility and integrity. It portrayed itself as a party following a steady course on an even keel. Its trump card was its leader, Jai Ram Reddy. A seasoned politician, Reddy had, especially since the 1992 election, emerged as a responsible, statesmanlike figure. A national poll gave him an astounding 80 per cent approval. His moderate yet insistent stance on important issues and his performance in parliament worked to the party's advantage. Fijian leaders, including Mara and Rabuka, spoke approvingly of him. But that, to his opponents, was the real problem. Conciliation and compromise to what end, they asked. Reddy's moderation they saw as weakness and timidity, reminiscent of the acquiescent politics of the Indian Alliance. They sought to discredit his political record by blaming him for the years of divisive and factional infighting in the National Federation Party. For the NFP, Chaudhry epitomised 'inconsistency, unreliability and unpredictability both in substance and style' (National Federation Party campaign material).

Personalities aside, there were some fundamental differences in approach and political philosophy that remained submerged in the campaign. One important difference between Reddy and Chaudhry lay in their approaches to the pace of political change. Gradualism was Reddy's preferred course of action; the favourite words in his political vocabulary being conciliation, consensus, dialogue and moderation. Expeditious change was Chaudhry's path; sacrifice, struggle, boycott and agitation the key words in his lexicon. When asked how long Indo-Fijians might have to wait for political equality, Reddy replied: 'I don't think time is important in politics; it is what you do' (*Islands Business*, January 1991). Indo-Fijians had suffered a great deal, but 'life goes on because of hope, that somehow, some day things will turn around and everybody will realise that we are all God's children and we're all meant to live and let live' (*Islands Business*, January 1991). Reddy's philosophical, even fatalistic, approach acknowledged the limited options available to his people.

Chaudhry was an intrepid, indefatigable fighter who entered national politics through the trade union movement; he was the long-serving general secretary of the Fiji Public Service Association. He was temperamentally different from Reddy. To him, power conceded nothing without a struggle and time did count for a lot in politics and in the life of a community. Change must come and, for Chaudhry, the sooner the better. 'We have to do something about this [racial constitution]', he said, 'because if we live under this constitution for the next 5–10 years, then they [Indo-Fijians] will end up as coolies' (*Islands Business*, March 1991). The same urgency—recklessness in the opinion of his detractors—informed his approach to the land issue. 'I don't believe in transferring the problems of our generation to the next generation', he said. 'We should try and resolve this issue. If it is not possible to have long term leases...then we better start talking about compensation. And Indians will have to accept the reality that they must move away from the land and find a livelihood elsewhere' (*The Review*, August 1991). This militant

Chaudhry was an anathema to his opponents, but, in an ironic way, he appealed to the dominant radical tradition in Indo-Fijian politics that had long been the province of the NFP.

The NFP seemed to have accepted the realities of communal politics and proposed to work within its framework. Jai Ram Reddy said in parliament in July 1992,

> [l]et us each be in our separate compartments if you like. Let communal solidarity prevail and I do not begrudge Fijian leaders for wanting to see that their community remains united. That is a very natural desire. Let the general electors be united. Let the Indians be united; let everybody be united, but from our respective positions of unity let us accept that we must co-exist and work together and work with each other. That is a more realistic approach (Parliament of Fiji, *Hansard*, 24 July 1992).

Labour's position differed. Although only a pale shadow of its 1987 form, denuded of its multiracial base, its leading Fijian lights having deserted the party, Labour still seemed to subscribe to the philosophy of multiracial politics, as opposed to communally compartmentalised politics of the type entrenched by the 1992 constitution. To that end the party fielded general elector and Fijian candidates. It was a token gesture, and the Fiji Labour Party's non-Indo-Fijian candidates polled miserably; but it still represented an act of protest against the racial constitution, whereas the NFP contested only Indo-Fijian seats.

In sum, the 1994 campaign was a curiously quiet, uneventful affair, with the ethnic groups locked into racially segregated compartments, debating issues of particular concern to their respective communities. There were few large rallies and virtually no campaigning through the media. Most people seemed uninterested and disenchanted. This parochial, tunnell-vision that rewarded ethnic chauvinism and communalism rather than multiracialism was one of the more deleterious effects of the 1990 constitution.

Polling occurred from 18 to 27 February. The SVT got 146,901 votes or 64 per cent of Fijian votes, a decline of 7 per cent from its 1992 figures. Its nearest rival was the Fijian Association with 34,994 votes or 15 per cent. The Fijian Association won all three Lau seats and the two in Naitasiri. Butadroka's Nationalists polled poorly, too, capturing only 14,396 votes (6 per cent), compared with its 1992 share of 10 per cent of all the Fijian votes. The All Nationals Congress, which had won 24,719 votes (10 per cent) in 1992, won only 18,259 (8 per cent) of Fijian votes. Gavidi's STV also recorded a loss, from 9,308 (4 per cent) votes to 6,417 (3 per cent) in 1994. Labour, which fielded just a few Fijian candidates, got only 555 Fijian votes in 1994. Independents did poorly, except the SVT-allied Ratu Jo Nacola from Ra, who won his seat comfortably.

The nationalists' agenda was appropriated by the SVT. Butadroka claimed with some justice that his trademark pro-Fijian policies had been hijacked by the party in power. Butadroka's running mate in the 1992 elections, Ratu Mosese Tuisawau, stood as an independent. But Butadroka had also lost ground and respect in his constituency with his antics in parliament (he was expelled for his virulent criticism of Mara's administration), his strident and now curiously antiquarian anti-Indianism, and his involvement in the Stephens affair. Gavidi's STV lost ground for similar reasons. His political integrity was in tatters over the Stephens affair, and his pro-western Fijian agenda was silently incorporated into the SVT's program. Tora's loss, and especially his loss of ground since 1992, was a surprise. Tora's sudden conversion to multiracialism was unconvincing, and the SVT fought hard to regain its strength in the west.

The real surprise among Fijians was the poor showing of the Fijian Association, except in Naitasiri (because of Kuli's rapport with his grass-roots supporters, the indifference of Tui Waimaro, Adi Pateresio Vonokula notwithstanding) and Lau. Among those who succumbed to the Fijian Association in Lau was the SVT's Filipe Bole. His support for Rabuka, despite Ratu Mara's well-known disregard for the man, cost him his seat. Mara was the paramount chief of the region. As president, Mara maintained outward neutrality, but as one Fijian observer put it, 'neither the acting chairman [Tevita Loga, Mara's traditional herald] nor Finau Mara [eldest son and a Fijian Association candidate], nor others would have dared move without prior consultation with Mara in his capacity as paramount chief' (*Islands Business*, February 1994). Why did the Fijian Association fail in its birthplace, Tailevu? Traditional politics probably played a part. The SVT lineup included Adi Samanunu Talakuli, the eldest daughter of the late Vunivalu of Bau (Ratu Sir George Cakobau), and Ratu William Toganivalu. The Fijian Association's lineup of chiefs lacked stature and authority. Some Fijians also suggested that

Kamikamica was damaged by Mara's endorsement. They believed that Mara harboured dynastic ambitions and supported Kamikamica, or anyone else, only until his son, Finau, was ready to assume the leadership. Others suggested that Tailevu was a traditionally conservative constituency, whose people found it hard to vote against a party sponsored by the chiefs. The SVT's allegation that Kamikamica had engaged in a 'calculated act of political sabotage' in his 'continuing remorseless and unbending ambition for political power in Fiji' (*The Weekender*, 2 February 1994) seemed to have stuck.

All this says little about the SVT's strengths, which were considerable. It fielded better, or, at least, better-known candidates, and, as the party in government, used the politics of patronage to its great advantage. There was no doubt that the SVT's trump card was Sitiveni Rabuka, who was returned by his electorate with one of the highest votes among Fijian constituencies. Many ordinary Fijians responded to him as one of their own—a man who had sacrificed much to promote their interests. They ultimately forgave him his lapses of judgment and inconsistencies. They saw him as a man who had suffered from disloyalty, bad advice from colleagues and intrigue from powerful forces outside government. Rabuka asked for a second chance, and the electorate responded.

Among Indo-Fijians, the total number of registered voters was 159,480. The NFP won twenty of the twenty-seven Indo-Fijian seats and captured 65,220 votes (55.5 per cent). The Fiji Labour Party got 51,252 votes (43.6 per cent). In the 1992 elections, the NFP had captured 50 per cent of the votes to Labour's 48 per cent. The NFP made a clean sweep of all the Vanua Levu seats and the urban seats. It also made gains in the sugar belt of western Viti Levu, to some extent because of the mill strike in September 1993 by the Sugar and General Workers' Union, which angered farmers. Other farmers turned to the NFP because they were suspicious of a compulsory insurance scheme proposed by the Labour-allied National Farmers' Union. However, Labour managed to retain its core support there. Part of Labour's problem was of its own making, but the NFP increased its support on the strength of its own performance, especially that of its leader. Many Indo-Fijians responded to his quiet tenacity.

The election returned both the NFP and the SVT with mandates. The Indo-Fijians had not renounced Chaudhry's style of agitational politics; they merely suspended it for the time being in favour of Reddy's more accommodationist approach. In that sense, Reddy's mandate was conditional; if his approach failed to produce timely results, the Indo-Fijians would return to Labour. A similar dilemma confronted Rabuka. The SVT leader told his campaign audience that he would never compromise on his goals to realise the aims of the coup. At the same time, he promised to promote national unity through the politics of inclusion. His task was made all the more difficult; members of his own party were aiming depose him at any opportunity. Rabuka may have taken his revenge, but would he have the last laugh?

## Notes

1 Typescript in the author's possession.
2 This quote is from a file of unpublished constitutional review papers owned by the author.
3 From Labour Party campaign literature in the author's possession.
4 From a copy of Reddy's budget speech in the author's possession.
5 Reddy's Budget Reply (typescript in the author's possession).
6 Typescript in the author's possession.

# 6

# Charting a new course

The 1990 constitution, decreed into existence by President Ratu Sir Penaia Ganilau five years after the military coups of 1987, was assumed by its architects to be a temporary solution to a troubled situation. Section 161 provided for its review within seven years, that is, before 25 July 1997. The constitution was undeniably a contested document provoking deep emotions and often diametrically opposed responses. The Indo-Fijian community rejected it, and made its repeal, or at least an impartial review, the central plank in their election campaigns in 1992 and 1994. Equally, on the Fijian side, there was fervent support for a document that was widely believed to entrench Fijian political dominance. Nonetheless, after the 1992 elections, which brought the SVT to power, the government initiated private discussions with the opposition on the nature and process of a constitutional review. Sitiveni Rabuka acknowledged the deep differences of opinion, but emphasised that 'these should not deteriorate into confrontational and tension-filled relations, if our political leaders exercise and develop relationships based on trust, understanding and respect for the laws of our country' (*Fiji Focus*, June 1992).

To start the review process, Rabuka appointed a cabinet subcommittee that was expanded to include opposition members after a discussion with Jai Ram Reddy and Mahendra Chaudhry on 9 June 1993. The three agreed that the review would be completed in time for the 1997 general election to be held under a revised constitution. Further, they agreed that the review would not be confined to the electoral provisions of the 1990 constitution but would be of a broad nature, covering the entire document and including 'a consideration of the system of government considered most appropriate for Fiji'. They agreed that the new constitution should be 'autochthonous', developed by the people within the country, unlike the 1970 constitution that was negotiated in London. They agreed further to think about some 'pillar principles' that 'would serve as the foundation for the promotion and reinforcement of national unity in Fiji' (Parliament of Fiji, *Hansard*, 14 September 1993).

The subcommittee appointed a multiparty Joint Parliamentary Select Committee (JPSC), made up of 11 government and nine opposition nominees, to facilitate the review. The JPSC would recommend to cabinet the size and composition of the review commission, assist the commission in its work and undertake initiatives to develop consensus about the new constitution. This was a significant achievement. After protracted private negotiations, the subcommittee recommended, and in September 1993 both houses of parliament unanimously agreed to set up a review commission. Parliament also unanimously approved its terms of reference, but progress was disrupted when the SVT government fell in November 1993. Early in 1994 the SVT, having returned to power with an increased majority, resumed discussion with the opposition parties.

The most important unresolved issues were the size and, more importantly, the membership, of the commission. In November, the cabinet agreed on an eight-member commission, chaired by a person from overseas who possessed 'vast experience in [a] multiracial, multicultural environment'—preferably someone from Malaysia—three Fijians, two Indo-Fijians, one Rotuman and one general voter, and assisted by two legal counsel, one from overseas and one local (*Fiji Focus*, June 1994). Subsequently, for reasons still unknown, the SVT suggested an 11-member commission, made up of a Chairman (Fijian), Deputy Chairman (Indian), two SVT nominees, one general voter, one NFP member, one Fijian Association member, one All Nationals Congress, one Rotuman and one state services representative. The government insisted that the commission consist of local people who represented major political parties or groups in parliament and who were familiar with local language and customs. 'Any foreign participation would be confined to the role of expert consultants and advisers only', because 'the exercise would only be meaningful if it was undertaken by people whose lives would be affected by changes that would be implemented and who had the relevant language and cultural understanding of the different sections of the Fiji's multiethnic and multireligious society' (Press statement).

It also proposed that the members of the commission be appointed by the major political parties represented in parliament, and not by other interest groups, such as, the Great Council of Chiefs, or the president, or the churches, because 'this would better facilitate communication with the Joint Parliamentary Select Committee and the public of Fiji as well as provide an impetus to the bipartisan consensus building process that was vital to this exercise'. The government envisaged the process having two stages. First, the commission would compile an interim report and submit it to parliament for consideration. Parliament's comments would then be incorporated by the commission in the final report. The exercise was expected to take about two years. Things turned out differently. The government's proposal for an eleven-member commission was soon realised to be too unwieldy and expensive. In the end, the JPSC decided on three members to undertake the review.

Similarly, the government's insistence that the chairperson should be an indigenous Fijian was rejected by the opposition, even though the person the government had in mind was the Chief Justice, Sir Timoci Tuivaga, who was willing to serve, if asked. The opposition wanted an independent outsider, and threatened to boycott parliament if the government refused to reconsider its position. Without some international participation, they said, the process would lack legitimacy and credibility.

A number of prominent individuals were identified, including Telford George, a former Chief Justice of Tanzania and Bermuda and member of the commission which had reviewed the constitution of Trinidad in 1974; Sir Robin Cooke, of the Supreme Court of New Zealand; Sir Graham Speight, a retired New Zealand judge and former President of the Fiji Court of Appeal; Eddie Durie, Chief Judge of the Maori Land Court; Sir Ian Thompson, former Fiji colonial civil servant living in retirement in Scotland; and Sir Paul Reeves, former New Zealand Governor General and Archbishop (*Daily Post*, 6 February 1996). Further negotiation between the government and the opposition narrowed the list to Thompson and Reeves, who were interviewed by Filipe Bole, chairman of the JPSC. Reeves was offered the chair.

As someone from the Pacific islands, with known sympathy for the Maori cause, and with his background in the church and experience of high public office, Reeves was acceptable to a wide cross-section of the Fiji community. As its representative on the commission, the government nominated Tomasi Rayalu Vakatora, a former senior public servant, senator, minister and Speaker of the House of Representatives; and the opposition nominated me, an academic specialist on Fiji history and politics. The commissioners received their warrant from the president on 15 March 1995. The two legal counsel, Alison Quentin-Baxter and Jon Apted, received theirs on 19 May. Quentin-Baxter was a retired Executive Director of the New Zealand Law Reform Commission with constitutional experience in the Marshall Islands and Niue. She was a great asset, with her tireless energy, her meticulous preparation and impeccable professionalism. Apted was resourceful and intelligent, with a sound understanding of the local scene. The commission secretary was another local lawyer, Walter Rigamoto, a Rotuman. The commission began its work in early June.

The terms of reference—a historic achievement of consensus and compromise, considering the bitterness generated by the coups—required the commission to recommend constitutional arrangements to meet the present and future needs of the people of Fiji, and promote racial harmony, national unity and the economic and social advancement of all communities. Those arrangements had to guarantee full protection and promotion of the rights, interests and concerns of the indigenous Fijian and Rotuman people, have full regard for the rights, interests and concerns of all ethnic groups, and take into account internationally recognised principles and standards of individual and group rights. The commission was expected to scrutinise the constitution, facilitate the widest possible debate on the terms of the constitution, and, after ascertaining the views of the people, suggest how the 1990 constitution could be improved to meet the needs of Fiji as a multiethnic and multicultural society. The terms of reference were wide-ranging, prompting some cynics to wonder what they actually meant and whether they could be reconciled into a workable formula. These thoughts also crossed the minds of those in the commission, who devoted a great deal of time to analysing the meaning of the terms of reference.

Unlike previous commissions of enquiry, such as the Street Commission of 1975, and others set up after the coups, the Reeves Commission (as it came to be known) was required to review the whole constitution, not only the electoral system and the composition of parliament. The review, then, was to be a fundamental, wide-ranging exercise, covering, besides the two critical areas just mentioned, the functioning of parliament, the relationship between the executive and the legislative branches, institutions of government and the mechanism for improving accountability and transparency, the administration of justice, citizenship, ethnic and social justice issues, rights of communities and groups, the operation of local government bodies, public revenue and expenditure, emergency powers, and a Bill of Rights, among others.

The commission adopted a carefully designed plan of action. The first stage would involve receiving submissions from the people of Fiji. Consultation would be open, transparent, thorough and inclusive. To ascertain the view of the people, and thus fulfill one of the requirements of the terms of reference, the commission decided to hold public hearings throughout the country to receive submissions. The opposition was not keen on a prolonged and public enquiry. Jai Ram Reddy had told parliament that 'this widest possible consultation is unnecessary' (Parliament of Fiji, *Hansard*, 22 September 1993). Mahendra Chaudhry agreed, adding that 'this was a concession that we made'. They perhaps feared that a public enquiry would revive old hostilities, politicise the review and derail the whole process.

Perhaps Reddy and Chaudhry were reminded of Rabuka's abortive 'government of national unity' proposal. A public enquiry would reveal nothing new: what the different communities wanted, or did not want, was already too well known to warrant detailed investigation—the commission could revisit the arguments by reading submissions given to previous enquiries. The commission did not share this view. It was determined to make its own independent assessment, although it had access to papers produced for earlier enquiries. It also knew that its report would lack credibility without public input. The people of Fiji should be bound into the review process, and not excluded from it—it was, after all, their constitution that was being reviewed.

The commission expected to hear discordant, even disquieting, voices from time to time; there would be public posturing and grandstanding; and some people might use the commission to promote their own causes. Some of our fears were realised, as both Mr Vakatora and I were vilified by people seeking free publicity for their personal and political causes. But that was the price of living in an open, democratic society. As it turned out, the consultation was exhaustive, and exhausting. From July to November, commission members travelled the country by car, boat and air, receiving over 800 oral and written submissions from individual citizens, community, religious, cultural and other interest groups, and all the major parties. A number of organisations were set up with the express purpose of making submissions. One, the Citizens Constitutional Forum, continues to do valuable work in educating the public about the constitution. Most of the submissions were made in open forum, and are available to the public; but some individuals spoke in confidence, and their presentations naturally form part of the closed record.

Supplementing these data were commissioned research papers on a range of issues. One set of papers dealt with local issues such as the performance of the economy, education, the relationship between state and religion, land tenure, the structure and functioning of Fijian institutions, gender relations, minority concerns and the like. The aim was to enrich commission members' knowledge of the local context in which the 1990 constitution functioned, and to deepen their understanding of some issues raised in the submissions. Another set, written by eminent scholars from around the world, focused on systems of power sharing in ethnically divided societies, alternative electoral systems, indigenous and human rights in international law, protection of fundamental rights, and so on. Both sets have been published (Lal and Vakatova 1997).

Early in the commission's deliberations, the need to view Fiji's constitutional experience in comparative perspective became clear. Malaysia, Mauritius and South Africa seemed to offer experiences and perspectives of particular relevance. Malaysia, which had grown close to Fiji since the coups—some of its legislation, for instance, regarding internal security, was adopted in Fiji—had experienced racial tensions, culminating in riots in 1969, but later emerged as an economic superpower in Southeast Asia. Its pro-indigenous (*bhumiputra*) policies, legislative protection of indigenous interests and their integration into the country's political system, the special place of Malay culture and the overarching role of Islam, the relationship between religion and state, all resonated with issues raised in submissions to the commission.

Mauritius, like Fiji, was a multiethnic island state, lagging behind Fiji in nearly all sectors of the economy when it became independent in 1968, just two years before Fiji. Three decades later it was ahead of Fiji in all sectors of the economy. The commission wanted to fathom the reason for this transformation and see for itself if there was any correlation between the constitutional system and economic performance. South Africa was an obvious choice, in the mid 1990s undergoing perhaps the most massive effort in constitutional engineering in modern times, steering a deeply divided and racially polarised society from its brutal apartheid system towards a non-racial, multiparty democracy. The commission wanted to understand the nature of the problems that arose out of the transition, particularly the use of the mechanism of a government of national unity to effect the change.

This comparative exercise was immensely educative, reinforcing the fundamental point that each country had devised unique constitutional arrangements to suit their particular social and political needs. But there were certain common threads. Everywhere, there was recognition of the need to share power among the various ethnic groups. Everywhere, there was explicit recognition of ethnicity. And everywhere, there was a strong commitment to an overarching sense of national unity, its importance underlined by a history of ethnic conflict and tension.

The commission's work received wide publicity in the media, particularly on the (recently introduced) television where it was a regular feature of the evening news bulletin for weeks. Predictably, submissions varied in tone and content, addressing some concerns and issues that were tangential to the commision's central project. The following sums up the thrust of what was presented to the commission. There was widespread recognition, among both indigenous Fijians and Indo-Fijians, that Fiji's political and social structures, instead of bringing people together, had kept them apart for more than a hundred years, so that people continued to live, think and work in racial compartments. Members of both groups noted that, in rural communities, Fijians and Indo-Fijians lived happily together, extending a helping hand to one another. Many Indo-Fijian individuals and groups expressed their commitment to working with Fijians towards restoring full democracy and establishing a genuinely harmonious non-racial and multicultural society, assuming, of course, that this was what Fijians themselves wanted. Racial cooperation was better than confrontation. Some adverted to the worldwide need to take account of the rights of indigenous peoples. Fijians, too, stressed that while indigenous interests were paramount, this should not affect the interests and traditions of other communities. No one should feel threatened in what was their own country. A multiracial society was one in which different communities respected one another, interacted, learnt each other's culture and languages and lived together in trust.

Some thought that a lasting solution would depend on foregoing racial politics and building mutual trust, while others argued strongly that Fiji must abandon the habit, introduced by the colonial government, of thinking, making decisions, legislating and carrying out other activities on a racial basis. The constitution should make people focus first on belonging to the country and only after that on belonging to a particular group. But that trust, some argued, should be built only on the confidence of the different ethnic group: their own identity should be built in relation to that of the other groups. While the Indo-Fijian population was increasing rapidly, there was genuine fear among the indigenous people that they would be swamped and Fiji taken out of their control. However, Fiji's biggest asset was that, despite each group's fears and mistrust, the ordinary people were basically decent and considerate, which had enabled Fiji to avoid violence so far.

Many Indo-Fijians expressed their commitment to social and economic advancement for all the people of Fiji. They urged that a new constitution should enable Fiji to solve its serious social and economic problems such as access to land, unemployment, poverty and homelessness, in a spirit of cooperation, trust, tolerance, sound planning, team work and the innovative and creative use of resources. The country's enormous potential could not be realised until its citizens were united in their diversity, and discussed such concerns as those of the Fijians about not being in the main economic stream and of Indo-Fijians about mushrooming squatter colonies on the fringes of the urban centres. The Indo-Fijian business community could take the initiative in training young Fijians in business and as apprentices. It was necessary to move away from the stereotype that all Indo-Fijians were educated and prosperous. Nor was it true that Indo-Fijians controlled the economy. The banking sector was not in their hands, nor was the gold mine. It was also wrong to suggest that Fijians had no significant role in the economy. They were not well-represented in the visible aspects of commercial life like shop-keeping, transport and tourism, but they owned of one of the country's most productive assets—land.

Many submissions pointed out that in many rural areas, members of the two communities spoke each other's language. Even so, a number of Indo-Fijians acknowledged that they could have done more to learn Fijian culture, tradition and language. Some Indo-Fijian schools already had a large number of Fijian students, and were promoting the teaching of Fijian to all students, but it was not an examinable subject for non-Fijians. Multiethnic schools encouraged communication and trust among the children. Although some schools were still categorised as 'Fijian' or 'Indian', almost 58 per cent of the 672 primary schools and almost 91 per cent of the 142 secondary schools were multiracial. However, stereotypes still took the place of knowledge. The state had to be a major player in promoting an understanding among the different communities of one another's language and culture.

The subject of a common name was raised in many submissions, which, it was said, was necessary to promote national identity. Among Indo-Fijians and a few Fijians, there was support for the name 'Fijian', but some thought that would be appropriate only if everyone spoke the Fijian language. Some Fijians took the view that 'Fijian' should be reserved for those registered in the *Vola Ni Kawa Bula*. Alternative common names were 'Fiji Citizens', or 'Fiji Islanders'. The suggestion that indigenous Fijians should be known as *'Taukei'* was deplored by some on the assumption that only members of other groups would be called Fijians, thus defeating the purpose, but welcomed by others on the ground that it would free up 'Fijian' for use by all.

The relationship between church and state was hotly debated. A number of Fijians, including the Methodist Church and many of its members, wanted Fiji to be declared a Christian state. Most saw no need to give reasons, but those that did suggested that the principles of the Christian faith would be enriched and protected by the government; Christianity would spread among non-Christians, and the introduction of new cults under the guise of religion would be stopped. With one or two exceptions, Fijians did not see the declaration of Fiji as a Christian state as affecting the freedom of non-Christians to practice their own religions. Many Fijians and predominantly Fijian religious groups expressed support for the Sunday ban. They thought that Sunday should be a day of rest, except for travelling and the provision of essential amenities.

Others, however, thought that the constitution should ensure that Fiji remain a secular state. Some saw an element of compulsion in declaring Fiji a Christian state as inconsistent with true Christianity. Privileging one religion over others would not be conducive to an atmosphere of trust and understanding. Religion should not be used by political leaders to further their own ends. The Sunday ban was opposed on grounds of principle, such as the conflict with freedom of worship and religious belief, and elements of inconsistency and hypocrisy. It also had socioeconomic consequences. Taken with a large number of holidays, the Sunday ban had caused a drop in production. The point was made that the ban was imposed by parliament, not by the constitution. It was therefore deemed to be a matter for parliament to resolve.

Citizenship was another issue that featured prominently in the submissions. The majority of those who addressed it, both Fijian and Indo-Fijian, opposed the idea of permitting dual citizenship. Belonging to a place required commitment. The Fijian view was that 'citizen' denoted someone who was entitled to land, a right which a person should not have in more than one place. Some, with backgrounds from all communities, however, favoured permitting dual citizenship, arguing that it would encourage skilled citizens who had chosen, or felt they had been forced, to live and work abroad to return to Fiji. Others thought that those registered in the *Voka ni Kawa Bula* should be allowed to retain Fiji citizenship even if they became citizens of another country.

Many, particularly women, considered that the citizenship rights of men and women should be the same. The foreign husband of a woman who was a Fiji citizen should have the same right of entry to Fiji and access to citizenship as the foreign wife of a male citizen, whether the right be citizenship by registration, or only permanent residence. They also thought that the child of a female citizen born abroad should have the same right to Fiji citizenship as the child of a male citizen. Such distinctions were seen to infringe international conventions. The policy reasons for treating men and women equally in matters of citizenship included the need to facilitate the return of women students who married overseas and the humanitarian need to allow a woman to choose whether to live in her own country or that of her husband.

There was strong support, among men as well as women, to enshrine gender equality in the constitution, and representatives of women's groups urged that laws and practices that discriminated against women be changed. These included rape laws, inadequate maternity leave and the absence of paternity leave, the absence of family support benefits, particularly for women, and the absence of laws against people trafficking. Many women expressed anxiety about the growing violence against women and children, particularly domestic violence, child abuse, rape and other crimes. These problems stemmed partly from the fact that women's aspirations clashed with men's cultural and traditional values. There would be less violence if women were recognised as having a real part in decision-making.

Evidence was produced to show inadequate participation of women in politics. The barriers were tradition, family commitments and an underestimation of women's capabilities, as well as men's intimidation and desire for power. Others stressed the need to recognise the equality of women at all stages of education, and to discourage gender stereotyping. Indo-Fijian girls were doubly discriminated against in the award of scholarships. Women and men should have equal remuneration and treatment, particularly in terms of promotion to senior positions in both public and private sectors.

Many submissions raised the question of land, which was sometimes seen as a more important concern than the constitution. Many Fijians wanted to be sure that their ownership would not be disturbed. Most Indo-Fijians agreed. A number of Fijians thought that some or all state-owned land should be returned to Fijians. Freehold land, alienated before Cession, should also be returned to its rightful owners. Some submissions insisted that the renewal of leases to Indo-Fijians should be conditional upon their accepting the principle of Fijian political paramountcy. As one submitter told the commission, 'the question of Fijian leadership in this country is an important equation in the debate [and] it would be naive to ignore that point'. To 'ignore the relation between tenancy and political power would be to misunderstand the post 1987 Fiji'.

Others disagreed. For Indo-Fijians, the main issue was not ownership but constitutional guarantee of security of tenure. They wanted the constitution to place some obligation on the government to provide land for those in all communities who became landless. For many tenants, a 30-year lease, as provided under ALTA, was insufficient to encourage good husbandry and land improvement. They wanted longer leases. Alternatively, if the land-owning *mataqali* wanted the land returned, the displaced tenant should be compensated to enable him to start again elsewhere. There was deep concern that many leases were on the verge of expiring and many were not likely to be renewed. They urged constitutional machinery to resolve the problem.

On the nature and character of representation in parliament, opinions divided sharply. Many indigenous Fijians saw themselves as having an inviolable, God-given right to govern Fiji for all time, since it was their leaders who had ceded Fiji to Great Britain in 1874. They argued that at independence Fiji should have been returned to the Fijian people and their chiefs. The newcomers, the *vulagi*, were entitled to remain in the country where they were born, to work and prosper, but they had no right to aspire to political leadership. Some Fijians saw the ownership of the land as giving them the right to control the state. As Sevoki Matanainiu, of the Taukei Movement, said, Fijians should have 86 per cent of the seats in parliament because they owned 86 per cent of the land (*Daily Post*, 3 April 1997). Unless Fijian paramountcy, understood as political control, was accepted by the other communities, some Fijians suggested, Fiji would be fated to go through another, possibly worse, crisis. They saw the 1990 constitution as near-perfect. It had been blessed by the Bose Levu Vakaturaga. Through the preponderant number of Fijians in parliament, it assured their political leadership, thus protecting their traditional way of life. For these reasons, many considered that the 1990 constitution should remain unchanged. It was suggested that other races' claim to equality of treatment was itself an abuse of the democratic right that those races had been accorded. The other races, with their superior commercial skills, should help the Fijians, not try to jump ahead of them.

Indo-Fijians saw the 1990 constitution as having been imposed on them. They regarded it as discriminatory in not allocating seats to communities on the basis of their population ratio. Consequently they saw themselves relegated to permanent opposition, to third-rate citizenship, to use their words: a state of affairs which did not reflect their earnest desire to coexist with all races and make a full contribution to the country and its government. They saw the 1990 constitution as dividing the people along racial lines, so that people focused on the advancement of their own community rather than that of the nation. Because the government was required to be an indigenous Fijian institution, it was perceived as having lost the ability to mediate fairly between the communities. Indeed, some regarded the constitution as a mandate for widespread arbitrary discrimination against them. They wanted the new constitution to heal the wounds—to include express recognition that there was a permanent place for them in the country of their birth.

The submissions were deeply moving in the transparency of thoughts and emotions they expressed. For the commission, listening to submissions was profoundly educative and humbling. The country listened again to a range of often diametrically opposed viewpoints. The commission had fulfilled an important role in restarting national conversation. And it had acquainted itself with a range of viewpoints across the entire spectrum. Armed with this evidence, it began to ponder its recommendations.

It is neither possible nor desirable to cover all areas in the commission's report. Here, two sets of issues will be discussed. The first, and perhaps the most critical, concerns the election to, and composition of, parliament. That question lay at the centre of the 'web'—Mr Vakatora's phrase—and was at the forefront of all the submissions, as the way power is acquired and used lies at the heart of politics. It was the one area of central disagreement between the major parties and communities. The second relates to the functioning of the institutions of government and issues of social justice and human rights.

From the outset, the commission believed that, unless the systemic nature of Fiji's constitutional problem were clearly understood, there was little hope of devising arrangements that would not give rise to the same problems in the future. From the evidence, the commission concluded that it was Fiji's constitutional arrangements that hampered the process of nation-building and impeded effective cooperation among the communities, which otherwise had shown remarkable tolerance and respect for each other's traditions. Fiji's constitutional problems, the commission concluded, arose from four features of the country's constitutional arrangements. Two were understandable responses to Fiji's multiethnic society: the principle that Fijian interests should be paramount, and the communal system of representation; and two reflected the Westminster system of government that Fiji inherited at independence: the role of political parties and the principle that a government must command the support of a majority in parliament. These four issues underpinned the 1970 as well as the 1990 constitution.

The principle that Fijian interests should always remain paramount was expressly enunciated by the colonial government from the early years of this century, partly reflecting genuine concern for the position of indigenous Fijians, partly serving to deflect the Indo-Fijian demand for equal political representation, and partly serving to guide political change at a pace acceptable to the colonial state. Nonetheless the principle became an accepted part of the political culture of Fiji. As Fiji moved towards self-government in the 1960s, the principle of political paramountcy became the focus of negotiations among the main political actors.

The Fijian view on the eve of independence was that their interests would be secure only if Fijians had political paramountcy as well. As other communities dominated the economy, Fijian leaders pointed out, it was only fair that Fijians should dominate in government. Indo-Fijian leaders agreed to the entrenched legislative protection of Fijian land ownership, culture and separate system of administration, but did not see the paramountcy of Fijian interests as involving the perpetual re-election of a predominantly Fijian government. If the democratic process gave them the opportunity, Indo-Fijian leaders saw no reason why they should not vote in a government in which they could participate. Differing interpretation of the meaning of Fijian paramountcy, then, was one contentious issue.

Another was the system of representation in parliament. From the very beginning, the electoral system in Fiji had been communal. This

139

arrangement grew out of the colonial government's view that separate representation of different communities was natural and desirable. And the system enabled the government to keep the communities apart as much as possible, accentuating its own role as an impartial and indispensable mediator. Until 1966, Fiji had only communal rolls, with voters in each community electing members from that community. Later, the communal rolls were complemented by cross-voting rolls, allowing members belonging to the three main communities to be elected by all voters. This system also represented a compromise between the Fijian and European desire for communal representation and the Indo-Fijian commitment to a non-racial common roll. The compromise spawned more problems than it resolved.

The third feature of Fiji's political arrangement was that all parties were essentially ethnic. The National Federation Party, formed in the aftermath of the strike in the sugar industry in 1960, was based in the Indo-Fijian community, attracting only a handful of Fijian supporters despite its non-racial political platform. The Alliance Party, formed in 1966 at the behest of Governor Sir Derek Jakeway, was a Fijian-dominated party supported by the General Electors Association and the Indian Alliance. The Alliance was more multiracial, but at each election the predominant ethnic basis of the two main parties was clear.

The final feature of Fiji's political arrangement was the Westminster system, where the prime minister is the leader of the party or combination of parties that commands majority support in the Lower House. The cabinet is drawn exclusively from that coalition or party. Through its direction of the departments and other government agencies, the government of the day has effective control of policy. If the party in power is defeated in a general election, control of government passes to the winning party.

These arrangements were reflected in both the 1970 and the 1990 constitutions. At the beginning, there were hopes for the development of multiracial politics. In the 1972 elections, both the Alliance and the National Federation Party made genuine attempts, with limited success, to attract voters from all communities; but communal politics gained the ascendancy. This was a logical consequence of the constitutional arrangement, combining the Westminster system with communal representation. The communal system provided little incentive or opportunity for voters or candidates to concern themselves with the problems of other communities. It followed that those elected from the national (cross-voting) seats were not regarded as really legitimate representatives. Third, political parties focused their energy on the community whose interests they were formed to promote. Those parties that were originally committed to multiracialism were inevitably driven back to promoting the interests of the community from which historically they derived their support.

Because the parties drew their support mainly from one community, government by one party was seen essentially as ethnic government. The defeat in a general election of the governing party by another party or coalition thus came to be seen as the defeat of one community by another. In 1987, when the Alliance was defeated by the NFP-FLP coalition, many Fijians thought that their community was defeated and their sacred institutions imperilled. Because so much weight was placed on political paramountcy, Fijians were unwilling to accept the outcome of the election, and saw the defeat of their party as a breach of the Indo-Fijians' tacit acceptance of that principle. By contrast Indo-Fijians saw no inconsistency in their recognition of the principle of Fijian paramountcy, as they understood it, and seeking to become government. The result was the military overthrow of the coalition government.

Yet the outcome of the 1987 election was entirely consistent with the nature of the 1970 constitutional arrangements. No democratic constitution could guarantee government to a particular party. Nor could it possibly guarantee that the majority party would always represent a particular ethnic community. The essence of a democratic system is the ability of elections to change the government, to maintain their accountability and responsiveness to the people.

The 1990 constitution embodied what Fijians believed to be the remedy for their predicament. That constitution was a drastic response to a drastic situation. Its underlying assumption was if Fijians had more than half the seats, they could govern in perpetuity. An indigenous Fijian party winning all 37 seats could form a government where splinter Fijian parties would submerge their differences and come together in the interests of the larger Fijian cause. And Rotumans and general electors could be counted on for support. That was the hope, but in fact there was considerable divergence of interests across occupations and regions, created by the effects of the money economy, which no amount of political engineering could hide. Even with weighted representation, Fijians could not form government without the support of independent members and members of another party. Nor was the governing coalition able to maintain its unity in all circumstances, clearly seen in the defeat of the SVT-led coalition in November 1993.

The lesson was clear. First, the goal of permanent Fijian political unity was unrealistic and efforts to pursue it had a high cost for Fijians themselves. Second, in the absence of unity, even a constitution as heavily weighted as the 1990 constitution could not prevent a minority of Fijians from joining with an Indo-Fijian party or parties to form a government. Third, trying to keep a predominantly Fijian government in office in perpetuity was not the best way to secure the paramountcy of Fijian interests. In short, the assumptions that underpinned the 1990 constitution had proved untenable, indeed counterproductive. Fiji would need a new course to move away from the *cul-de-sac* of communal politics.

The commission was convinced after listening to submissions that the people wanted all communities to play some part in the cabinet, and that voters should be able to cast votes for at least some candidates from communities other than their own. They disagreed on the means of achieving that end and the pace that should be adopted in the direction of multiethnicity, but it was agreed that this broad goal was widely shared. The commission agreed that progress towards the genuine sharing of power was the only way to resolve some of Fiji's constitutional problems, the only way to attain racial harmony, national unity and the social and economic advancement of all communities. Constitutional arrangements that promote multiethnic government should be the primary goal.

Such arrangements, moreover, should protect the rights and interests of all citizens, particularly of the indigenous communities. And they should provide incentives to parties to strive for multiethnic cooperation, and for the political process to move gradually but decisively away from communal representation. The principle of Fijian paramountcy should be recognised, as in the past, in its protective role, in securing effective Fijian participation in a multiethnic government, and in securing the fruits of affirmative programs of social and ethnic justice based on a distribution of resources broadly acceptable to all. Fijian interests should not be subordinate to those of other communities. Ultimately, however, the best guarantee of the interests of all communities was a constitution that gave all parties a strong inducement to view the important interests of each community as national interests.

This goal of an inclusive, democratic, open and free multiethnic society is reflected in a number of the commission's early recommendations. Fiji should be named The Republic of the Fiji Islands, which would give all Fiji citizens, if they wished, the opportunity of calling themselves 'Fiji Islanders'. The constitution should accord Fijian, Hindi and English equal status and, wherever possible, offer services to the public in all three languages. The preamble should be broadly acceptable to all citizens, touching on the history of Fiji's multiethnic society and its shared beliefs and values. Perhaps most important, the values and principles which should be taken into account when forming governments should be stated in a compact, an artefact of moral, as distinct from legal, force.

These included respect for the rights of all individuals, communities and groups, including those protecting the traditional ownership of Fijian land and the observation of lease arrangements between landlords and tenants; the right to freely practice religion, language, culture and traditions; the right of the indigenous communities to governance through separate administrative systems; political freedom and full and equal citizenship rights for all; respect for the democratic process; fair and inclusive government and the need to negotiate in good faith to reach agreement to resolve differences and conflicts of interests; recognition of the principle of the paramountcy of Fijian interests as a protective principle to ensure that the interests of the Fijian community are not subordinated to those of other communities; and the need for affirmative action and social justice programs to secure equality of access to opportunities, amenities and services for the Fijian and Rotuman people, as well as other communities, and for all disadvantaged groups, to be based on an allocation of resources broadly acceptable to all ethnic communities.

These principles were given concrete constitutional form in the commission's recommendations on the structure of government. They represented significant shifts from the 1990 and 1970 constitutions. To begin with, the commission recommended that the Bose Levu Vakaturaga should not only be recognised in the constitution (as in 1990), but that its composition, powers and functions should be further specified. There was widespread support for this view, reflecting the respect that institution was accorded. Some Fijians wanted to return the Bose Levu Vakaturaga to its original status, restricting membership predominantly to chiefs and according a privileged role to the descendants of those who had ceded Fiji to the United Kingdom.

The commission regarded that view as impracticable and anachronistic. It recommended instead that the Bose Levu Vakaturaga should consist of a mix of members nominated by the three confederacies and those elected by the provinces, besides five ex-officio members including the president, the heads of the three confederacies, and the minister for Fijian affairs. The Bose Levu Vakaturaga should continue to be an advisory body, though with the important functions of nominating candidates for the office of president, and exercising veto power over amendments of the entrenched legislation relating to Fijians, Rotumans and the Rabi Island community or any other legislation that the attorney general certified as affecting Fijian land or customary rights. To exercise its functions impartially, the Bose Levu Vakaturaga should be independent not only from government but also from any political party. It should have its own secretariat and relative financial autonomy as well as electing its own chairperson. The Indo-Fijian community wanted a body similar to the Bose Levu Vakaturaga for itself. The commission recognised the need for such a body but felt that this was a matter for the Indo-Fijian community to take up in the first instance. It could be conferred statutory or constitutional status if it proved its utility as a representative body of Indo-Fijian opinion.

The commission recommended the retention of the office of the president, with much the same powers as the governor general in the Westminster tradition. Executive power would rest with the cabinet, and the president would be bound to act on the advice of ministers. The ceremonial role of the presidency would continue to be important, with the incumbent expected to symbolise the unity of the nation, command the loyalty and respect of all the communities and be impartial in the discharge of duties. It would be clearly spelt out on which matters the president could act in his or her 'own deliberate judgment', but these instances would be within the bounds of the conventions of the parliamentary system of government.

Most submissions agreed that the president should continue to be an indigenous Fijian, an important recognition of Fijians as the indigenous people of the land, but they suggested that this be balanced by the provision that there should be a non-Fijian vice president. The president (and the vice president, who would be the president's running mate as in the United States) would be elected without debate by the Electoral College, comprising both houses of parliament, from a list of three to five names submitted by the Bose Levu Vakaturaga. A President's Council of 10–15 distinguished citizens from all ethnic communities and walks of life would provide their well-informed, non-partisan views on issues of national importance, without in any way imposing constraints on the actions of the cabinet.

The commission recommended the retention of the bicameral Westminster system which had been in existence in Fiji for nearly 30 years, but suggested important changes in the composition of the two houses as well as the method of election. Both houses should be elected. The Upper House, to be renamed Bose e Cake, should comprise 35 members, two each from the 14 Fijian provinces, one from Rotuma and six appointed by the president on the advice of the Electoral Commission to represent communities and groups unrepresented in parliament (religious and cultural organisations, women, youth). The commission recognised that members of all communities have a strong sense of territorial identity through birth and residence as well as shared or complementary interests.

In rural areas, most people were able to speak both Fijian and Hindi; indeed, in several places, some Indo-Fijians indicated their desire to make their submissions in the Fijian dialect of the area. For these reasons, the commission recommended that members representing the provinces in the Bose e Cake be elected by voters from all communities resident in the province, to strengthen the sense of common identification with the province and their economic, and sometimes social, interdependence. Provincial concerns would be articulated from provincial rather than racial perspective. In terms of its powers and functions, the Bose e Cake would be similar to a house of review in the Westminster tradition.

The arrangements for electing members of the House of Representatives understandably attracted the greatest attention nationally and internationally. The commission approached the delicate issue with certain objectives in mind: they should encourage multiethnic governments; comply with international standards of equal suffrage; be based on a more open system of representation, and provide a gradual but decisive means of moving away from the present arrangements. Applying these criteria made it clear that communal representation was anachronistic and generally contrary to international practice. A study of the voting systems of 150 of the world's 186 sovereign states by the International Parliamentary Union in 1993 showed that in only 25 states are some members elected or appointed to the legislature to represent particular groups; but in each case, the proportion of special seats is very small.

Many submissions supported the existing arrangements, and many Fijians wanted to see them even more heavily weighted in favour of the indigenous community. Equally, many submissions from all communities wanted at least some seats to be filled on a non-racial basis. Many advocated a return to the cross-voting seats under the 1970 constitution, but that arrangement was fraught and only marginally successful in bringing about more conciliatory politics. The commission recommended that a 70-seat Lower House, to be called the Bose Lawa, made up of 45 seats elected from open constituencies (with no restriction of race for voters or candidates) and 25 from reserved seats: Fijians (including Pacific Islanders) 12; Indo-Fijians 10, general voters 2 and Rotumans 1.

Communal representation is not inconsistent with international standards, especially if it operates within the framework of individual choice and the principle of equal suffrage, but the commission saw the reserved seats as a transitional measure. Hence any deviation from the principle of equality could be accommodated within the 'margin of appreciation' that international law allows to states in applying human rights standards. The allocation of reserved seats is broadly based on population figures, taking account of historical and other factors that have affected the present and past allocations of communal seats. The point was that the allocation should be seen to be fair. The 25 reserved seats represented approximately 36 per cent of the seats in the Bose Lawa and the open seats 64 per cent, the minimum necessary to allow them to spur the development of multiethnic politics. As a further incentive to the emergence of multiethnic governments, the commission recommended that 45 open seats should be elected from 15 three-member constituencies, the boundaries drawn in such a way as to ensure that the constituencies are heterogeneous while taking traditional criteria into account, such as geographical features, administrative and recognised traditional areas, means of communication and mobility of population. That is, they should be composed of members of different communities to force political parties to appeal for votes from communities other than their own. The chances of candidates of a community-based party succeeding would depend on the extent of support from other communities. The level of heterogeneity would naturally vary, given the nature of population distribution, but the principle of multiethnicity should be borne in mind when drawing constituency boundaries. The commission took as the measure of heterogeneity the inclusion within the constituency of a mixed population ranging from a more or less equal balance between Fijians and Indo-Fijians, to a proportion as high as 85–95 per cent of one community. The average distribution was 60 per cent of one community and 40 per cent of the other. The evidence before the commission suggested that it was entirely possible to draw such boundaries.

The electoral system also plays an important role in promoting multiethnic cooperation. Fiji, like most ex-British colonies, inherited the British voting system at independence, best known as first-past-the-post, in which the winning candidate is the one who gets the greatest number of votes. A logical system when the choice is only between two candidates, first-past-the-post is widely considered unfair where there are more than two candidates. It also denies voters the possible range of preferences. Because of the disadvantages of plurality systems, various modifications have been proposed over the years to ensure that a winning candidate gets an absolute majority of votes cast. Several of these systems were put forward to the commission for its consideration.

Acknowledging the critical role of electoral systems in determining political outcomes, the commission identified and ranked a number of criteria against which available options could be evaluated. These, in order of importance, included the encouragement of multiethnic government; recognition of the role of political parties; incentives offered for moderation and cooperation across ethnic lines; effective representation of constituents; effective voter participation; effective representation of minority and special interest groups; fairness between political parties; effective government; effective opposition; proven workability; and legitimacy.

All electoral systems met some of these criteria, and some more than others. The single transferable vote, which was recommended by the Street Commission in 1975, for example, mitigates against the winner-takes-all outcome of the first-past-the-post, and achieved better proportionality of seats to votes. But by requiring an extremely low threshold to get elected in a three member constituency, a successful candidate would need no more than 25 per cent—and by privileging the representation of community interests, it failed to meet the commission's most important criteria: the promotion of multiethnic governments. The list system's proportional representation allocates seats to parties in proportion to the number of votes cast for the party. While it had considerable merit, its weakness was that by treating the whole country or major region as a single constituency, it failed to provide links between the voter and his or her member. It also provoked fears of small parties exercising disproportionate influence.

In the commission's view, the alternative vote, also known as preferential vote, best met all the criteria. The alternative vote is based on the same principle as second ballots, but avoids the need for a second election at a later date. It is in effect a refinement of the first-past-the-post system in that it requires voters to rank candidates in order of preference. To be elected, a candidate must have a majority of the votes cast, that is, 50 per cent plus 1. If no candidate reaches the threshold when first preferences are counted, then second and third preferences are counted and allocated. The process of elimination continues until one of the candidates has obtained the required quota. The alternative vote system provides incentive for vote pooling by requiring the winning candidate to obtain more than 50 per cent. In heterogeneous constituencies, this threshold increases the need for a candidate to have multiethnic support. The system allows parties to trade preferences.

Again, only moderate parties with conciliatory policies would agree to trade preferences, and persuade their supporters to honour the agreement. The system therefore encourages such parties. Constituents are effectively represented at least insofar as candidates represent territorial constituencies, and citizens are given considerable opportunity to affect the outcome by expressing preferences. As a majoritarian, rather than a proportional system, alternative vote is likely to encourage the emergence of a strong party or pre-election government. The commission recommended that the alternative vote system be used in multi-member constituencies, but there was nothing to stop its use in single member constituencies.[1]

The commission recommended the retention of the Westminster system. The people were familiar with its workings and conventions. Nonetheless, its adversarial nature, pitting an 'Indian' opposition against a 'Fijian' government, elicited comment in the submissions. The commission noted that in Fiji, opposition criticism of a government proposal, no matter how valid or rational, was often portrayed essentially as Indo-Fijian criticism of Fijian performance. People asked the commission to suggest ways of minimising the harmful effects of this aspect of the Westminster system and to allow the house to use the talents of all its members.

Fortunately, Commonwealth countries, including New Zealand, have devised such ways by setting up sector committees that permit all members of the Lower House, except ministers or assistant ministers, to take part in national decision-making. Sector committees are structured in such a way that all departments and other government agencies come within the supervision of some committee. The commission recommended that in addition to the existing Standing Committees (such as the Standing Select Committee on Sugar and the Public Accounts Committee), there should be five standing Select Committees, each dealing with one sector: economic services, social services, natural resources, foreign relations and administrative services. These committees would scrutinise all areas of government activity, and consider bills referred to them by parliament. Their overall membership should reflect the balance of the parties in the house, with the chair and the deputy chair to come from opposite sides of the house. All these mechanisms are designed to achieve an open, representative, inclusive and multiethnic government that protects the interests and addresses the concerns of all communities and groups. That was the only way all the people of Fiji could aspire to realise a prosperous and united future.

While questions surrounding the election of parliament occupy centre stage in any constitutional review, other areas impinge on the daily lives of the people. These include provisions for the acquisition and deprivation of citizenship, fundamental freedoms and a Bill of Rights, the independence and functioning of the judiciary, the enforcement of accountability in the public sector, and equal access to state services. Often in these areas, the commission was required not so much to formulate new proposals as to modernise or revise the existing ones in the light of new international conventions and practices.

To illustrate, the 1990 constitution already had a Bill of Rights, called fundamental rights and freedoms, adapted with few changes from the one present in the 1970 constitution. But the independence Bill of Rights was in a form developed by the Foreign and Commonwealth Office and was included, with only slight variations, in the constitutions of most former British colonies. It reflected British caution about including individual rights in a judicially enforceable constitution. Individual rights and freedoms were seen as already enshrined in common law. The emphasis was not on affirming their existence but on protecting them from unjustified interference by the state.

The commission recommended that in keeping with modern trends, the constitution should affirm rights and freedoms in positive terms, that these should be judicially enforceable, binding the legislative, executive and judicial branches of government at all levels, and that they should not conflict with international human rights standards but rather give effect to them where appropriate. It recommended that a three-member Human Rights Commission be created to educate the public about the nature and purpose of the Bill of Rights, make recommendations to government about matters affecting compliance with human rights and exercising any other functions conferred by the Act. The commission adopted a similar approach to citizenship. Fiji's existing citizenship laws reflect the thinking of an earlier generation and were in some important respects archaic. The independence constitution and its 1990 counterpart allowed non-citizen women the automatic right to acquire Fiji citizenship on marriage to a male citizen, but did not accord the same privilege to non-citizen husbands. Most women's groups who made submissions were adamant that discrimination against women and children had to go, and the commission agreed.

In the Westminster system, a vital corollary to the power of politically appointed ministers to direct government policy is the expectation that the administration of that policy will be carried out economically, efficiently and effectively by politically impartial state services. Although the objectives of economy, efficiency and effectiveness in state services had a long history in Fiji, they were never expressly required in the constitution. Because they were fundamental to the functioning of all state services, the commission felt that they should be reflected in a constitutional provision. A related issue was the 'fair treatment' of each community in the number and distribution of entry appointment. The 1970 constitution directed the Public Service Commission to 'ensure that, so far as possible, each community in Fiji receives fair treatment in the number and distribution of offices to which candidates of that community are appointed on entry'. The 1990 constitution compelled the government to ensure that each level of each department comprised not less than 50 per cent of Fijians and Rotumans, and not less than 40 per cent members of other communities. But this quota was not observed, nor was it possible to achieve it at every level within every department.

Indo-Fijians complained of a significant reduction in their numbers in the state services, particularly at the senior levels. They expressed concern at their falling representation in the police force and their almost total absence from the armed forces. Whatever the reason—occupational preferences, active discouragement, emigration—the complaint was empirically well-founded. The commission concluded that while efficiency, economy and effectiveness should be the principal objectives in managing state services, some more appropriate account must be taken of the overall representation of different ethnic groups.

To that end, the commission proposed a new general provision in the constitution. In recruiting and promoting members of all state services—including the public service, the police force and the military forces—and in the management of those services, the following factors were to be taken into account: ensuring that government policies are be carried out effectively; achieving efficiency and economy; making appointments and promotions on the basis of merit; providing men and women and members of all ethnic groups with adequate opportunities for training and advancement; and all levels of services broadly reflecting the ethnic composition of the population, taking into account occupational preferences.

Closely related to the provision of state services was the issue of ethnic and social justice. Section 21 of the 1990 constitution enjoined the government to introduce affirmative action programs for the Fijian and Rotuman communities, notably in the areas of education, commerce and participation at the higher levels of the public service. These policies had an effect. In 1985, Fijians made up 46.4 per cent of established civil servants, Indo-Fijians 48 per cent, and general voters and expatriates 5.6 per cent. The corresponding figures in October 1995 were Fijians 57.3 per cent, Indo-Fijians 38.6 per cent, and general voters and expatriates 4.11 per cent. In 1995, of the 31 permanent secretaries, 22 were Fijians, 6 were Indo-Fijians and 3 general voters. Indo-Fijians accepted the principle of affirmative action to redress imbalances, but wanted to include disadvantaged members of all communities, not just the indigenous people. Their submission drew attention to the growing levels of poverty among sections of their people, and their growing numbers in squatter settlements.

The commission agreed that the government needed to continue implementing policies and programs to reduce inequalities between different ethnic communities, but since there were areas in which other communities were also disadvantaged, social inequalities should not be neglected. It was recommended that a social justice and affirmative action program be implemented for Rotumans and Fijians and other ethnic communities, and for men as well as women. This program would ensure effective equality of access to education and training, land and housing, participation in commerce and all aspects of service of the state at all levels, and other opportunities, amenities and services essential to an adequate standard of living. The program should be authorised by an artefact (following parliamentary debate) which would specify the goals of the program, identify the persons or groups it was intended to benefit, and outline the means by which those goals would be achieved, and highlight performance measures and criteria for the selection of the members of the group entitled to participate. In short, it was the commission's view that, in order to be effective, affirmative action policies should be transparent, properly debated and carefully monitored.

For state services and institutions to be effective and impartial, they needed to be subject to strict rules of accountability. The commission received many submissions proposing constitutional provisions to prevent official corruption and achieving higher ethical standards from those holding important offices of state. They were not accusations against ministers or state servants; they were about public confidence in government and the integrity of its leaders. Existing statutes, regulations and orders contained ethical standards and rules which applied to state servants, members and officers of statutory bodies, but the commission was convinced of the need to go further. It therefore proposed an Integrity Code for the president, the vice president, ministers and all members of parliament, and all constitutional office holders. Such a code would require them not to place themselves in positions where they could have a conflict of interest, compromise the fair exercise of their public or official functions and duties, use their offices for private gain, allow their integrity to be called into question, endanger or diminish respect for, or confidence in, the integrity of government, or demean their office or position. These principles were to be enshrined in an Act of Parliament, which would make detailed and specific provisions to deal with the various kinds of conflicts of interest in Fiji's particular circumstances. The commission also recommended that the Office of Ombudsman be strengthened, allowing it to investigate allegations of corruption or mismanagement of public office. In an important and innovative stand, the commission recommended that a new Constitutional Offices Commission be created; this body would directly appoint the Solicitor General, the Director of Public Prosecutions, the Secretary General to Parliament, the Supervisor of Elections and the Commissioner of Police, and would put forth recommendations to the President on the appointment of the Ombudsman and the Auditor General.

A future constitution, the commission felt, should be generally acceptable to all citizens; guarantee the rights of individuals and groups and promote the rule of law and the separation of powers; recognise the unique history and character of Fiji; encourage every community to regard the major concerns of other communities as national concerns; recognise the equal rights of all citizens; protect the vital interests and concerns of the indigenous communities and all the other groups, within the inclusive and overarching framework of democracy.

## Note

[1] Subsequent experience shows that political parties, including the Labour Party, would trade preferences with anyone in order to win, including their sworn opponents.

# 7

# A time to change

The 1990s was a decade of unexpected political change in Fiji, confounding conventional wisdom about power sharing arrangements in that troubled country. For the sheer momentum and unpredictability of events, it rivalled the 1960s, Fiji's decade of decolonisation—a time of industrial strikes where violence was threatened, keenly contested elections and by-elections, and tense conferences about which constitutional systems suited Fiji's multiethnic society. The 1990s, too, Fiji's decade of progressive political democratisation, had its tension and turbulence, false starts and extended detours as its people grappled with the unsettling aftermath of the coups and struggled to devise a constitutional order suited to its situation.

The decade began on a divided note, as the architects of the coups of 1987 attempted to frame a constitution to entrench Fijian political control within a nominally democratic framework. That goal was enshrined in an interim constitution promulgated on 25 July 1990. Contested and opposed by Indo-Fijians and others marginalised by it, and denounced by the international community, who were affronted by its disregard for universal human rights conventions, the constitution was reviewed by an independent commission five years later. The commission recommended a more inclusive, non-racial system of representation while protecting the legitimate interests and concerns of the different communities. Two years later, most of the commission's recommendations, except for the significant reversal of the proportion of open and reserved seats, were incorporated in a new constitution approved unanimously by parliament and blessed by the all-powerful Great Council of Chiefs. Within ten years, Fiji had travelled the gamut from coup to constitutionalism like few other countries.

In May 1999, Fiji went to the polls under the revised constitution. 'Fiji's general elections now under way are expected to see the three-party coalition led by outgoing prime minister Sitiveni Rabuka emerge as the largest block in the new House of Representatives', wrote one respected observer after voting began, echoing virtually every observer of the Fijian scene. The report went on: 'The coalition conducted the most coherent campaign, making the most of the advantages of incumbency, and Rabuka was clearly the dominant figure in campaigning' (*Pacific Report*, 10 May 1999).[1] The Fiji voters delivered a dramatically different verdict, electing by a landslide a newly formed, fractious, 'People's Coalition' consisting of the Fiji Labour Party, the Party of National Unity (PANU) and the Fijian Association Party (FAP), with Labour winning 37 of the 71 seats in the House of Representatives, enough to govern alone. The other coalition of the Soqosoqo ni Vakavulewa ni Taukei (SVT), the National Federation Party (NFP) and the United General Party (UGP), suffered a massive defeat, with the NFP losing every seat, and the SVT winning only 8. The shock caused by this would be felt for a long time.

Ironies abounded. Against all odds and all expectations, an Indo-Fijian, Mahendra Pal Chaudhry, was appointed prime minister, a prospect that would have appeared implausible just a few days earlier. More baffling still was that Chaudhry had formed a coalition with the Fijian Association, whose overtures for political support to form a government in 1992 he had rebuffed. Ratu Sir Kamisese Mara, whom Chaudhry had regarded as the evil genius behind the country's recent political troubles, was now hailed as an ally, a statesman providing sage advice to an inexperienced, hastily cobbled together administration representing divergent agendas and speaking with discordant voices. On the other side of the divide, NFP's Jai Ram Reddy had joined hands with SVT leader Rabuka whom he had refused to support—but whom Chaudhry had supported—for prime minister a few years back.

The two dominant figures of contemporary politics, widely praised for their leadership in the constitution review, became generals without armies. Rabuka resigned from parliament to become (a commoner) chairman of the Great Council of Chiefs and the Commonwealth Secretary General's peace envoy to Solomon Islands. From coup-maker to international peace negotiator—it was a remarkable journey. For Reddy, also widely respected for his contribution to the country's healing, the results were a fateful replay of history. His party, under A.D. Patel, had played a leading role in Fiji's independence struggle but was consigned to the wilderness of the opposition benches for a generation. Now once again, he and his party were dealt a crushing blow and seemed destined to be consigned to the political margins after helping deliver the best constitution Fiji had ever had and laying the foundations of a truly multiracial democracy. Parties which had played a marginal or negligible role in formulating the new constitution were now poised to enjoy its benefits. The vanquished of 1987 had emerged victorious in 1999.

The conduct of the campaign and its outcome were determined by specific provisions of the new constitution. The first important feature was the provision for electing members of parliament, in particular the House of Representatives (the Senate being an appointed body). Of the 71 seats in the house, 46 are elected on a reserved, communal basis, with 23 contested by Fijian communal candidates, 19 by Indo-Fijians, 3 by general electors and 1 by the Council of Rotuma. For these seats, the candidates, as well as the voters, belong to the same ethnic category. The remaining 25 are open (common roll) seats, with ethnic restriction for neither voters nor candidates. These open seats are an innovation for Fiji, designed to lead gradually but decisively away from communal to non-racial politics. Under the 1990 constitution, all seats were communally reserved for the three ethnic communities (37 for Fijians, 27 for Indo-Fijians, and 5 for general electors). The 1970 (independence) constitution had a curious mixture of communal and cross-voting national seats where the ethnicity of the candidates was specified but all voted for them. The way in which the open seats were contested proved crucial to the outcome in some constituencies and helped determine the overall result.

The 1997 constitution also provided for a new alternative, or preferential, voting system, to replace the archaic first-past-the-post system inherited at independence. The alternative voting system was recommended by the Constitution Review Commission. The ballot paper required voters to vote either above the line, accepting the party's allocation of preferences, or below the line, where they could rank the candidates themselves. Most voted above the line, and this had an important bearing on the outcome of the election.

The third feature of the constitution which affected the outcome of the election was the mandatory provision for power sharing, entitling any political party with more than 10 per cent of seats in the lower house to a place in cabinet (in proportion to its percentage of seats). The party with the most number of seats provides the prime minister, who allocates portfolios in cabinet. Because of this provision for a multiparty cabinet, the parties in the winning People's Coalition formed only a loose coalition among themselves, leaving the details of power sharing and leadership to be decided after the elections. This tactic gave them flexibility and internal leverage. The NFP, SVT and UGP, on the other hand, formed a binding pre-election coalition in a more conventional mould.

The campaign was the most relaxed in living memory. Trading preferences with other parties dampened what would have been a fiery campaign. For once, race was relegated to the background because both coalitions were multiracial. The constitutional provision for mandatory power sharing also made political parties wary of being too aggressive towards each other because of the possibility of working together in cabinet later. The multiparty cabinet concept also erased the winner-takes-all mentality. The long and difficult negotiations preceding the promulgation of the new constitution had created goodwill and understanding and cross-cultural friendship among candidates facing each other in the election. The fact that the constitution had been approved unanimously by the parliament, endorsed by the Great Council of Chiefs and warmly welcomed by the international community also had a calming effect.

The fear that rights of the indigenous Fijians could be eroded if a non-Fijian ruled had often been used to mobilise opposition against that prospect, as happened in 1987. People were generally ignorant—or uninformed—about the way their rights and interests were protected in the constitution. That was no longer true. The new constitution was homegrown, devised in a transparent manner after wide consultation and in full glare of national publicity and international scrutiny. This was not the case with the 1970 constitution, which was negotiated in secrecy, approved in London and never subjected to a vote. The 1990 constitution was also promulgated by presidential decree with no popular participation.

For the first time, the legitimate needs and concerns of all communities were protected in a manner broadly acceptable them. The Great Council of Chiefs, whose constitutional role was recognised, could veto legislation that affected issues of concern to the Fijian people; it nominated both the president and the vice president; the ownership of Fijian land according to Fijian custom was recognised along with their and the Rotuman people's right to governance through separate administrative system. The compact, a set of principles which all governments were enjoined to observe, stipulated that where the interests of the different communities were in conflict, 'the paramountcy of Fijian interests as a protective principle continues to apply, so as to ensure that the interests of the Fijian community are not subordinated to the interests of any other community'. And all communities were assured that affirmative action and social justice programs would be 'based on an allocation of resources broadly acceptable to all communities'. Clarifying the principles and procedures of governance helped greatly in allaying fears and doubts.

## Political parties

Twenty-one political parties contested the 1999 election.[2] Many were obscure in origin and purpose and insignificant in their impact. If they were known at all, this reflected their entertainment value rather than their vision. Among these were the Natural Law Party, the Coalition of Independent Nationals Party, the Viti Levu Dynamic Multiracial Democratic Party, the Tawavanua Party, the National Democratic Party, and the Farmers and General Workers Coalition Party. The main actors were in the two coalitions, and in the Christian Democratic Alliance, which emerged on the eve of the campaign.

### The SVT/NFP/UGP coalition

This was a predictable coalition of three self-described mainstream parties representing the three main ethnic communities, standing on the basis of a firm pre-election agreement about power sharing. The members of the coalition had worked together, and they promised to continue their dialogue and consensus. Sitiveni Rabuka and Jai Ram Reddy, leading the two main parties, had contributed significantly in securing the approval of the new constitution in parliament. Rabuka had invited Reddy to address the Great Council of Chiefs to ask for their blessing of the constitution. The two had set up a joint parliamentary committee to resolve the complex issue of expiring leases under the Agricultural Landlord and Tenant Act (ALTA). Rabuka and Reddy, so different from each other in training and temperament—one a soldier, open and intuitive, the other a lawyer, reserved and cautious—enjoyed a remarkable personal rapport, which they promised to translate into continuing cooperation.

Both leaders extolled the virtues of a pre-election coalition. Reddy said that a coalition that shares common goals, ideas and policies is more likely to succeed than a post-election multiparty government of hitherto mutually hostile forces.

> [Another] compelling case is the need to bring together the different racial groups as partners in the electoral process in order to reduce communal tensions that have historically characterised our elections of the past. We want to put an end to the long years of political rivalry between our different communities and usher in a new era of political cooperation—consistent with the aims and objectives of the constitution. The valuable experience we have acquired during the making of the new constitution and the immense goodwill that has been shown by the Fijian people can be made the basis for solving many of our difficult problems such as ALTA, crime, unemployment, health and education. They cannot be solved through confrontation but by working together (*Daily Post*, 26 March 1999).

The coalition agreement, signed by Rabuka, Reddy and UGP leader David Pickering, provided that the leader of the SVT, whoever it might be, would be the coalition's nominee for prime minister, while the NFP leader would become deputy prime minister, with the UGP being guaranteed a cabinet seat. Second, the parties agreed to share the 25 open seats, with SVT getting 14 and NFP 11. The two parties agreed to give their first preference to each other's designated candidates for the open seats, and not field parallel candidates or support independents or other candidates. The coalition would last until the next election, with the parties working together as coalition partners even if one party won enough seats to govern alone. Finally, the agreement provided for regular consultations to develop policy or resolve difficulties, but agreed to 'respect particular party positions in agreed areas where special group interests may be affected'.

This escape clause was necessary because there were areas where the two parties had diametrically opposed positions. The privatisation of public assets was one, and it highlights the difficulty for the coalition in mounting an effective campaign as a unit. What one partner advertised as a major achievement, the other saw as a public policy disaster. The SVT government had sold 49 per cent of Amalgamated Telecom Holdings Limited for F$253 million to the Fiji National Provident Fund, and 51 per cent of the National Bank of Fiji to Colonial Mutual Insurance Company for F$9.5 million, ostensibly to promote competition in the private sector. It had also sold 17 per cent of Air Pacific for F$26.8 million to foreign airlines 'to strengthen the airline's international network and [increase] tourist arrivals', and 51 per cent of the Government Shipyard for F$3.2 million to improve its 'competitiveness and [win] international orders' (Ministry of National Planning Information 1998). These sales, the government argued, would free up resources for growth in the private sector and enable it to 'focus more on improving the efficiency of its operations in the priority sectors, i.e. core and essential services'. The NFP, on other hand, opposed the privatisation of state enterprises that were yielding high returns or covered strategic resources, such as the international airport and shipping facilities, or those that were undertaken purely to fund recurrent fiscal deficits. It supported only those privatisation efforts where the state had no legitimate economic interests or the enterprises were unprofitable or relied on permanent grants and subsidies. The People's Coalition was unambiguous in its opposition: 'strategic utilities such as water, electricity, telecommunication and civil aviation facilities must remain in public hands as viable units' (People's Coalition campaign material).

Another issue dividing the parties was the status of state land. There are two types of state (formerly crown) land: Schedule A (52,513 ha) refers to land owned by landowning *mataqali* deemed to have become extinct by the time of Cession in 1874; Schedule B (43,113 ha) land which was unoccupied and had no claimants when the Native Lands Commission met. This land was managed by the state. In the early 1990s, facing pressure from landless Fijians and with a view to gaining political mileage, the government devised a bill to return this land to Fijians and provide for land-management to be transferred to the Native Land Trust Board, which also managed native land on behalf of Fijian landlords. The NFP criticised the government's proposal. It also opposed the policy of purchasing freehold land and giving it to the Fijians. It had been particularly vocal in denouncing the setting up of the Viti Corps, a government initiative to provide agricultural training to Fijian youth on a freehold property it had purchased for F$7 million. Other areas of disagreement included strategies for creating employment, strengthening economic growth and poverty alleviation.

The coalition agreement compromised both parties. The SVT could not highlight its pro-Fijian policies for fear of alienating supporters of its coalition partner, while the NFP had to soften its public opposition to the government. They were caught on the horns of a dilemma. As ethnic parties they were expected to champion the sectional interests of their communities; and yet, as parties which had worked together to fashion a new constitution and lay the foundations of a new multiracialism. They could not afford to adopt an 'ethnicist' position which might have sharpened their appeal among supporters because this would hurt the larger cause of reconciliation. The two parties were not standing on the joint record; they were standing on their promise to work together in future. It was a critical distinction that was lost on the electorate.

## The People's coalition

The People's coalition was the other main multiracial coalition. Unlike the SVT/NFP/UGP coalition, it was loosely structured, and details of the agreement and internal understandings about power sharing were never released to the public. The coalition consisted of the Fiji Labour Party, the Party of National Unity and the Fijian Association. Each had its own history and agenda, but they were united by one common, overriding ambition: to remove Rabuka from power and (for Labour) to supplant Reddy and the National Federation Party as the party of the Indo-Fijians.

The Fiji Labour Party was formed in 1985 as a multiracial party backed by the powerful trade unions. Dr Timoci Bavadra, an indigenous Fijian medical doctor, was its founding president and leader, with the powerful

Fiji Public Servants Association leader Mahendra Chaudhry as its mastermind and general secretary. Labour won the 1987 election in coalition with the NFP, only to be deposed in a coup a month later. The partnership did not last long, the rift erupting into a bitter disagreement over participation in the 1992 election. NFP participated, while Labour decided not to, until the last minute. Labour's support for Sitiveni Rabuka as prime minister following the 1992 elections, drove the two parties further apart. Although they returned to make a joint submission to the Constitution Review Commission, the rift was widening. By the mid 1990s, Labour was a shadow of its earlier self, with most of its founding members having left for other parties, including many Fijians. By the time of the election, it had enticed some back. The FLP, although supported predominantly by Indo-Fijians, had continued to field Fijian candidates in previous elections. And it kept nurturing its support base among workers and farmers and the trade unions.

The spectacularly misnamed western Viti Levu-based Party of National Unity was the brainchild of Apisai Tora, the quintessential maverick of Fiji politics. In a political career spanning nearly four decades, Tora had been a member of nearly every political party in Fiji, beginning with the Western Democratic Party in 1964, progressing to the National Democratic Party, the National Federation Party, the Alliance, the All National Congress and the Fijian Association Party. He had been a founding member of the nationalist Taukei Movement, and an enthusiastic supporter of the coups. But throughout his tortuous—not to say tortured—career, he had been a fierce champion of western Fijian interests, which, he argued, had been neglected in a government dominated by chiefs of the eastern establishment. PANU was Tora's latest vehicle to redress the longstanding grievance of the western Fijians and to secure them an appropriate place in the Fijian sun. All the nation's wealth-generating industries were concentrated in the west: sugar, tourism, gold and pine as well as the international airport and the hydro-electric power stations, Tora argued; and he wanted a commensurate share of national power.

PANU had the blessing of prominent western chiefs, including the Tui Vuda—the paramount chief of western Fiji and vice president—Ratu Josefa Iloilo, Tui Nawaka Ratu Apisai Naevo, Tui Sabeto Ratu Kaliova

Mataitoga, Tui Vitogo Ratu Josefa Sovasova and Marama na Tui Ba Adi Sainimili Cagilaba. The list was impressive, but the chiefs' support did not carry as much influence as before (see *The Review*, May 1998). Tora broached the idea of a coalition with the SVT first, and wanted a seat-sharing arrangement that would recognise and consolidate his influence in the west. He was rebuffed by western Fijian members of the SVT, especially Isimeli Bose and Ratu Etuate Tavai. Tora, they felt, was a spent force, his reputation for integrity and probity irreparably tainted by his impressive record of political bed-hopping. Moreover, the seat-sharing formula sought by Tora would have ended SVT's influence in western Viti Levu, a prospect no serious party aspiring for national leadership could countenance. Tora then turned to Labour, which responded favourably. It was a coalition of convenience; Labour gave Tora a wider platform on which, relying on his cunning, he no doubt hoped to enlarge with his own agenda. Tora promised Labour western Fijian support and assistance in resolving the issue of the expiring leases. The land issue was serious. On the eve of the election, Ba chiefs, who command the largest province, wanted 87 per cent of the leases not to be renewed (34,634 out of 39,725 ha) and in Sabeto, Nawaka, Nadi and Vuda, the chiefs wanted 92 per cent of the leases not to be renewed (12,728 out of 13,704 ha). Tora held—or seemed to hold—powerful cards.

The Fijian Association was the third member of the People's Coalition. It was formed in the early 1990s by Fijians opposed to Rabuka, ridiculing his leadership and attacking his moral character. Its founder was Josefata Kamikamica, an affable, mild-mannered but politically naive long-term head of the Native Land Trust Board and a member of the Mara-led post-coup Interim Administration (in which he had served as finance minister). He unsuccessfully challenged Rabuka for prime minister in 1992, and failed to get elected in 1994 and in later by-elections. After his death in 1998, the Fijian Association was led by Adi Kuini Bavadra Speed, the remarried widow of the founding Labour leader and herself one-time leader of the Fiji Labour Party and president of the All National Congress. The party's social philosophy was broadly similar to Labour's. In fact, nearly all its leading Fijian candidates were former members or friends of the Labour Party. But the party also contained a strange assortment of political refugees from other parties, with their own agendas and ambitions, united by the overriding desire to see Rabuka defeated. Sometimes the Fijian Association gave the impression of having a 'schizophrenic personality',[3] of saying one thing and doing another. One of its parliamentarians, Viliame Cavubati, was standing for the SVT while another, Dr Fereti Dewa, missed out on selection and launched a scathing attack on the party leaders. Its parliamentary leader, the ever-unpredictable Ratu Finau Mara, had left politics for a diplomatic career.

The People's Coalition had few common understandings, which invited attacks from the rival coalition. Who would lead the coalition if it won? 'The party with the most seats', the People's Coalition responded. Would that leader be a Fijian? The answer was similarly vague. The coalition had an equally flexible arrangement about allocating seats in the open constituencies. In some constituencies, they supported a common candidate, while elsewhere it fielded parallel candidates. Where it fielded parallel candidates, the coalition partners were given their second preference. This worked well for the most part, but created problems in some places. PANU, for example, expected to be allowed to field candidates in western constituencies with substantial Fijian population, but Labour disagreed and fielded its own, poaching some of Tora's prominent supporters and potential candidates, among them Ratu Tevita Momoedonu. Tora's own seat was contested by Labour, whose candidate beat him. Outmaneouvred, Tora refused to attend any of People's Coalition rallies. Towards the end of the campaign, he became a vocal critic of the Labour Party, chiding Labour president Jokapeci Koroi for not forgiving Rabuka for his past actions and accusing Chaudhry of treachery (*Fiji Times*, 7 May 1999). Tora refused to give preferences to his coalition partner, the Fijian Association Party, which had fielded candidates against his own. But by then, he mattered little. For once, the Machiavellian politician had been marginalised.

## Veitokani Ni Lewenivanua Vakaristo/Christian Democratic Alliance (VLV/CDA)

This party was launched on 27 March, on the eve of the election, by various Fijians opposed to Sitiveni Rabuka and his government. Its support came from three sources. First, there were those who opposed the 1997 constitution. Rabuka and his party had 'failed the Fijian people miserably',[4] the VLV charged. Rabuka had given away too much; he had 'exploited the indigenous Fijian institutions for his own glorification, even to the extent of selling out on the rights and interests of Fijians'. Unless the 'core interests' of the Fijians were addressed, there would be no political stability in the country.

We remind the PM of the VLV's primary platform that unless there is stability in the indigenous Fijian community, there will be no stability in this country in the future. It will all be fruitless and a waste of effort for all who have been trying to build and make Fiji a better place for all to live in.

In essence, they wanted to restore those provisions of the 1990 constitution that would have kept power in Fijian hands and supported Fijian paramountcy.

Other members and supporters came from sections of the Methodist Church, who wanted to turn Fiji into a Christian state (*Daily Post*, 31 March 1999). The very public blessing given to the party by the affable but malleable president of the Methodist Church, Reverend Tomasi Kanailagi, and the presence within it of such fire-breathing figures as former president Manasa Lasaro and Taniela Tabu, was powerfully symbolic. These people wanted the Sunday ban reintroduced, which reversed the stance the church had taken when Dr Ilaitia Tuwere was president in the mid 1990s. Tuwere had argued that turning Fiji into a Christian state would not 'make it a better place for everyone to live in. It will neither further the cause of Christianity not adequately meet the present wish to safeguard Fijian interests and identity'. And attention to 'man's careless disregard of the environment' was 'more urgent than Sunday observance' (*Daily Post*, 31 March 1999). Much depends on the character and vision of the person at the helm of the church. Nonetheless, religion is close to the heart of many Fijians, and most would not oppose the Christian state proposal. But others wanted to manipulate this deep religious attachment for their own ends.

The VLV claimed the support of 'members of the chiefly establishment'. To prove it, they made traditional approaches to Ratu Mara (Tui Nayau) and Adi Lady Lala Mara (Tui Dreketi), as well as Tui Vuda Ratu Josefa Iloilo. Most people believed that the president silently supported the party and encouraged his former supporters to do likewise.[5] Close members of his own family were contesting the election on the VLV ticket, including his daughter and son-in-law, and Poseci Bune, who was expected to 'strengthen and consolidate the Mara/Ganilau dynasty' (*Daily Post*, 29 March 1999). Fairly or unfairly, the president was accused of harbouring dynastic ambitions. Many Fijians remarked on Mara's cool relations with Rabuka, and his desire to see the prime minister defeated. Many founding members of the Fijian Association were known to the president as members of the Diners Club formed in the early 1990s with whom he shared his experiences and reflections on politics. Rabuka had defeated Lady Lala for the presidency of the SVT, which was not forgotten or forgiven. And Rabuka's claims, made before and during the election, that he had been used to stage the coup, raised questions about who else was involved, including members of the chiefly establishment which now supported the VLV. Rabuka had said that he was the 'fall guy' who refused to fall. His comment, in Lau of all places, that a commoner candidate could be more accessible than a chiefly one, raised further questions about his loyalty to chiefs (*Daily Post*, 7 May 1999). Mara's relations with Rabuka, never warm, had become decidedly chilly.

As the campaign proceeded, the VLV attempted to distance itself from its more extreme positions, and proclaimed its commitment to socially progressive policies. These included reorganising and restructuring regional development, improving the 'economic, social and human conditions in the rural areas' by assisting the provinces to implement 'infrastructure plans and projects, industrial, business and commercial plans and projects, agriculture, forestry and fisheries plans and projects, and social/human development plans and projects' (whatever these phrases, allegedly written in New York by an expatriate former Fiji public servant (Peter Halder), might mean), facilitating Fijian ownership of business, industry and commerce in each province and assisting Fijian landowners to 'utilise their lands for their own economic development and upliftment' (*The Review*, 14 April 1999). Bune, an experienced civil servant and former representative at the United Nations, got himself elected as party leader over Ratu Epeli Ganilau, the army commander who had resigned to contest the Lau open seat; but his elevation was contested by powerful party insiders who questioned his background and personal and moral credentials.[6] Nonetheless, the VLV fielded some well known and experienced candidates, including Ganilau and Adi Koila

Mara Nailatikau, Fijian academic Asesela Ravuvu, trade unionist Salote Qalo, and lawyers Kitione Vuataki and Naipote Vere.

Among the smaller Fijian parties, the Fijian Nationalist Vanua Tako Lavo Party was the most prominent. Led by longtime Fijian nationalist Sakiasi Butadroka, it was the latest reincarnation of the original Fijian Nationalist Party founded in 1975 to keep 'Fiji for the Fijians'. Twenty years later, it had changed little, except in name. The party rejected the 1997 constitution as a sell-out of Fijian interests, and wanted Rabuka punished for betraying the aims of the coup, which, they said, was to entrench Fijian political control. Its manifesto proclaimed that 'in addition to the normal guarantees for 75 per cent support from the Great Council of Chiefs for amendments concerning the Fijian people, we will ensure that 100 per cent support will be needed from all 14 Provincial Councils before any changes can be made to the iron clad guarantees affecting the Fijian people'. The name of the country would be changed from the Fiji Islands to Fiji because 'we want to be identified overseas as Fijians not Fiji Islanders' (*Daily Post*, 16 April 1999). The Fijian language would be taught in all schools, crown land returned to the indigenous people, and special bodies would be set up to exploit natural resources in the interest of the Fijian people. Fine words, but the party was now a caricature of its former self, not a force of consequence. Some leading members (Isireli Vuibau) had joined other parties, while ex-Taukei Movement member Iliesa Duvuloco was embroiled in financial difficulties. After the elections, Butadroka changed his trademark blood-red bow tie signifying violence if Indians ever challenged Fijian right to rule, to a black bow tie, mourning the political loss 'of the Fijian race'.

## Issues

For the SVT/NFP/UGP coalition, the main question was which party or coalition was best placed to provide political stability. Reddy spoke for the coalition.

> Experience around the world shows that political stability is a precondition for economic and social progress. Without political stability we will not be able to achieve anything. Political stability will lead to enlightened and progressive policies which, in turn, will generate business confidence, investment, economic growth and, above all, jobs for our unemployed (Reddy's final campaign address, 3 May 1999).

The NFP had always been the majority party of the Indo-Fijian community, while the SVT 'is without doubt the majority Fijian party representing the widest cross-section of the Fijian community', and the UGP was the largest party of the general electors. This coalition, he said, broadly based, representative, and with a record of working together was 'best placed to provide that political stability which will form the foundation for progress on economic and social issues'.

The SVT paraded its achievements, reminding Fijians of its pro-Fijian activities: more scholarships for Fijians, financial assistance, the promise to revert crown land to Fijian landowners. It reminded them of the new hospitals and health centres in Kadavu, Lami, Nabouwalu, Rabi and Rakiraki; improvements in infrastructure, including better shipping services to the islands under the Shipping Franchising Scheme; completion of major bridges; rural electrification; improved water supply in rural areas; the poverty alleviation scheme (F$4.4 million per year); and better housing for low income earners. But these achievements did not impress the voters, who remembered the scandals that had brought the country into disrepute and close to bankruptcy. There was widespread suspicion that a well-connected few had done well, rather than the bulk of the citizens. In western Viti Levu, opposition parties said publicly that their region had been neglected, as in the past, and that the bulk of the development projects had gone elsewhere.

The SVT claimed credit for 'wide consultation in the comprehensive review and promulgation of the new constitution, which laid the foundation for a united, free and democratic multiracial Fiji' (Soqosoqo ni Vakavulewa ni Taukei campaign material). It claimed credit for Fiji's readmission to the Commonwealth, and for restoring Fiji's link with the British monarchy. The Fijian electorate was unmoved. Many thought that the revised constitution had somehow whittled down the Fijian position and deprived them of rights. The government claimed credit for establishing the 'framework for a multiparty government', when most Fijians wanted a Fijian government, with some participation from the other communities, not equal partnership. The opposition Fijian parties, with diverse agendas and ideologies, united to condemn the SVT for compromising Fijian interests.

Rabuka's firm and decisive leadership had indeed been instrumental in negotiating the constitution. Even his closest colleagues in cabinet had opposed the report of the Constitution Review Commission, and had tried to have the constitution amended at the last minute. Eight of the fourteen Fijian provinces had rejected the report. The hero of 1987 had become the villain of 1999, deserted by close supporters, friends and high chiefs with agendas of their own. They all wanted him defeated.

The NFP presented Rabuka to sceptical Indo-Fijian audiences as the leader best suited to take Fiji into the next millennium. Rabuka responded by apologising for the pain the coup had caused the Indo-Fijian community, and espoused an inclusive vision.

> I believe we cannot build a nation by tearing people down. No matter how they arrived in Fiji, they are a part of Fiji society. This is their land to till and make productive. We owe it to the indentured labourers, to cotton planters for what we have now. Let us leave our differences aside, have common interests in our hearts to build a beautiful Fiji (Speech in Labasa, 10 April 1999).

Rabuka appeared genuine in his contrition, but it came late, and in the heat of an election campaign it sounded expedient. As one observer put it, 'commitment to multiracialism and forgiveness for sins past' sounded all too vague. 'It is feel-good politics that blisters under the blowtorch of the Fijian Association Party-Labour call for new direction' (*Fiji Times*, 3 May 1999).

The promulgation of the new constitution became the main campaign platform for the NFP. Much had been achieved through dialogue and discussion with a mainstream Fijian party, and it promised to continue that approach. If the Indo-Fijian people wanted to resolve the land lease issue, they could only do so with the support of the main party of the Fijian people. It urged voters to take a longer-term view. Much had been accomplished, but much remained to be done. The NFP praised Rabuka as the man who had risked his political capital among his own people. They acknowledged his past misdeeds, but as Reddy said, 'this is the same person who has shown, by leading the revision of the constitution, that he believes in genuine multiracialism, not just in parliament but more importantly in government' (Reddy's final campaign address, 3 May 1999). He continued,

[w]e are not in a partnership with token Fijians and general voters, as in 1987, after which the coups took place. These parties will have the full force of their racial groups behind them. This coalition will have real political authority and social backing to tackle the problems of our country, for example crime and ALTA (Reddy's final campaign address, 3 May 1999).

NFP wanted to eschew the confrontational politics that had 'only result[ed] in misery for people'. Instead, they wanted to pursue 'moderation, reconciliation and tolerance of all races, regions and cultures that grace this beautiful country of ours'. Reddy reminded voters of his party's record in opposition: 'The country knows that we have been in the forefront of bringing these issues (corruption, mismanagement of the economy and inefficiencies) to the attention of the public, whenever the need has arisen'. Nonetheless, as Stewart Firth remarked, 'no answer could explain to an average Indian the reason why NFP leader Jai Ram Reddy formed a coalition with Sitiveni Rabuka's party' (*Fiji Times*, 18 May 1999).

The NFP heavily criticised Labour's allocation of preferences. In 22 seats, Labour gave its first or second preferences to the VLV, a party whose policies Labour had characterised as 'abhorrent, contrary to the spirit of our constitution and against the interests of the Indian community' (Fiji Labour Party campaign material). The VLV would reintroduce the Sunday ban, make Fiji a Christian state and change the constitution. The NFP placed the VLV last, and despite its competition with Labour it placed that party above the VLV 'as a matter of principle or morality'. For Labour, however, the election was not about principle and morality: it was about winning. To that end, it put those parties last that posed the greatest threat. Among these parties was the NFP, its main rival in the Indian communal seats. Labour's unorthodox tactic breached the spirit and intention of the preferential system of voting, where like-minded parties trade preferences among themselves and put those they are morally at odds with last. Political expediency and cold-blooded ruthlessness triumphed. Reddy was right about Labour's motives when he said that Labour wanted 'to get rid of Rabuka and the SVT [and Reddy and the NFP as well] at all cost'.

The constitution, by which the NFP had placed such store, was for Labour an accomplished fact and a non-issue. It made no mention of it in the manifesto. When this issue was brought to the fore, Labour belittled Rabuka's and Reddy's roles, saying that the constitution was the work of the Constitution Review Commission and the Joint Parliamentary Select Committee. In any case, why should Rabuka be praised for rectifying a grievous mistake he had made in the first place. As Sir Vijay Singh put, 'in restoring the democratic constitution', Rabuka 'did the Indians no favour'. He 'restored what he had stolen in the first place. He is deserving of some mitigation. If you were a criminal in court and you did some right thing, the court will deal with you lightly but it won't reward you' (*Fijilive*, 19 May 1999). It was a harsh, unforgiving judgment on Rabuka, which did not take account of the fact that he had accomplished despite the difficult circumstances and the powerful opposition from within his own party. Moreover, Rabuka was not alone in carrying out the coups. Some of Sir Vijay's own former colleagues in the Alliance Party (and now Rabuka's bitter opponents) had joined the colonel in 1987 to overthrow the 1970 constitution. But these subtle points did not register.

Labour reminded the electorate of SVT's sorry record in government, and implicated the NFP in the mess, calling it the Rabuka-Reddy record. Labour catalogued the ills of the SVT government: mismanagement of public office, corruption at the top echelons of government, alarming crime rates, high unemployment levels, enforced redundancies in public enterprises brought about by privatisation and corporatisation, the high cost of living in an economy deep in recession with two consecutive years of negative growth, and dreadful infrastructure. This, Labour said, was the true record of the SVT government. The electorate understood. The sight of redundant workers at Nadi airport while the election was in progress reinforced the image of the government as uncaring and arrogant. The NFP said little; for Labour the pictures of the redundant workers were a godsend. 'The NFP', Labour president Koroi remarked, 'has been an ineffective opposition, frequently and actively supporting the repressive measures of a government whose sole aim is to remain in power permanently' (*Daily Post*, 2 April 1999). The electorate believed her.

Labour also promised policies and initiatives of its own. It would remove the 10 per cent value-added tax and customs duty from basic food and educational items, review taxation on savings and raise allowances for dependents, provide social security for the aged and destitute, and lower interest rates on housing loans. If elected, Labour promised to repeal legislation requiring farmers to pay back the F$27 million cash grant and crop rehabilitation loan made to drought-stricken farmers in 1998; establish a Land Use Commission, in consultation with landowners and tenants, to identify and access vacant lands; and oppose privatisation of strategic utilities such as water, electricity, telecommunications and civil aviation. 'We also believe that the overall control of the exploitation of natural resources such as forestry and fisheries must remain in state hands to maintain their sustainability. We will, therefore, reverse all moves to restructure and privatise them'.

Labour's partners broadly shared its policy platform, but their main target was Rabuka. The Fijian establishment, in whose name he had carried out the coup, jettisoned him as an ambitious commoner unfit to govern, a man who had overreached his authority and station. He had to be defeated almost at any cost. For Chaudhry, removing Reddy and his party was a priority.

## Results

Voting in Fiji was compulsory for the 428,000 registered voters, but only 393,673 voted. Of the votes cast, 8 per cent were invalid. There were roughly equal number of invalid votes among Fijians (8.7 per cent) and Indo-Fijians (8.5 per cent). The percentage of Fijians not voting was slightly higher (10.9 per cent) than among Indo-Fijians (7.5 per cent). The Labour Party won 37 of the 71 seats in the House of Representatives, and thus was entitled to form a government in its own right. Its coalition partner, the Fijian Association Party, won 11, PANU 4 and the Christian Democrats 3. The UGP won 2 seats, the SVT 8 and the NFP failed to win a seat. Fijian Nationalists won 2 seats and independents 4.

The Indian communal seats saw a two-way contest between Labour and the NFP. Labour won 108,743 of the 165,886 Indian communal votes cast (65.6 per cent of first preference votes) and the NFP 53,071 (32 per cent). Independents and other parties got 4,030 (2.4 per cent). Labour fared well in rural and urban constituencies, its electoral dominance evenly spread. Among the Fijian parties contesting the communal seats, the SVT won 68,114 or 38 per cent of (first preference) Fijian votes, VLV 34,758 (19.4 per cent), Fijian Association Party 32,394 (18 per cent), PANU 17,149 (9.6 per cent), independents 7,335 (4.1 per cent), Nationalist Vanua Tako Lavo Party 16,353 (9.1 per cent) and Labour 3,590 (2 per cent). Labour's poor performance among Fijians should be seen in context. Although it fielded some Fijian candidates, Labour left Fijian constituencies largely to its Fijian partners. When the votes in the open seats are taken into account, there is evidence of large Fijian support for the party. There, of the 360,085 valid votes cast— 428,146 were registered of whom 393,673 voted—Labour won 33.3 per cent of the votes, SVT 21 per cent, VLV 9.8 per cent, NFP 14.4 per cent, Nationalists 4.2 per cent, Fijian Association Party, 10.8 per cent, independents 2.1 per cent, United General Party 1.3 per cent and PANU 2.7 per cent.

Among general voters, 11,981 voted from a total of 14,029. That is, 14.6 per cent did not vote and of those who did, 8.2 per cent were invalid. The United General Party won 5,388 votes (49 per cent), Fijian Association Party 1,052 (9.6 per cent), independents 3,346 (30.4 per cent) and the Coalition of Independent Parties 1,156 (10 per cent). The strong support for independents centered on personalities (Leo Smith and Bill Aull who were prominent sitting parliamentarians).

Why the massive swing to Labour? The NFP argued that Indo-Fijian voters had taken revenge for the coups, that its pre-election coalition with Rabuka cost them the election. If NFP had not allied itself with the SVT and not revealed its hand, it would not have carried SVT's baggage. It would then have been able to mount an effective campaign in its traditional constituency and win enough seats to become a player in parliament. There is a grain of truth in this assertion. Certainly Labour advertised its campaign as a continuation of a brutally interrupted experiment of 1987, with Dr Timoci Bavadra's official portrait adorning many a campaign shed in western Viti Levu. Rabuka's public apologies unwittingly revived memories of disrupted careers, lost incomes and broken lives.[7] The NFP's pre-election coalition may have cost it votes, but would an alternative strategy have made much difference?

The answer is not at all clear. In the public mind, Reddy was already hitched to Rabuka through the constitutional review, and any attempt by the two leaders to distance themselves from each other, after having worked so closely for so long, would have been counterproductive to the purported aims of moderation and reconciliation they espoused. If Reddy had publicly distanced himself from Rabuka, Labour would not have let the matter rest. They would have prodded and provoked and demanded to know why Reddy was not with the SVT leader. On the other side, the Fijian nationalists, unhappy with the new constitution, would have accused Reddy of treachery, and of using Rabuka and the Great Council of Chiefs to amend the constitution to suit the interests of his own community. The Fijian supporters of the SVT would have felt used and discarded.

Reddy argued that his party had taken the correct decision to ally with the SVT. The coalition, he said, was based on fundamental principles.

> You don't abandon your coalition partners because they have done something wrong or they may be suddenly becoming unpopular. But I didn't see it that way. I saw the SVT as the mainstream Fijian party. They were founded by the chiefs. They seemed to have the support of the Fijian people. The important thing is that all these things we did with the utmost good faith. We did it because we believed in something. We believed that Indian and Fijian people and everybody else must be brought together in government (*The Review*, June 1999).

He had been honest with the electorate. His coalition decision was not 'a grievous error of principle as well as strategy', as some commentators noted, but a principled and courageous one.[8]

The NFP's problem was not so much in the message as in its failure to take it effectively to the voters. In hindsight, its focus on the constitution—great achievement that it was—to the virtual exclusion of any other issue was probably a mistake. Selling an untested constitution, however good, to a sceptical, suffering electorate was not the same as criticising a demonstrably flawed one, as it had done successfully in 1992 and 1994. The fact that it could not use its solid performance as an opposition party, now that it was in partnership with the party in government, weakened its campaign. In short, the NFP was caught in a trap. A frontal attack on the SVT would have polarised the main communities, revived old hostilities and taken the country back to the tired politics of ethnic confrontation. By holding fire on the SVT, the NFP opened itself to the charge of complicity and collaboration.

Labour's message was sharper and more effective, its criticism of government relentless. Its focus on the bread and butter issues of employment, better health, social welfare and accountable government sat well with the electorate. Moreover, it had an extensive network to communicate that message. The Fiji Public Service Association, of which Mahendra Chaudhry was the head, covered the public sector unions. The National Farmers' Union, of which Chaudhry again was the head, galvanised the farming community. And the Fiji Teachers' Union, headed by Pratap Chand, a Labour candidate, reached out to primary and secondary teachers who play a pivotal social role in the community. They shape opinion and influence events. Farmers, workers and teachers were thus covered. The NFP's structure was less focused. Its once powerful working committees had become moribund, its decision-making and consultative function taken over by the Management Board. This change made the party more businesslike, but damaged its links to the grassroots.

Labour appealed to people who were desperate, direct victims of government policies—400 redundant employees at the Civil Aviation Authority, 15,000 garment factory workers and their families, squatters and residents of low-cost Housing Authority flats, people threatened with job losses at the Fiji Electricity Authority, Telecom Fiji, the Fiji Sugar Corporation and in the public service, already reeling from the 20 per cent devaluation of the Fijian dollar. NFP's appeal was less focused. The Indo-Fijian community, whose interests it sought to protect, was increasingly divided in its aspirations. The middle class, a constituency traditionally receptive to its message of gradual progressive change and with a keen eye on the long term, had been declining through migration. Many had left since the coups while Labour's base of workers, farmers and teachers remained intact. For them, the immediate social and economic concerns were more important than saving for a rainy day. As one observer put it, the 'NFP's achievements on the constitution and talk of racial harmony were abstract issues while Labour promised tangible gains' (*The Review*, June 1999). Such 'tangible gains' included reducing prices, increasing exports and creating jobs. The NFP was perceived as a rich person's party, not caring about the concerns of ordinary people.[9]

In the sugar belt, the heartland of the Indo-Fijian community, Labour outmanoeuvred the NFP. The National Farmers' Union had displaced the NFP-backed Fiji Cane Growers' Association as the most effective voice of the farmers. Ironically, it was the NFP which had paved the way for Chaudhry's entry into sugar politics after the coups, handing over to him a constituency that had long been the party's own but which Chaudhry would convert into his own solid base. To the drought-stricken farmers, Labour promised relief and concrete proposals: addressing the problem of milling inefficiencies, improving the transportation system, exploring diversification into agro-based industries, and writing off the F$27 million crop rehabilitation loan. Labour told the farmers that Reddy had opposed the cash grant, which patently misrepresented his position. The NFP cried foul, but the damage was done. The sugar belt turned to Labour as never before.

Rabuka's defeat was caused by several factors. His government's scandal-ridden performance was one. For many ordinary Fijians, life had not improved much since the coups. As Tamarisi Digitaki put it, at the grassroots level

> [t]he standards of living have remained largely unchanged from ten years ago. While his [Rabuka's] government's performance on the national and international fronts has been commendable, it is in the rural areas that the goods have failed to be delivered. Poor roads, water supply, communication services, education facilities and shipping services to the islands only give rural people more reason to vote the government out of office (*The Review*, February 1998).

Rabuka conceded that the complacency of his parliamentarians and a dormant party structure cost him votes, saying that 'while party leaders were busy resolving national issues, no one was really looking into bread and butter issues affecting its supporters' (*The Review*, June 1999). Labour and its partners capitalised on this disenchantment affecting rural Fiji.

Rabuka's pursuit of moderate, conciliatory politics was always going to risk being outflanked by more extremist parties. Parties that court moderation in an ethnically divided society tempt fate. Rabuka was accused of selling out Fijian interests, just as Reddy was accused of playing second fiddle to the Fijians. Further, Rabuka was not fully in command of his party. The 23 Fijian seats are contested on provincial lines, and candidates are selected in consultation with provincial councils. In some cases, candidates preferred by the party were overruled by the provincial councils, an example being the replacement of the highly regarded Education Minister Taufa Vakatale by Jone Kauvesi for the Lomaiviti Fijian seat. Provincial concerns take priority over party interests. These problems of divided loyalties are set to plague Fijian politics as long as elections are fought from within provincial boundaries.

The political fragmentation of Fijian society distressed many Fijians, and Rabuka regarded this as a major cause of his defeat. 'Gone are the days when Fijians worked in accordance with what was required of them from their elders. Now when an order is given from an elder, they are asked to give the reason and if they are satisfied, then they can act' (*Daily Post*, 27 March 1999). He was referring to the influence of urbanisation, multiracial education and the challenges and opportunities of a multiethnic society. The use of the provincial boundaries for electing members to parliament accentuated provincial rivalries and sentiments, to the detriment of a centralised party structure. The decline in the number of Indo-Fijians through emigration and a lower birth rate diluted the fear of Indian dominance, which had long unified politics in Fiji. Finally, the absence from the national stage of strong and powerful chiefs—a Ratu Mara or Ratu Penaia or Ratu George and Ratu Edward Cakobau—opened up opportunities for others. It is unlikely that Fijian society will see the likes of these on the national stage in the near future.

## The race to be prime minister

As the count proceeded and a change of government appeared likely, most people wondered what Rabuka's next move might be. The SVT leader conceded defeat with exemplary grace and dignity. His words are worth recalling not only because of their symbolic importance but also as a measure of the man Rabuka had become. The people of Fiji had demonstrated to themselves and 'to the watching world that we have embraced democracy fully by the way the election was held and by the very nature of the result'. He congratulated the Labour Party, and told his supporters: 'Take heart that we have fought the good fight. We have given all that we could. Let us now, without rancour and bitterness or any sort of division, congratulate our fellow citizens who have won the day'. Rabuka lamented the apparent block voting by the Indo-Fijian community, but urged the new government to 'govern us all'. He would lend support when necessary, promising to be 'vigilant to ensure a just, accountable and honest government'. He urged the people 'to move to the centre ground, the middle ground', to 'genuinely come together to work for the common good of all our people'. It would be a terrible tragedy to 'dismantle the progress that we have made together'. Rabuka thanked Reddy for his support. Reddy knew the risks he was taking in coalescing with his party, but as leader with 'deep conviction and strong principles, he courageously stuck to our agreement and it has cost him and his party dearly'. Not all was lost. 'I now give my assurances to him and his loyal supporters that their sacrifice and contribution in helping to lay the framework for lasting national unity, stability and progress in our country has not been in vain'.

To the Fijian people, he said,

> [w]e must find a way to come together to allow our collective voice to be heard. And to be a force in shaping the future of our country. We have allowed ourselves to splinter into different groups working against our common interest. We know the wise words that a house divided amongst themselves cannot stand. We have a lot of houses, our collective *yavu* and *vanua* have become divided. And the result is our voice in Government has been diminished (Rabuka, unpublished speech).

Rabuka promised to keep a watchful eye on the government, but before parliament met, he resigned his seat. In a stunning move, Rabuka was then elected chair of the Great Council of Chiefs by polling—the first time in history that chiefs had used secret ballot—32 votes to Tui Vuda Ratu Josefa Iloilo's 18. Rabuka described his victory as 'a sign of the chiefly support I have' (*Daily Post*, June 1999). His name was moved by Adi Litia Cakobau from the leading chiefly family of the Kubuna confederacy and seconded by Ratu Tevita Vakalalabure, the Vunivalu of Natewa.

Labour's victory put Chaudhry in the driver's seat. Within hours of the election results becoming known, Chaudhry convened his Labour parliamentary caucus, which elected him as the party's nominee for prime minister. Soon afterwards, he was appointed prime minister by Ratu Mara. Chaudhry's other coalition partners were not consulted or informed, and they reacted angrily, claiming that Chaudhry's appointment was a breach of an implicit agreement to have an ethnic Fijian as prime minister. Adi

Kuini Bavadra Speed, the Fijian Association leader, asked Mara, through Ratu Viliame Dreunimisimisi, to revoke his decision and appoint her as head of government, because she was the leader of the largest 'Fijian' party in the winning coalition. Poseci Bune, the VLV leader, began canvassing the possibility of heading a broad coalition of Fijian parties in opposition. Tora threatened to pull out of the coalition altogether. The Fijian Nationalists proposed to march against the government.

Nothing happened. Chaudhry offered Speed the post of deputy prime minister, which she accepted after Mara asked her to support Chaudhry, and after Labour threatened to invite VLV into cabinet. Speed capitulated, quoting Mara's advice: 'It was basically appealing to us as leaders to consider the importance of cooperation rather [than] be at loggerheads with the new government' (*Fijilive*, 19 May 1999). Speed had been outmanoeuvred. She could sit on the opposition benches with Rabuka, possibly as leader of the opposition, or become deputy prime minister. She chose the latter. Speed also opposed the VLV's inclusion in the cabinet, but was overridden. It was widely believed, but difficult to prove, that Mara wanted Bune and Adi Koila Nailatikau in the cabinet: that might have been the condition of his surprisingly warm public support for Chaudhry. Be that as it may, both were offered and both accepted cabinet posts, as did members of PANU, despite Tora's objections. Later, Chaudhry praised Mara for his critical role in getting the Fijian dissidents to support his government. In truth, Mara did what the constitution obliged him to do: to appoint as prime minister the member of the House of Representative who, in his opinion, commanded majority support. Chaudhry's numbers bolstered his position—he was unassailable; he could govern on his own. But a confluence of interests brought Mara and Chaudhry together. The eastern chiefly establishment had felt ignored by the Rabuka administration; it was now in a position to be represented in cabinet. Mara's waning influence was also reinvigorated. For Chaudhry, the presence of the president's daughter in cabinet, and Mara's public support for his government, shored up Labour's credibility among Fijians who might otherwise have distrusted an Indo-Fijian prime minister. Dislike of Rabuka brought the men together—my enemy's enemy is my friend.

In his first broadcast as prime minister, Chaudhry was at pains to emphasise his government's broad non-racial appeal. He stressed repeatedly that he was prime minister 'not for any[one] community' but 'for everybody'. He pledged his commitment 'to complying with the requirements of the constitution for the equitable participation of all communities in government', promising to 'ensure that all communities fully benefit from the nation's economic development'. He would be 'guided by the wisdom and counsel [of the Great Council of Chiefs] on all matters affecting the interests and welfare of indigenous Fijians and Rotumans'. The business community too had nothing to fear. 'In working to uplift the conditions of life of the poor, the workers, and the less privileged in our society we are not being anti-business. We're just being pro-people'. His government believed in development with justice. 'But we are equally committed to laying down economic policies that will encourage investors and business to grow' (Chaudhry, Address to the Nation, 19 May 1999).

Chaudhry acted astutely in forming his cabinet. Eleven of the seventeen ministers were ethnic Fijians, a gesture of reassurance to the Fijians that their interests were adequately protected. However, he himself controlled the key portfolios of finance, public enterprises, sugar industry and information. His Labour ministers controlled foreign affairs, education, labour and industrial relations, commerce, business development and investment, national planning, local government, housing and environment, justice, regional development and multiethnic affairs and women, culture and social welfare. Chaudhry knew that his success at the next election would depend on his handling of the domestic social and economic agenda. People reacted cautiously and approvingly, though some Fijian nationalists, as well as a few defeated SVT parliamentarians, wanted to oust Labour from power immediately (*Daily Post*, 28 May 1999). Rabuka was approached by people within his own party, including former senior ministers, to lead a 1987-style coup, but he rejected their overtures outright (Personal communication with Rabuka). Things had changed, he said; the majority of the Fijian people had rejected the SVT, and the overwhelming sentiment in the country was to give the new government a chance to prove its mettle. 'Fijians would not be fooled again', a searching editorial in a Fijian weekly wrote. It was typical of the reaction throughout the country.

> Sakiasi Butadroka and supporters of the Nationalist Vanua Tako Lavo Party are being mischievous and misleading in trying to scare the Fijians into believing the Indians have taken over Fiji…Buta is saying Ratu Mara and Mahendra Chaudhry are selling the rights of the indigenous Fijians. But we all know that no one on their own can sell the rights of the Fijians. No one who is not a Fijian, even if he or she is head of the government, can remove the rights of Fijians to their land and resources. This will only happen if the Fijians themselves agree to it (*Volasiga*, 31–6 June 1999).

The editorial then drew attention to the problems facing the Fijian people, which, it added, had little to do with other groups. 'When we look at our schools and their academic results, we see it is mainly the Fijians who are failing their exams. That's because there are weaknesses in our family life and within Fijian society'. The majority of those breaking the laws were Fijians. The biggest victims of sexually transmitted diseases were Fijians. Teenage pregnancies and single mothers were disproportionately Fijians. 'Who then is Butadroka fooling in Fiji. We are trying to catch up on the difficulties in life we are now facing and to reverse the general opinion that we are lagging behind'. To many Fijians, then, Chaudhry was not an adversary but an ally. It was their own leaders, drunk on power and dulled into complacency, who had deserted them

Parliament opened on 15 June. In his opening address, the president outlined the government's policies for its first term. The government's 'two crucial and central challenges' were to 'further strengthen the bonds of unity in our multiethnic and multicultural society' and to 'promote economic growth and social progress'. These challenges, Mara said in a televised speech,

> …are to be undertaken with a strong sense of social justice to ensure that development benefits all in our society, including the poor, the disadvantaged and all those who, through no fault of their own, need the helping hand of the state. Government will implement affirmative action and social justice programmes to secure for all citizens and communities equal and equitable access to opportunities, amenities and services to better their lives.

Over the next year or so, the Chaudhry government had its hands full, attempting, albeit not always successfully, to deliver on its large, uncosted promises or explaining why it could not, at least for the time being.

Chaudhry made a concerted effort to assure the Fijian community that he would not undermine their interests. Soon after the election, he addressed the Bose Levu Vakaturaga, only the second Indo-Fijian leader (after Jai Ram Reddy) to do so, seeking their blessing and expressing his gratitude 'for their immense contribution in laying the foundation for freedom, democracy, unity and development in our country' (Ministry of Information Press Release, 8 June 1999). His government agreed to honour a request by the BLV to transfer all state Schedule A and Schedule B to the Native Land Trust Board. The decision was widely praised in the Fijian community. The government also pledged to continue the special annual education fund of F$4.5 million for Fijian education, and initiated programs to ensure that people on remote islands 'are not denied the benefits of development'.

But it was not all plain sailing. Chaudhry's own transition from a trade union leader to a national leader was rocky, leading to confrontation with the media. His cabinet was weak and inexperienced and often spoke with discordant voices. Deputy prime minister Adi Kuini Speed's ill-judged remarks during her maiden speech, that people should pray for Chaudhry's conversion to Christianity, embarrassed the government. Adi Kuini's decision to make Navosa, where she was a high chief, a separate province was rejected by Chaudhry who told her to 'focus on issues which would bring Fijians together and not disunite them' (*Fiji Times*, 4 June 1999). Adi Kuini was seen by some as a loose cannon—erratic and autocratic—but she was not the only one in cabinet who harboured personal ambition. Others also saw Chaudhry as a vehicle for their own agendas. The opposition benches, occupied entirely by Fijians and general electors, promised to play rough and hard, adopting expediently extremist positions to sabotage government initiatives, especially in the eyes of the Fijians whose support they needed to recover.

Meanwhile, away from the public gaze, disgruntled groups began to gather to explore ways of ending the life a government that had begun in such optimism.

# Notes

1  These words are from the *Pacific Report*, but they are echoed in most reports on the election.
2  These were the Fiji Labour Party, National Democratic Party, National Federation Party, the Soqosoqo ni Vakavulewa ni Taukei, Fijian Association Party, General Voters Party, General Electors Party, Vanua Tako Lavo Party, Vitilevu Dynamic Multiracial Party, Party of National Unity, Veitokani ni Lewenivanua Vakaristo Party, United National Labour Party, Party of Truth, Natural Law Party, Coalition of Independent Nationals Party, Nationalist Vanua Tako Lavo Party, Farmers and General Workers Coalition Party, and Lio On Famor Rotuma Party.
3  I owe this description to Robert Norton.
4  All the quotations come from the Party's campaign literature.
5  When Ratu Mara was confronted with this allegation, he said his 'conscience was clear'.
6  Among them was Colonel Inoke Luveni and Manasa Lasaro. They argued that Bune did not meet any of the criteria the party had laid down for leadership. These stipulated that the leader must come from a chiefly family and should be the offspring of a marriage, must not be divorced or separated from his wife and have a stable and happy family, not have 'produced children' outside of marriage, be a Christian and a regular churchgoer, and must believe that Fiji should become a Christian state and that the Sunday Ban be reimposed (see *Daily Post*, 21 April 1999).
7  Rabuka offered the first of many apologies at his coalition rally in Lautoka on 26 April 1999. At that meeting, he also said he was 'supposed to be the 'fall guy' but I'd like to tell them that I am the fall guy that refuses to fall'. His implication was that others high in the Fijian hierarchy were involved in the coups.
8  Among those who saw the coalition as an error was Sir Vijay Singh (see *Fiji Times,* 18 May 1999).
9  Reddy acknowledged this perception in his first post-coup press conference, but he saw this 'partly [as] the result of very successful propaganda', noting that in recent years, his party had extended its base to include as candidates trade unionists, teachers and women.

# 8

# George Speight's coup

Around 10am on 19 May 2000, seven armed gunmen, led by George Speight, stormed the Fiji parliament taking Prime Minister Mahendra Chaudhry and his ill-fated government hostage. May 19 marked the government's first anniversary in office. The seizure of parliament followed a series of protest marches by a variety of aggrieved Fijian nationalist groups and defeated politicians opposed to the People's Coalition government and committed to its overthrow. Still, the hostage crisis seemed improbable. Speight, a part-Fijian failed businessmen, due to be arraigned in court on a bankruptcy charge, was a little-known player on the local scene. And, unlike 1987, no recognisable group or institution claimed immediate responsibility for the deed, including the recently revived Taukei Movement headed by the perennial dissident Mohammed Apisai Tora. In 1987, the Royal Fiji Military Forces, under then Lt Col. Sitiveni Rabuka, took responsibility for the coup and was, in turn, held accountable for it. A case could be made that the 1987 coup was carried out on behalf of, and blessed by, the Fijian establishment, including the Methodist Church and sections of the Great Council of Chiefs. In 2000, George Speight and his men carried out a coup against the Fijian establishment, or at least without their overt blessing. If 1987 was about shoring up indigenous Fijian power and preserving Fijian political unity, Speight's intervention had the effect of fostering Fijian political fragmentation on an unprecedented scale. George Speight's dramatic intervention altered the fundamental dynamics of Fiji—and indigenous Fijian—politics.

The hostage crisis left in its wake an impressive list of casualties. The 1997 constitution, approved unanimously by a parliament dominated by indigenous Fijians, blessed by the Great Council of Chiefs and warmly welcomed by the international community, was abrogated, albeit briefly. One of the coup supporters' demands was that the constitution be revised to entrench Fijian political supremacy. Ratu Sir Kamisese Mara, president of the republic, a central figure in contemporary Fijian public life and a paramount chief in his own right, was asked by the army to step aside, while the Republic of Fiji Military Forces assumed executive control of the country. After he was presented with a customary forgiveness-seeking *tabua* (whale's tooth), Mara was sent under the cover of darkness, guarded by soldiers, on a patrol boat heading towards the Lau Sea. It was a sad end to a distinguished though not uncontroversial career, marking the final eclipse of the long reign in Fiji politics of powerful paramount chiefs tutored for national leadership by the colonial government in the years following World War II. The democratically elected government headed by Mahendra Chaudhry was unceremoniously and unconstitutionally dismissed. While the prime minister endured the longest period of captivity in modern Pacific islands history, his freedom—or lack of it—was curiously overshadowed by other struggles for power taking place in Fijian society.

The crisis also ruined the reputation of once sacred institutions of Fijian society in previously unthinkable ways. Among them was the military, with a proud record of service in the jungles of the Solomons in World War II, in Malaya against the Chinese communist insurgents in the 1950s, and as peacekeepers in the Middle East in the 1970s. In the face of the coup, the army stood divided and confused, unable, or, worse still, unwilling, to uphold the constitution or protect the security of the state. The security forces were shown to be infected by the virus of provincialism and regionalism.[1] It took a great deal of personal courage on the part of its leaders, in particular Commodore Bainimarama, to restore a semblance of order and professionalism in the army, but this came at great cost. The sight of Fijian soldiers shedding Fijian blood during the attempted mutiny of November 2000 has left deep scars in the collective memory of the nation.

The Great Council of Chiefs, who had sought in recent years to enlarge its role and status as the guardian of national, and not only indigenous Fijian interests, failed the test of national leadership. They sympathised with Speight's self-defined ambition for the Fijian people, but then backed President Ratu Sir Kamisese Mara to lead the country out of the crisis. They vacillated while the country awaited their wise counsel, which never came, or came too late. Their deliberations were embroiled in traditional confederacy and provincial politics, their proceedings dominated by younger, more assertive chiefs wanting their own place in the Fijian sun, leading to further division and fragmentation. As army spokesman Col. Filipe Tarakinikini put it, the chiefs were 'riddled with personal agendas', and were incapable of impartial, decisive action (*The Australian*, 4 June 2000).

However it is looked at, the hostage crisis-cum-coup was a disaster for Fiji. The economy, which was just beginning to recover from the downturn of the 1990s, was once again poised at the precipice. Investment ceased, factories closed and hundreds of workers, often at the bottom of the economic ladder and therefore the most vulnerable, were been laid off, especially in the handicraft, garment and tourism industries. Investment in the improvement of essential services—health, education, water supply, electricity—stopped, and thousands of Fiji citizens queued up at foreign embassies to migrate, taking with them skills the country could ill-afford to lose.

Some costs, though, were less easily measured. Within the indigenous Fijian society, for instance, old assumptions about the traditional structure of power were questioned in novel and potentially significant ways. It is almost a truism now to say that this crisis, as it unfolded, became more about intra-Fijian rivalries than about race. Even George Speight himself admitted that 'the race issue between Fijians and Indians is just one piece of the jigsaw puzzle that has many pieces' (*Fiji Sun*, 10 June 2000). In this respect, it was unlike the crisis of 1987, which was seen largely as an ethnic conflict between Fijians and Indo-Fijians. Then, there was much sympathy for the Fijian 'cause' across the Pacific whereas now there was outright condemnation.[2] Some have argued that Speight represented the interests of the Kubuna confederacy against the long ascendancy of the traditional hierarchies of the Koro Sea. Fijian political analyst Jone Dakuvula's claim to this effect brought upon the local television station broadcasting his remarks the wrath of the Fijian mob allied to George Speight, as they pillaged its premises and killed a policeman on duty.

Then, as the crisis dragged on, the western chiefs, long aggrieved about their absence from the national centre of power threatened—yet again—to secede from the state of Fiji, failing which they promised to settle for a much-cherished and long-demanded fourth confederacy, the *Yasayasa Vaka Ra*. The west, they said, drove the engine of the national economy. Sugar, pine, gold and tourism are produced from its soil, and they wanted representation in national councils proportionate to their contribution to the national economy. The east–west divide exists, but it is not a sharp, clear line, extensively criss-crossed now by marriage and kinship ties that blur distinction of old. The threatened secession of western Viti Levu was followed by a declaration of partial autonomy by the province of Cakaudrove proposing to set up a separate Tovata state, but the declaration lacked conviction or authority (*Sunday Times*, 11 June 2000). The declaration was probably a stunt, but it did indicate the willingness of the Fijian people to contemplate ideas that would have been unthinkable in the twentieth century.

Race relations were severely strained just at the point when things looked to be on the mend in the wake of the successful review of the constitution. The wounds of the crisis—reflected in the images of looting and violence on the streets of Suva, the fleeing of terrorised Indo-Fijians from parts of the Rewa delta to safe havens in western Viti Levu, the destruction of schools and desecration of places of worship, the unruly Fijian mob roaming the neighbourhoods around the parliamentary complex—would take a long time to heal. The attempted coup raised deeper questions than I can deal with here, questions about culture and history and identity. The Fijian, the *taukei*, the indigenous owner of the land, who has lived side by side with his/her Indo-Fijian neighbour, still regards him/her as a *vulagi*, a foreigner, welcome to stay and enjoy the hospitality of the host but who must always be aware of whose house it is (*New York Times*, 8 June 2000). Even the chiefs of western Fiji who opposed Speight, and had—or should have had—a better understanding of Indo-Fijian fears and aspirations, wanted Fiji to be declared a Christian state so that Hindus, Muslims and Christians could all solve their problems in the proper Christian way. They blamed Australia and Britain for introducing Indians into Fiji; this revealed a lack of appreciation of the Indians' role in Fiji's economic development—without their labour Fijians might have shared the fate of some dispossessed and marginalised people in parts of the Pacific. Indo-Fijians, now fourth or fifth generation, were hurt to be still regarded as outsiders in the land of their birth, threatened with the denial of equal citizenship and equal protection under the law.

Sometimes, those who applauded the indigenous Fijians for maintaining their culture and tradition asked the Indo-Fijians to subjugate theirs in the cause of assimilation. Salman Rushdie, writing about the Fiji crisis makes a telling point. 'Migrant people do not remain visitors forever', he has written. 'In the end, their new land owns them as their old land did, and they have a right to own it in their turn' (*New York Times*, 14 June 2000).

The 2000 crisis was far worse than its 1987 counterpart in terms of violence and damage to property. In 1987, the army was held responsible for the maintenance of law and order. To its credit, it did manage to contain the mobs. In 2000, the mobs had free reign, directed, if they were directed at all, by invisible hands in the parliamentary complex, armed and energised by Speight's racial rhetoric, terrorising the rural Indian countryside for food and fun, as they did in the hinterland of Nausori. The main targets unsurprisingly were Indo-Fijians in outlying rural areas; their cattle slaughtered and root crops stolen. After 1987, some 100,000 migrated from Fiji, most of them Indo-Fijians, mostly to Australia, New Zealand, Canada and the United States. It is often said that there is hardly an Indo-Fijian family in Fiji that did not have at least one member outside the country. Kinship became a multinational or transnational corporation, sustaining those left behind on money remitted from abroad. 'I would rather be a dog in America than an Indian in Fiji', said a broken man whose house had been demolished and his possessions taken by Fijian mobs.

The public face, though not certainly the principal instigator, of this crisis was George Speight. A businessman with a career littered with failures in Australia and Fiji (and possibly elsewhere as well), the 45-year old Speight wandered on the fringes of the local commercial circles on the eve of the coup (*Fiji Times*, 23 May 2000). He had been sacked by Agriculture Minister Poseci Bune as Chairman of the Fiji Pine Commission and the Hardwood Corporation. Shortly before he stormed parliament, he had been negotiating on behalf of the American company Trans Resources Management to win a tender for harvesting the country's massive mahogany forests valued at over F$300 million (*Sunday Times*, 11 June 2000). The government chose the Commonwealth Development Corporation, who had a proven record in the exploitation of natural resources. Speight was declared an undischarged bankrupt and was about to face court proceedings when he launched his assault on parliament. Clearly, Speight had his own private grievances, which he carefully hid behind a fiercely nationalist rhetoric. Like Sitiveni Rabuka in 1987, Speight portrayed himself as a faithful servant of the Fijian cause, an anointed saviour of the Fijian 'race'. Speight, however, was no Rabuka, as even his most ardent supporters admitted. Indeed, an important reason why the international community—as seen in Australian Foreign Minister Alexander Downer's reaction—was so severe in its condemnation of Fiji was because George Speight had presented himself as the face of indigenous Fijian nationalism. A part-European of Fijian descent, head shaved, Speight was articulate, engaging, bantering with the international media, reading emails and Fiji news on the internet before his press conferences; for all that, he remained an unconvincing Fijian hero, though probably not in his own eyes.

George Speight was not acting all on his own. If he were, the crisis would have had a limited and inconsequential life. He was the front man for others. Behind him, in the shadows, were individuals and groups, writing his speeches, drawing up position papers, building up his support base, and orchestrating the crowds—people who had little to lose but everything to gain from the overthrow of the Chaudhry government and from the mayhem that followed. Among them were politicians defeated at the last elections or otherwise excluded from power, seeking redress and probably revenge. Apisai Tora and Berenado Vunibobo come readily to mind. The Fijian opposition leader Ratu Inoke Kubuabola was there as well, and so, strangely enough, were factional leaders of Fijian political parties in coalition with Chaudhry's Labour Party. Fijian Association Party's Adi Kuini Vuikaba Speed was the deputy prime minister, but

Ratu Cokanauto Tua'akitau was seen with Speight's group. Apisai Tora, the founder of the Party of National Unity, wanted Chaudhry's head, but three members of his party were in the cabinet.

Speight was also supported by people like himself—young businessmen on the make, who rode the gravy train of the 1990s, benefited from opportunistic access to power, secured large, unsecured loans from the National Bank of Fiji, but who then found their prospects for continued prosperity dimming on the election of a new government. Prominent local businessmen-cum-politicians in the previous SVT government supported the destabilisation campaign. For them, it was important that the Chaudhry government went before it managed to entrench itself. In this group of the ambitious and upwardly mobile, I would also include what I call the 'children of 1987'. This group included those who had benefited from the post-coup racially based affirmative action programs—sanctioned by the 1990 constitution—in the award of scholarships, promotions in the civil service and training opportunities. They were the children of privilege, sons and daughters of the well connected. Many of them had come of age in the mid 1990s, at the height of SVT government's reign.[3] This new generation of fast-tracked Fijian middle class had a narrow, limited experience of multiculturalism, and little taste or patience for it. They contrasted starkly with an earlier post-independence generation of the 1970s, which grew up working in a multicultural environment, dedicated to professionalism and the principles of good governance, under governments publicly committed to a unifying vision.[4] The 'children of 1987' did not understand nor approve of the spirit of the 1997 constitution.

While the indigenous Fijian middle class, or at least sections of it, provided the brains for Speight's agenda, the Fijian social underclass contributed the brawn. The bedraggled unemployed, unskilled Fijian youth—armed with sticks, knives, bamboo spears, stones and sometimes guns looted, burned and trashed Suva, terrorised the countryside, and acted as human shields for Speight and his men—had little understanding of the larger, hidden personal agendas and complex forces at work. They were in some sense the human casualties of globalisation and economic rationalism, and, more immediately, the victims of the structural reform policies pursued by the Rabuka government in the 1990s. They could not understand why they remained behind, mired in poverty and destitution, while others had moved on. Without hope and without a future, they fell easy prey to George Speight's mesmerising rhetoric and easy solutions: getting rid of the Indians, reverting to tradition and putting Fijians in political control would mean all would be well. Speight gave them a purpose, an explanation, a mission and a brief spot in the Fijian sun. They in turn responded enthusiastically to his clarion call of racial solidarity.

How did this crisis come to a head? To understand this, it is necessary to look at events over the previous 12 months, beginning with the 1999 general elections that took place under the revised 1997 constitution. As shown before, Chaudhry's Labour Party won 37 of the 71 seats in its own right. Together with his other coalition partners, Party of National Unity (PANU), Fijian Association Party (FAP) and Veitokani ni Levenivanua Vakaristo (VLV), the People's Coalition won altogether 58 seats. The unexpectedly convincing victory was due to two factors: an effective campaign against the outrages and excesses of the Rabuka government, of which there were many, and a sharp, carefully calibrated focus on the bread and butter issues affecting ordinary working and middle class people. Labour promised to roll back the structural reform programs of the Rabuka government that had caused massive unemployment, introduce minimum wages, lower interest-rates, provide social security for the elderly, and resolve the long-festering issue of expiring agricultural leases. These uncosted but electorally appealing policies were effective on the hustings, but they came to haunt the party when it came to power. The opposition National Federation Party (NFP), Fiji's oldest political party who had long been the champion of Indo-Fijian interests, did not win a single seat, and opportunistically kept the government's heel close to the fire. To counteract criticism and keep its support base from fragmenting, the Chaudhry government embarked on a hectic program of legislative reform, setting up commissions (Education and Human Rights), instituting inquiries (into corruption), staffing statutory organisations with competent staff (Housing Authority).

The appearance of movement and change was impressive, but it also embroiled the government in a hugely counterproductive tussle with the media. Small issues were magnified in an atmosphere already rife with suspicion and distrust about the government's motives. Why did Chaudhry appoint his own son, not a civil servant, as his personal assistant on the public payroll? Here was a man who, as long-term secretary of the Fiji Public Service Association, had given scathing assessments of nepotism and corruption in previous governments, but once in power, had begun to ignore his own wise counsel about transparent governance and public accountability. There was nothing illegal in the appointment: a prime minister can, of course, appoint anybody he or she wants. But the perception of the government favouring its own was created, which stuck despite repeated denial. Fijian civil servants, appointed under the Rabuka government when ethnicity and loyalty were privileged over merit and seniority, complained about being unconsulted or marginalised in important decision-making.

Faced with intensifying opposition, the governed battened down the hatches. To every question and all opposition, it chanted—to its opponents with constant, arrogant regularity—the mantra of having a mandate to do what it had promised in its election manifesto. The government did have a mandate, but its mandate was one among many mandates in Fiji. The parliament is not the sole source of all power in Fiji: the Native Land Trust Board has its mandate to look after native land, the Great Council of Chiefs has its own mandate under the constitution, and the army has its own. It was the failure, or perhaps the unwillingness, to balance the complex equation of competing mandates that compounded the government's problems. Chaudhry's own forceful personality, forged in the long years spent in the trade union movement, also played its part in galvanising the opposition. Chaudhry was a highly intelligent and resourceful person, tenacious and uncompromising (confrontational to his opponents)—a born fighter who was a painful thorn in the side of the Rabuka government for years. He was feared by Fijians, but not trusted. He was a strong and decisive leader of a generally weak cabinet, and his opponents, rightly or wrongly, saw his unmistakable imprint on every policy decision of the government

Another problem facing the government was the fractious nature of the People's Coalition itself. As mentioned, the coalition was a loose structure made up of four parties: Labour, PANU, FAP and VLV. Some of these parties espoused philosophies directly contradictory to Labour's. But what they all had in common was their adamant opposition to Sitiveni

Rabuka. Opposition to a common enemy, then, rather than commitment to a common agenda, brought the disparate groups together. And when Rabuka was defeated, the difficulties of internal cohesion came to the fore, almost immediately after the election. Chaudhry rightly took steps to become prime minister: his party had an outright majority in parliament. The FAP cried foul, accusing Labour of reneging on a deal that a Fijian, one of its own members, would be chosen prime minister by the coalition.[5] Chaudhry was helped unobtrusively and opportunistically by Ratu Mara who urged the Fijian parties to rally behind him, but Chaudhry's ascension also split the coalition. A faction of the FAP disregarded Adi Kuini's leadership and informally aligned itself with other Fijian opposition parties, eventually going so far as to back George Speight. Tora became a fierce rabble-rousing critic of the government, expressing his disgruntlement by leading a revived Taukei Movement.

The issue that united the Fijians was land. Land, as I have said before, has always been a sensitive issue in Fijian politics. The question always has been the use rather than the ownership of land. Now, 83 per cent of all land in Fiji—3,714,990 acres—is held in inalienable rights by indigenous Fijians, 8.2 per cent is freehold, 3.6 per cent is state freehold and 5 per cent is crown or state. Much of the country's agricultural activity—in particular sugar cultivation—is carried out on land leased from Fijian landowners. The country's 22,000 cane growers, the overwhelming majority of whom are Indo-Fijians, lease native land under the Agricultural Landlord and Tenant Act. This Act, which came into existence in 1969 provided for 30-year leases, whose renewal was negotiated between the tenants and landlords on the expiry of the leases. These leases were beginning to expire, and some, but by no means all, landlords want their land back—either to cultivate the land themselves, rezone it for commercial or residential purposes, or use the threat of non-renewal to extract more rent. They were led by the head of the Native Land Trust Board, Marika Qarikau. He was, by all accounts, a hardline, abrasive nationalist who has used every means available to push his agenda, from addressing the provincial councils to using the network of the Methodist Church, to rallying Fijian landowners behind him and against the government. The NLTB was Qarikau's power base, and he, too, claimed a mandate: to protect native Fijian land. Three weeks after the coup, Qarikau circulated a 20 page 'Deed of Sovereignty' which demanded, among other things, the return of all state and freehold land to native ownership.

Chaudhry did not contest the landowners' desire to reclaim their land. Nor, on other hand, could he—or any other government for that matter—ignore the human plight of the tenants, unskilled, uneducated, poor, evicted from land their families had cultivated for four or five generations. The government offered the displaced tenants F$28,000 to start afresh in some other occupation, and about F$8,000 to the landlords who repossessed their former leasees' land to become cultivators themselves. Meanwhile, it also resuscitated the idea of a Land Use Commission, mentioned in his party's manifesto but with a history going back nearly forty years, to work with landowners to identify idle land and to put it to productive use, including, if possible, for resettlement of the displaced tenants. With the NLTB on a warpath, the government went directly to the Fijian landlords. Early in 2000, it sent a delegation of Fijian landowning chiefs to Malaysia to familiarise themselves with the work of a similar commission there. The chiefs returned impressed but, by then, Qarikau had already orchestrated a move among the provincial councils to reject the concept outright. Poseci Bune, the agriculture minister, recalled the malicious misinformation spread among the people. In one province, he was told the Land Use Commission was a ploy by Chaudhry to bring Indians to Fiji. Apparently Air India had expressed an interest in opening an office in Suva. But this was a false front. The main aim behind setting up an Air India office was to bring Indians from India to settle on land identified for development by the Land Use Commission. Faced with this malicious propaganda, the government then did what it should have done in the first place: it took the proposal to the Great Council of Chiefs, which approved it in principle but asked the government and the NLTB to develop it further cooperatively. It was a hard fought victory for the government.

Just when the government seemed to be gaining the upper hand, as shown by approval levels in the polls, Tora's Taukei Movement resurfaced in western Viti Levu, fuelling and galvanising extreme Fijian opinion against the government. The Cakaudrove Provincial Council passed a vote of no-confidence in the government, and others followed. Ratu Tevita Bolobolo, Tui Navitilevu, formed a landowners' council, Matabose ni Taukei ni Vanua, attacking the government and threatening non-renewal of leases. Ratu Tevita had lost to Labour in the 1999 general election. Taniela Tabu, former Taukei Movement stalwart and a trade unionist with a chequered career, formed the Viti National Union of Taukei Workers and attacked the Chaudhry government for 'Indianising the public service'. The charge was baseless—the upper echelons of the public service, and nearly 90 per cent of the permanent heads of government departments, were dominated by indigenous Fijians—but proved effective among many Fijians already distrustful of the government. The Christian Democrats labelled the government—in which it was partner—anti-Fijian over its hesitation to renew the work visa of expatriate Fiji TV head Kenneth Clark, because the Fijian provinces held the majority shares in the company headed by Clark.

The protest movement, small and disorganised at first, gained momentum and focus as May drew near. The government continued to repeat the refrain of mandate and refused to acknowledge that trouble was in the offing, dismissing the marches as the work of a few miscreants and misguided people. The police commissioner Isekia Savua's public warning to the government to raise its political antenna to catch the grumbling on the ground was ignored, so he claimed, and Savua was chastised for daring, as a public servant, to advise the government on questions of policy.

Convinced that its policies were beginning to bear fruit and were popular with the electorate, who had learned the hard lessons of 1987, the government adopted a business-as-usual approach as tension mounted around the country. Ignoring all the warning signals, it sent the commander of the military forces, Commodore Frank Bainimarama, to Norway on an official trip. The police commissioner was on holiday, and the president was in Lau celebrating his eightieth birthday. When the parliament met on 19 May, marking the first anniversary in government, no special security precautions were taken; no special police forces were deployed around the parliamentary complex. The police force focused on the protest marchers downtown heading towards Government House to present a petition to the president. At 10am Speight and his men stormed parliament, led by 20-year SAS veteran Major Ilisoni Ligairi and members of the Counter Revolutionary Warfare Unit he had set up

at the request of the 1987 coup leader Sitiveni Rabuka.
At 1.20pm that day Speight spoke to a stunned nation.

> People of Fiji in their desire to achieve self-determination and control of their
> future destiny in all matters pertaining to their livelihood and the affairs of the
> Republic of the Fiji Islands. We executed our actions this morning, there were a
> small number of us but as I speak and as I sit to make these announcements to
> you I speak on behalf of every individual member of the indigenous Fijian
> community. Through these actions I am stressing ownership, am asserting control
> and I am asserting executive power over Fiji. We have revoked the constitution and
> have set that aside. We have revoked the powers of the President of the Republic
> of Fiji. The executive control of this country of ours currently resides in my hands
> (*Fijilive*, 19 May 2003).

Soon afterwards, he announced the make-up of his administration. All,
without exception, were known nationalists, including many 'children of
1987'. Ratu Timoci Silatolu (FAP, Rewa) was appointed prime minister,
Ratu Naiqama Lalabalavu (SVT Cakaudrove) was made minister for Fijian
affairs, Ratu Rakuita Vakalalabure (SVT, Cakaudrove), minister for home
affairs. Three others had no portfolio: Simione Kaitani (SVT Lomaiviti),
Isireli Leweniqila (SVT, Tailveu), Levani Tonitonivanua (Nationalist,
Serua). Speight himself had his eye on the presidency, but that was not
officially announced. A fuller list, announced two days later, demoted
Silatolu to deputy prime minister, but added the more recognisable names
of Berenado Vunibobo, Ratu Tu'uakitau Cokanauto and Ratu Inoke
Kubuabola. Whether these individuals had agreed to serve in the Speight
administration was not known, but there was no doubt that they sang the
same nationalist tune as the architects of the coup.

Speight had hoped for a speedy acceptance of the proposals. A meeting
of the Great Council of Chiefs would be convened, the proposed list of
names presented and endorsed, the hostages released, and the country
run by a Taukei Civilian Administration. But events took a different,
perhaps unexpected, turn. Late in the afternoon of 19 May, as a rampaging
mob burned and looted Suva, President Ratu Sir Kamisese Mara declared
a State of Emergency. 'There are democratically recognised avenues for
airing grievances in accordance with the laws and the Constitution', Mara
told an anxious national television audience. 'I urge all those who lay
claim to be leaders of this dissenting group to follow lawful means in
raising their dissent'. His words fell on deaf ears. The president lacked

the power to enforce his will. The army was still in the barracks, divided in its loyalty, and the police force was confused, under-resourced and effectively leaderless—and, in the view of some, guilty of colluding with Speight's supporters.

After being persuaded that Rabuka did not have foreknowledge of the coup, Ratu Mara engaged him as his mediator with Speight. Rabuka was an occasional golfing partner of Speight's and the hijackers had reportedly trained on his estate in Vanua Levu. Some of them were from his own province of Cakaudrove. As events unfolded, Rabuka's lack of active support in the May uprising became clearer; outwardly, he was almost a bystander in the unfolding drama. Of all the major players on the Fijian side, he was the only one then who stood uncompromisingly by the constitution. Mara suggested through Rabuka that Chaudhry should voluntarily step down in favour of an indigenous Fijian. Deputy Prime Minister Tupeni Baba was the name Mara had in mind as the Fijian replacement. Speight welcomed the suggestion, but asked Mara to step down as well. When Rabuka conveyed that demand to Mara, the president agreed to oblige but only if the Great Council of Chiefs backed that demand. Speight also wanted to meet the president but Mara refused unless the hostages were released first. As Mara recalled, 'he was going to tell me that if I don't follow what he says, he will start executing hostages one-by-one and when I said what does he really want I was told that he wants me to step down and allow his group to run the country. I said I will not be able to oblige'. But while refusing dialogue under duress, in a nationally televised address Mara gave Speight and his supporters his 'personal guarantee as executive head of the Republic that the issues you have raised will be dealt with fully and your position as the indigenous community will be protected and enhanced'.

This was an important victory for Speight: the president had conceded the need to amend the constitution to 'protect and enhance' Fijian interests. But Mara wanted to achieve that goal through constitutional means. More was still to come. Mara also hinted that Mahendra Chaudhry might not be reinstated as prime minister. 'I can't say that I will put back the government that caused all these problems...What I intend to do is to talk to them (government members) and say "you've seen what has happened" so what's your possible solution' (*Fiji Sun*, 23 May 2000).

Whatever Mara's motives, his public doubts about Chaudhry's return to government served to strengthen the hostage takers' resolve that their goal was now within reach. Unwittingly or otherwise, the president had shown his hand. He was—or was seen to be—essentially on the same side as the broad spectrum of Fijian nationalists; they differed only in their methods.

While Mara sought to assert his executive authority, Speight began to build a human fortress around him by transporting in hundreds of supporters from southeastern Viti Levu—men, women and children. They sang and danced and cooked food on the grounds of the parliamentary complex—food (cattle and root crops) stolen from Indo-Fijian farmers in the Rewa delta and brought to Suva in police vans. The carnival atmosphere kept up the spirit of the gradually increasing crowd, but their presence in large numbers also ruled out a hostage rescue operation. When the police force sought to control the crowd at the parliamentary complex, they were chased away by armed youths. The crowd gave the impression of a growing groundswell of support for Speight, especially to the international community; Speight himself emerged as an articulate and effective manipulator of the media.

With the deadlock between Mara and Speight, all attention shifted to the meeting of the Great Council of Chiefs convened on 23 June. What transpired in that deeply emotional meeting is not known, although it was later reported that the Tailevu chiefs presented a *tabua* to the Great Council of Chiefs to seek forgiveness for George Speight's insulting remarks about them. Speight wanted the chiefs to justify their decisions, saying they had lost touch with the grassroots whom he now claimed to represent. After two days of talk, Ratu Mara was able to sway them to his side. He assured the chiefs that he would return the country to normalcy but would address the concerns that Speight and his supporters had raised with him, though by what authority he did not say.

The chiefs agreed. They expressed full confidence in the president and the vice president, endorsing Mara as the leader of his proposed interim administration but asked that his proposed council of advisors include some of Speight's group. The chiefs asked for the hostages to be released immediately and all stolen arms to be surrendered to the army. They also recommended a pardon for all those involved in the hostage takeover. And finally, they urged Mara to

> ...give full and urgent attention to the grievances as raised by the various *taukei* groups during the recent protest marches with special attention given to ensuring that the position of president and prime minister together with other senior government positions (unspecified) shall always be held by indigenous Fijians and Rotumans (Council of Chiefs, press release 23 June 2000).

Speight had got most of what he wanted, but he was still unsatisfied. He had not wanted a pardon but complete amnesty; there was always the hint that he expected to hold office in a new government. Mara agreed to consider it, but only after a proper trial. Speight was not satisfied with an amendment to the 1997 constitution as the chiefs had recommended; he wanted it abrogated. And, knowing Mara's political cunning, he wanted the president to step down as well, fearing that he might appoint to his council of advisors people personally loyal to him.

Mara proceeded with his plan to assume executive control. With Chaudhry incarcerated, the Labour coalition had elected Ratu Tevita Momoedonu as its interim leader and spokesman. Mara swore him in as acting prime minister 'solely to enable me to take three steps' (*Fijilive* 29 May 2000). The first was to advise the president under Section 99(1) of the constitution to dismiss all cabinet ministers, paving the way for him to appoint a caretaker prime minister and other advisors. The second was to advise the president to prorogue parliament, buying him time to 'set things in order'. And the third was for the acting prime minister to tender his resignation, handing over executive authority to the president to run the country in the absence of a prime minister, a cabinet and a sitting parliament. Ostensibly to save the constitution, the President sacrificed the prime minister and his duly elected government. Chaudhry, Mara said, 'is not only absent from duty but also he's unable to perform the functions of that office'. He invoked Section 106 of the constitution: 'The president may appoint a minister to act in office of another minister, including the prime minister, during any period or during all period when the minister is absent from duty, or is for any other reason unable to perform the functions of the office'. Mara's action was constitutionally flawed. The constitution, following the normal Westminster convention, severely limited the power of the president to act without ministerial advice. The constitution did prescribe the circumstances in which the president may act in his or her own deliberate judgement, but as far as the dismissal of a prime minister is concerned, Section 109(1) of the constitution explicitly stated

> [t]he president may not dismiss a prime minister unless the government fails to get or loses the confidence of the House of Representatives and the prime minister does not resign or get a dissolution of parliament.

Chaudhry was a hostage; he had not vacated his office, and he still enjoyed the confidence of the House of Representatives—he was still prime minister. But Mara had assumed otherwise 'as a matter of political reality', to use the fateful words of Chief Justice Sir Timoci Tuivaga who had advised him.[6]

In hindsight, it seems that Chaudhry's fate was sealed the moment Speight and his gunmen entered parliament. Sadly for him, neither the president nor the chief justice were prepared to stand by the constitution or the democratically elected government. The chief justice's behaviour invited the wrath of the Fiji Law Society which accused him of acting hastily in assuming that the 1997 constitution was in fact abrogated. His authorship of the Administration of Justice Decree, a decree that abolished the highest court in the land, the Supreme Court, and made the chief justice a judge of the Court of Appeal of which he was previously not a member and where he would now take precedence when the court sat, was severely criticised by the society. 'The eyes of the profession, the nation and the world are upon the judiciary', Peter Knight, the President of the Law Society, reminded the chief justice. 'It cannot be seen to openly condone criminal activity. It should as a matter of record [note] that it will continue to occupy and function in its judicial role in the same uncompromising manner as it had done prior to 19 May'.[7] The chief justice remained unmoved.

Ratu Mara's action was equally controversial, having decided on his own shortly after the takeover of the parliament that the 1997 constitution needed to be amended to accommodate the wishes of the Fijian nationalists. Yet, two years before, the president had praised the constitution as a fair and just charter for the nation. Perhaps Mara sensed that the Fijian opinion generally supported Speight's position, and, as in the past, he wanted to be where his people were. As Mara so often said, a chief without his or her people's support was not a chief. In 1982, Mara had behaved in a similar manner, refraining from condemning a motion passed by the Great Council of Chiefs demanding Fijian control of parliament. Be that as it may, Mara's action dismayed many, among them the United Nation's Special Envoy Sergio Vieira de Mellor and Commonwealth Secretary General Don McKinnon who were reportedly 'stunned by Mara's endorsement of Speight's nationalist views' (*Sydney Morning Herald*, 25 May 2000). And Pratap Chand, the minister for education, reminded Mara that the effect of his intervention would be to 'legitimise the overthrow of a constitutional and democratically elected government by terrorists' (*Fijilive*, 29 May 2000). But Mara was determined to pursue his course of action while the world speculated on his motives.

On the streets, where Speight's men marauded freely; these constitutional manoeuvres mattered little. On 28 May, they trashed the local TV station that ran a program drawing attention to the partial, provincial base of Speight's support. And in the melee that followed, a police officer was shot dead and shots were fired at the president's residence. The following day, Speight's supporters planned to march from the parliamentary complex to the president's house demanding his resignation; the march called off at the last minute on the advice of the army which feared a violent conflict after hearing rumours of Lauans gathering in Suva in support of their paramount chief. Despite his public pronouncements, the president's authority was weak. The police were outgunned; the army was divided and unwilling to back the president fully.

Part of the reason, according to Commodore Frank Bainimarama, was that emotionally many soldiers were in Speight's camp but did not support the methods he had used. Many were not prepared to risk their lives for a man, Ratu Mara, whom they distrusted for a variety of reasons. They regarded Mara as the man who stood between them and the goal of Fijian paramountcy—an autocratic leader who, in Speight's words, was 'imposing his will and controlling the Great Council of Chiefs through fear as he has done to the cabinet, the civil service, the *vanua* over the years, despite the will of the people' (*Fiji Sun*, 10 June 2000). Speight, like many others in Fiji, suspected that the president harboured dynastic ambitions, that he supported the Chaudhry government because his own family members were in it. Mara, for them, was a part of the problem not a part of the solution; he had to go. When that decision had been reached, four senior army personnel, lead by the commander as well as

Ratu Mara's son-in-law and former army commander Ratu Epeli Ganilau, approached Mara late on 29 June in the traditional Fijian way, presented him a *tabua* in forgiveness, and asked him to step aside.

Commodore Bainimarama assumed executive leadership and imposed martial law at 6pm on 29 May. An immediate curfew was imposed. A new military council was appointed to run the country for up to three years during which a new constitution would be drawn up and elections would be held under it. The army named former commander and Mara's son-in-law Ratu Epeli Nailatikau as its choice for prime minister. But it was a poor choice that added fuel to fire. Speight and his supporters saw in his nomination the continuation of the Mara dynasty and the Fijian establishment although Nailatikau himself came from a high-ranking chiefly family of Bau. Speight's group had at first welcomed the military's intervention. 'I suppose for the maintenance of law and order and for the safety of the lives of the public that was the only option for the military to take', Ratu Timoci Silatolu told Radio Fiji on 30 May. 'And we are keen to negotiate with them, someone who understands the hostage situation—an institution that is totally Fijian'.

The optimism of a breakthrough, however, was short lived: Speight's group wanted the new interim administration to be dominated by their followers. The opposition forced the army to delay naming its military council and withdraw Nailatikau's name.

As the third week of the crisis ended, the impasse continued. The military attempted to consolidate its support among the provinces by promising that their demands for political paramountcy would be accommodated in the new constitution. George Speight himself did not find a place in the civilian administration although his supporters did. But Speight had made other achievements: most significantly, the acceptance by a broad cross-section of the indigenous Fijians that the 1997 constitution, and the spirit that underwrote it—the spirit of multiethnic cooperation, of equal rights under the law, of equal citizenship, of enlarging the common space through representative democracy—could not be sustained in a country divided along racial lines for so long.

Fiji had travelled that route before under the 1990 constitution, ending up in a *cul-de-sac*. Speight and his supporters wanted self-determination for the indigenous Fijians, but they had had autonomy—and veto power in parliament—over matters of internal governance since independence. They had their traditional chiefly institutions intact, including the Great Council of Chiefs, and other separate administrative systems set up for their governance under the Fijian Affairs Act. Invoking international conventions on the rights of indigenous people was similarly unhelpful. The clear inference from them was that at the national level, the political and other rights of indigenous peoples are on exactly the same footing as those of other members of society. These conventions saw the special rights of indigenous peoples as distinct communities as supplementing the fundamental human rights and freedoms they already enjoy and share with other citizens. Nothing in these conventions gave an indigenous people superior or paramount rights in taking part in the government of the country. Fijian nationalists want Fijian paramountcy recognised as a right, but there was no basis on which the paramountcy of Fijian interests or Fijian political paramountcy could be elevated into a right.

Concepts of 'self-determination' and 'sovereignty' gave no support to that proposition. They wanted numerical dominance in a democratically elected parliament. But no constitution could guarantee political paramountcy of a particular ethnic group in a multiethnic state unless, of course, it abandoned all claim to be democratic. The 1990 constitution was weighted in favour of Fijians, but even it could not regulate the distribution of political power among Fijian parties. For that reason it could not ensure that Fijians would always be able to form an exclusively or predominantly Fijian government. Rabuka's government fell in 1993 because of political fragmentation among indigenous Fijians, and it fell for a similar reasons in 1999.

The army imposed martial law and returned the country to a semblance of normalcy. Power was handed to an interim administration. The rebels were rounded up.

George Speight was tried for treason and received life sentence. Many of his co-conspirators were also sent to prison for varying lengths of time. Soldiers who participated in the mutiny have also been punished but there is a lingering suspicion in Fiji that many people who worked behind the scenes, even some of the masterminds, have escaped punishment and are enjoying the fruits of Speight's handiwork. In April

2004, the chiefs sentenced to imprisonment for their role in the mutiny of November 2000 were released on compulsory supervision order after serving a only week in jail. And the government proposed a new legislation, 'Outside Dispute Resolution', which would absolve chiefs from criminal prosecution if they were deemed to have intervened to resolve a dispute, even if their participation was illegal. Creating two sets of laws, one for the chiefs and one all others, was myopic and dangerous, as was the proposal to increase the powers of the Great Council of Chiefs from its currently advisory role. They would one day return to haunt Fiji.

## Notes

1   See Col. Filipe Tarakinini's statement on *Fijilive*, 4 June 2000: 'The army is just a reflection of society, so what is happening there [fragmentation] is happening in the army as well; you can't deny that'.

2   With some eccentric exceptions as the Maori lawyer Anthony Sinclair who said, without irony, 'we believe that revolution is a legitimate part of the democratic process' (*Fijilive*, 3 June 2000).

3   Representatives of this group would include Rakuita Vakalalabure, Saimone Kaitani, Timoci Silatolu and Filipe Tuisawau.

4   This group would include Josefa Kamikamica, Savenaca Siwatibau and Mosese Qionabaravi.

5   This is confirmed by Chaudhry's deputy Tupeni Baba who thought the party had agreed to have him (an indigenous Fijian) as prime minister. See his book, Tupeni, Unaisi and Field 2005).

6   The quote is from the Chief Justice's letter to Peter Knight, President of the Fiji Law Society, 14 June 2000.

7   A copy of this letter dated 9 June is in the author's possession.

# 9

# In George Speight's shadow

On 25 August 2001, Fiji once again went to the polls, under the 1997 multiracial constitution that George Speight and the Fiji military forces had declared abrogated, but which had been upheld by the High Court and subsequently by the Fiji Court of Appeal. The holding of the elections was a significant achievement in the circumstances. Nonetheless, instead of resolving the country's political difficulties and healing wounds, it ended up polarising ethnic relations even further, embroiling major political parties in an acrimonious debate about power sharing mandated by the constitution.

A record twenty-six, mostly indigenous Fijian, political parties registered to contest the elections, but only eighteen fielded candidates for the 71-seat lower house. Interim Prime Minister Laisenia Qarase's Soqosoqo ni Duavata Lewenivanua (SDL), launched on the eve of the elections, won 32 seats, deposing Mahendra Chaudhry's Fiji Labour Party who won 27. The coup-supporting Conservative Alliance Matanitu Vanua (CAMV), among whose successful candidates was George Speight himself, won 6 seats, the National Federation Party one and the breakaway New Labour Unity Party (NLUP), formed by Dr Tupeni Baba, deputy prime minister in the People's Coalition government, and independents won two each. The smaller splinter parties failed to make an impact. What was surprising was the failure of more established parties which had fared well in the past, including the Fijian Association Party (FAP), a senior partner in the People's Coalition government, and the Soqosoqo ni Vakavulewa ni Taukei (SVT), the party in power for much of the 1990s.

George Speight, awaiting trial for treason, cast a long shadow over the campaign. Indigenous Fijian political parties competed with each other to court his supporters, promising to fulfil his agenda of enshrining Fijian political paramountcy in perpetuity. Otherwise, there was little public enthusiasm for the election. The electorate was genuinely pessimistic and apprehensive. On the Indo-Fijian side, there was a pervasive feeling of fear and anxiety; the memory of May 19 was still fresh. 'Fijians will do whatever they want', a voter told me. 'What's the point of voting?' The low voter turnout—78.6 per cent—and a surprisingly large number of informal votes, indicated indifference and protest. On the Fijian side where the voter turnout was equally low, there was dismay and disillusionment at the large number of parties, with divergent and sometimes diametrically opposed agendas, despite the efforts of the Methodist Church to forge a semblance of political unity. Public confidence in the most important institutions of the state was at its lowest ebb, their reputation for professionalism, independence and integrity tainted or otherwise compromised. Among them was the police force. The *Daily Post* summed up the popular perception.

> The force remains under-paid, badly equipped, lacking in skills, demoralised, lacking in a leader with the moral authority to preach to his men and women, let alone the people of Fiji. The force under Mr [Isikia] Savua has been linked with complicity in last year's political crisis. Many a police officer has said that the police did not act when they were needed during the riots in Suva city because they had not received the relevant instructions from the top (*Daily Post*, 21 August 2001).

Isikia Savua was eventually cleared of illegality and complicity in the coup by a closed tribunal headed by Chief Justice Timoci Tuivaga, but without abating public scepticism. One observer called the inquiry 'a fraud' facilitated by the chief justice, a 'person who has come under attack from legal sources in Fiji and internationally for facilitating the abrogation of the constitution and for continuing to frustrate legal challenges to the abrogation of the constitution' (*Fiji Sun*, 11 August 2001). Labour Party president Jokapeci Koroi accused Savua of having 'deliberately misled the government by giving assurances that there was nothing to worry about. Mr Savua must go' (*Fiji Sun*, 13 August 2001). Savua continued for a while as police commissioner, with a tarnished reputation, until he was posted to the United Nations as Fiji's permanent representative.

The army, too, was diminished in public esteem. It managed to restore law and order after the hostages were released from 56 days of incarceration, but not before it was shown to be infected by the dangerous virus of indiscipline, insubordination and provincialism. Members of the army's Counter Revolutionary Warfare Unit, established by Sitiveni Rabuka after the 1987 coups, was instrumental in the execution of the coup. Several senior military figures professed public sympathy for Speight's agenda but disapproved of his method, though precisely what method they would have approved they did not specify. In November 2000, a section of the army mutinied, killing five soldiers and injuring scores of others. The brutal violence that the army used to quell the mutiny remains a source of great bitterness and tension in the Fijian community—who were unable to comprehend the possibility of the Fijian army ever fighting Fijian civilians. President Josefa Iloilo granted immunity to the regular soldiers, while mutineers were tried and sentenced to various periods of imprisonment.

Another institution that lost credibility in their independence and integrity in the immediate aftermath of the coup was the judiciary, with a local daily newspaper pleading with the judges to 'wake up, grow up and, importantly, stop bickering' (*Fiji Times*, 29 August 2001). The role Chief Justice Tuivaga, played or did not play—the advice he gave the president in resolving the crisis which later proved to be unconstitutional, his early acceptance that the constitution had been abrogated, his authorship of a decree abolishing the Supreme Court—became matters of intense public dispute, leading the Fiji Law Society to call for his immediate resignation. The chief justice rebuked judges who disagreed with his interpretation or otherwise showed independence, and rewarded those who sided with him. His unexpectedly harsh attack on Justice Anthony Gates of the Lautoka High Court, who had upheld the constitution, was typical. Tuivaga accused Gates of not 'recognising and respecting the hierarchy of administrative power and authority with the judiciary of this country', and advised him to 'explore other work environment where the rules of administrative propriety do not apply' (Fiji High Court File CJ/WF/9 as cited in *Fiji Times*, 28 August 2001). Tuivaga defended himself. 'I have been chief justice for 20 years, in the driver's seat, and I know what is good for this country and what I did was good for the country' (*Daily Post*, 1 September 2001). He had accepted the *de facto* government as 'a matter of political reality', and intervened to 'ensure that the maintenance of law and order and justice in this country was not to be frustrated by any ineffective administrative court machinery' (Supreme Court File CJ/WF/9). The Court of Appeal, however, thought otherwise.

The social costs of the political crisis were visible. These included poverty, joblessness, prostitution, growth in the population of squatter settlements fringing major urban centres, people evicted from expiring leases living in makeshift camps in Valelawa in Vanua Levu and at the Girmit Centre in Lautoka, women from broken homes, single mothers, unemployed with the closure of garment factories established under lucrative tax regimes in the 1980s. Since the crisis of 2000, there was a marked increase in the suicide rate, particularly among women (*Pacnews*, 31 August 2001). Many workers suffered from pay cuts and reduced working hours, thus completing the vicious cycle of poverty and despair.

The economy, which was beginning to show signs of growth after the 1999 elections, suffered a severe downturn, with a projected 1 per cent growth rate. Foreign investment once again dried up, and many local big businesses yet again moved their financial assets overseas. A few large ones are now operating in Fiji as foreign companies. Investor confidence, severely shaken by the crisis and continuing uncertainty about Fiji's political stability, took a dive, while the economy suffered from the huge cloud over the sugar industry, which provided over 40 per cent of the country's export earnings and 15 per cent of the gross domestic product, and employed nearly 150,000 people (P. Lal 2000). The anticipated loss of preferential access to the European Union was one problem.

But the more immediate issue was the fate of farmers whose leases under the Agricultural Landlord and Tenant Act (ALTA) began to expire. The government and the Native Land Trust Board wanted ALTA to be replaced by the Native Land Trust Act (NLTA) because they saw ALTA as favouring tenants—making the termination of expiring leases more difficult and remuneration for landlords less attractive. The essential difference between the two was that NLTA provided for rolling 5–30-year leases, rather than minimum 30-year leases, giving landowners the opportunity to reclaim their land earlier if they so chose. Under ALTA, the rent was assessed at a fixed 6 per cent of the unimproved capital value, while under NLTA, it was to be assessed at the current market value and a percentage of production, to the benefit of landowners. Other provisions of the Act generally favoured the landowners. The land problem is inevitably politicised, both by the leaders of the farming community and by those representing the landlords, to the detriment of the economy. In many cases where leases were not renewed, land was lying fallow, slowly turning to bush, while the displaced tenants, dismayed to see their life's work ruined, sought shelter in refugee camps and looked for alternative employment.

The fabric of national society was strained. While ostensibly things looked calm—people went about their business, intermingled in the workplace, on the sports field, around the *yaqona* bowl, more so in parts of Fiji not directly traumatised by the events of 19 May—but hidden behind the rhetoric of multiculturalism and reconciliation lay deep suspicions and raw prejudices, more widespread now than in Fiji's recent past. People who once had genuinely moderate views sought shelter and succour in extremist ethnic camps. Many Indo-Fijians, although politically opposed to Mahendra Chaudhry, supported him as 'their only hope' against the Fijian nationalists. Many Fijians similarly supported Laisenia Qarase. Some might see the widening divide between the two ethnic groups as confirming the historical pattern of race relations in Fiji history, but that would be a mistake. The two communities have cooperated in the past; the prominent example being in the review of the 1990 constitution. And there was genuine regret on all sides at the racial turn Fiji politics had taken.

I have already said that in Fiji, race relations tend to get polarised at election times. The race card has long been a part of the zero-sum game politicians have played. A semblance of normalcy returns as political tempers cool. While relations were tense, it would be a mistake to draw a picture of two solidly united groups, at the edge, at each others' throat, ready to explode. The truth is that both the communities are internally divided by class, regional origins and culture. Not all Fijians, for instance, wanted the 1997 multiracial constitution revoked, nor Fiji to be turned into a Christian state. Some demanded special affirmative action programs for Fijians, while others did not. Some wanted George Speight and his co-conspirators pardoned while others insisted on a proper trial. The deeper cracks, the confederacy and dynastic politics which surfaced in the aftermath of the coup, are still there, papered over for the moment. Fijian leaders recognise that the political unity of all Fijians under a single banner is an evanescent dream. Fijians rallied behind Rabuka in the early 1990s only to fragment later. Large numbers supported Qarase in 2001 but over a dozen Fijian political parties, including the newly launched the National Alliance Party, will contest the general elections scheduled for 2006.

Strong support for Chaudhry among Indo-Fijians should be read in a similar light. They rallied—and continue to rally—behind him because of the spectre of violence and discrimination that threatens them at the hand of the Fijian nationalists. But deep divisions exist. In the 2001 election campaign, more than in previous ones, there was open talk of the difference between Gujaratis and the descendants of the girmitiyas, and between North and South Indians. The National Federation Party was portrayed as a party of the Gujaratis and the South Indians. Several community leaders spoke with dismay about the damage reference to regional and cultural origins during the election campaign had done to social relations at the local village level. Whether, or how, the internal frictions and divisions manifest themselves in future political realignments would be watched with interest.

The turnout at the polls in 2001 was low; a mark of fear, apathy, indifference and protest and, possibly, the absence of fear of non-collectable fines for not voting. Many Indo-Fijian voters also stayed away because of intimidation, fearing reprisal from Fijian landlords as well as the nationalists if they voted for Labour, which everyone assumed they would. The percentage of invalid votes was a staggering 11.69 per cent compared to 8.69 in 1999. The campaign itself lacked the verve and excitement normally associated with election campaigns in Fiji. There were a few large rallies in selected centres, but most of the campaigning was done in small pocket meetings. Television advertisement played a larger role this time than before, featuring party manifestos and policy positions. There was lengthy debate among leaders of all the major parties, though this generated more heat than light. Interestingly, all the major parties used the internet, several with their own web sites, publicising their manifestos and accomplishments. The internet was largely for overseas supporters and fundraisers as few outside the major urban centres in Fiji had access to computers. The calibre of candidates among Indo-Fijians was markedly inferior to the 1999 line-up, featuring a lacklustre list of retired schoolteachers and public servants and others looking for a second career. This was in contrast to the calibre of Fijian candidates, especially in the SDL, which featured accomplished, if politically inexperienced, professionals most of whom had served in the interim administration. Fijians saw a future in politics; Indo-Fijians did not, at least not with any expectation of taking a leading part in the nation's affairs. Many had sent their families abroad, and they themselves would migrate if they could.

The road to the August elections began with the hijacking of the Fijian parliament on 19 May 2000 holding members of the People's Coalition government hostage for 56 days. George Speight and his wide circle of supporters, defiant and uncompromising, sought to have themselves installed as the new government, preferably with the endorsement by the Great Council of Chiefs. A number of appointments to an interim administration were in fact announced but then abruptly withdrawn and lists revised when negotiations failed. The besieged president, Ratu Sir Kamisese Mara, sought, albeit unconstitutionally, to wrest control of the unfolding events, offering an olive branch to the rebels with the promise to review the constitution to take account of their concerns. He failed because the rebels saw him as a part of the problem—an aging, imperious leader unwilling to give up power, out of touch, seeking personal advantage for himself and harbouring dynastic ambitions. Unable to stamp his customary authority, Mara vacated office under armed protection on 29 May, allowing the army to impose martial law and a curfew in the urban areas.

Following Mara's resignation, the army installed a military government headed by Commodore Voreqe (Frank) Bainimarama. He became executive head of government, and was advised by a Military Court of Advisors. Their main aim was to secure the release of the hostages and the return of stolen weapons. After a long and frustrating series of meetings with the rebels, the military managed to negotiate the Muanikau Accord, which freed the hostages. The rebels were promised amnesty if they surrendered the arms stolen from the military's armoury. But when the rebels reneged, making further impossible demands from their new holdout at Kalabu, the army, its reputation already bruised and battered by the hostage crisis, its inaction the subject of derisive comment about its much-vaunted professionalism, retaliated with a brutality that shocked the Fijian community. The army eventually subdued the rebels and established a semblance of law and order, but its brutal tactics left a legacy of bitterness among Fijians, planting the seed for a violent mutiny several months later.

On 3 July, the interim military government announced a 19-member cabinet to run the country till 2002; it hoped that by then a new constitution would be in place and fresh elections could be held under it. The military saw the main task of the interim administration as rehabilitating the economy, and drawing up the terms of reference for a new constitution review commission. The commission would 'consider particular constitutional issues of concern to indigenous Fijians', including strengthening the role of the Great Council of Chiefs 'in the national affairs of the state', a race-based affirmative action for Rotumans and Fijians, and recognition of traditional and customary laws of the indigenous community (*Pacnews*, 3 July 2001). The commission began hearings in mid August 2000, but met immediate public opposition, both for the manner in which it was appointed, by an unconstitutional interim administration without consultation with the major political parties, and for the composition of its membership. The four Indo-Fijians on it were all Christians, representing only a tiny percentage of the Indo-Fijian community, and none enjoyed the confidence of the community at large. The chair of the commission was Asesela Ravuvu, a long time advocate of Fijian paramountcy and one of the vocal hardline Fijian nationalists. His presence and unguarded utterances compromised the commission, with the Indo-Fijians boycotting the hearings *en masse*.

The commission was suspended in January 2001 following a high court ruling upholding the 1997 constitution and declaring its appointing authority, the interim administration, illegal. Nonetheless, a small four-member subgroup prepared a summary report that, for the most part, blamed the Indo-Fijians for the problems facing the Fijian people. The Indo-Fijians were characterised as *vulagi*, visitors, who should, but did not, accept their proper culturally sanctioned role to serve, or at least be subservient to, the *taukei*, the owners of the land. Indo-Fijians used 'democracy, equality, and human rights to discourage and outmanoeuvre Fijian political efforts and aspirations to regain that nationalism and the power which had been ceded in 1874', the report argued. The Indo-Fijians, moreover, 'did not consider the Fijian people's demands for the paramountcy of their interests and the return of all government authority into Fijian hands'. The solution to Fiji's political problems? Fijians 'must rule it [Fiji] and feel secure that they shall not be dominated in their own house. This is the only solution to long-term political stability, peace and prosperity'. The political leadership of the country should always remain in Fijian hands, the authors argued 'within a time frame to allow others to be eventually assimilated and accepted as Fijians'.[1] Laisenia Qarase promised to be guided by the spirit of the report, adding provocatively that since Fijians owned 83 per cent of the land, they should have proportionate dominance in parliament.

On the economic front, the government promised a number of initiatives to revive the stagnant economy. It proposed to lower the corporate tax rate for all tax payers, introduce investment and accelerated depreciation allowances, lower duty rates on construction materials and capital items, permit exporters access to world priced inputs, introduce a duty suspension scheme for all regular exporters with a record of compliance. Four months later, following the example of the post 1987 initiatives, the Qarase administration embarked on a 'Look North' policy, seeking export markets and fresh investment input from East Asia (*Fiji Times*, 5 December 2000). Fiji backed Japan's effort to become a permanent member the United Nations Security Council, and supported China's membership of the World Trade Organization. China gave the Royal Military Forces F$1.8 million dollars, and Japanese aid similarly increased. But not for long. The financial crisis humbled the Asian tigers and the promised large-scale investments did not materialise. Given the imperatives of international financial investment, it is fair to surmise that they never will.

These initiatives were overshadowed by, or subsumed under, the interim administration's 'Blueprint for the Protection of Fijian and Rotuman Rights and Interests, and the Advancement of their Development', presented to the Great Council of Chiefs by Qarase on

13 July 2000. The blueprint proposed to transfer all crown or state land to the Native Land Trust Board, set up a Land Claims Tribunal to 'deal with long-standing historical land claims' for 'land acquired for public purposes', establish a Development Trust Fund for Fijian training and education, give Fijian landowners more royalty for resources extracted from their lands, the payment determined by the cabinet and not parliament, exempt Fijian-owned companies from company tax for a period of time, reserve 50 per cent of the licences (import, permits) for Fijians as well as 50 per cent of government contracts. These initiatives were not new. Many such schemes had been tried in the past and had failed, but the administration was less concerned about the internal coherence and viability of its proposal. It was more attuned to the blueprint's appeal among Fijian voters.

In May 2001, the administration announced a 'Blueprint for Affirmative Action for Fijian Education'. Long on vision and rhetoric but short on specifics, the blueprint proposed a ten-year affirmative action program for the 'development of a new generation of indigenous Fijians, proud of their traditions and cultural heritage, and imbued with a hunger for education for individual development and success; and of a national society with indigenous Fijians competing successfully in all fields of endeavour towards national socioeconomic development'. The aim was to

> ...develop and transform all Fijian schools into centres of cultural and educational excellence to promote, facilitate and provide the quality education and training Fijian students need for their own individual development, and to adequacy equip them for life in a vibrant and developing economy. To inculcate into Fijian parents the understanding that education is the key to success in life and to therefore place the education of their children highest on their list of priorities.

These would be realised through the establishment of an advisory Fijian Education Board, strengthening community participation, providing access to quality education and training at all levels, upgrading the qualification of Fijian teachers, mounting special programs to meet the needs of Fijian school leavers, strengthening education in rural areas, and providing for a system of review to monitor the progress of the aims of the blueprint.

As shown in earlier chapters, Fijian education has long been a national problem. Failure rates, especially at secondary and tertiary levels have been alarming for years, despite nearly four decades of affirmative action. An estimated 90 per cent of Fijian students dropped out between 1988 and 2000. In 1988, 11,000 Fijian children enrolled in class one, but thirteen years later, only 1,247 were in form seven. There has been little proper accounting for the failure rate, and the allocation of more money would not necessarily solve the problem. The interim administration's 'racial' approach neglected certain complexities of educational activity in Fiji. Only Fijian schools, so designated, were eligible for funds earmarked for Fijian education. Yet, there were many non-Fijian schools which Fijian children attended; in some instances—Pandit Vishnu Deo Memorial School in Samabula, DAV Girls College and Suva Sangam High—they comprised the largest numbers. Yet, these schools did not qualify for special assistance, discouraging Fijian parents from sending their children to non-Fijian schools, shielding them from a competitive learning environment they would inevitably encounter later in life.

The interim administration had its critics who saw the blueprint as Qarase's ploy to pay off militant elements who were behind the 19 May event. Dr Isimeli Cokanasiga of the Fijian Association Party argued that the blueprint would 'not benefit Fijians who were hardworking, successful, talented, smart and ambitious', but those who were 'blue-blooded, losers, lazy, dumb and ambitious' (*Fiji Times*, 13 November 2001). Qarase was undeterred. His policies, backed by all the advantage of incumbency and the state purse, proved popular among Fijians and accounted for the party's victory in the elections. Buoyed by popular support and unable to form a united Fijian political front, Qarase, a politically inexperienced merchant banker of mixed record, launched his own political party, the Soqosoqo ni Duavata ni Lewenivanua, in May. Qarase targeted the Fijian voter as his first electoral priority, and brazenly committed the public purse to that end.

There was much movement and activity on the Labour side as well. Released from captivity, the members of the deposed government pleaded their cause to the international community already outraged by Speight's coup. Australia, New Zealand and the United States responded with trade and 'smart' sanctions banning coup supporters from entering their countries. In July, Labour filed a case in the Lautoka High Court before Justice Anthony Gates challenging the abrogation of the constitution. It argued that the attempted coup of May was unsuccessful, the declaration of a state of emergency invoking the doctrine of necessity by President Ratu Sir Kamisese Mara unconstitutional, and the purported abrogation of the 1997 constitution void. The People's Coalition government remained the legitimate government 'in view of the [inability of the] interim military government and Speight's group to reach an agreement on governing the country'.[2] For its part, the interim administration argued that the applicant, Chandrika Prasad, a farmer fleeing terror in Muaniweni in southeastern Viti Levu, who had sought temporary shelter at the refugee camp at the Girmit Centre, and in whose name Labour had instituted the legal proceedings, had no *locus standi* to mount the court case. His action was an 'abuse of process', 'scandalous, frivolous and vexatious'.

Justice Gates, however, thought otherwise. He agreed that the coup had failed. 'It never achieved any legitimacy', he declared, because it had breached established procedures for amending the constitution. He then turned to the contentious 'doctrine of necessity', on which the state had rested its case. The doctrine justified extra-legal intervention in exceptional circumstances, through military takeover, for instance, to preserve peace, order and a semblance of government when the state is paralysed. But it could not be used to legitimise or consolidate the extra-legal usurpation of the power of the state. 'The doctrine does not permit necessity to be used as a means of subverting the existing constitutional structure either by abrogating the existing legal order or by bypassing the path laid out for lawful amendment'. 'Whatever is done however should be done in order to uphold the rule of law and the existing constitution', Gates ruled. 'Necessity cannot be resorted to in order to justify or support the abrogation of the existing legal order. The doctrine is valid only to protect not destroy'.

The interim administration, too, was illegal, in Gates' opinion. The 'rule of law means that the suspended state of affairs and the constitution return to life after the stepping down of a responsible military power and after the conclusion of its work for the restoration of calm for the nation. The nation has much for which to be grateful to he military, and may yet have further need for its assistance to maintain stability. There is no constitutional foundation of legality for the interim administration'.

The pre 19 May parliament was still in existence. Ratu Mara still remained president. The '*status quo* is restored. Parliament should be summoned by the president at his discretion but as soon as possible'.

Gates' was a courageous decision that caught the interim administration, and most people in Fiji, by surprise. Nonetheless, to its credit, and against the advice of some hardliners, the administration agreed to appeal the decision before the Fiji Court of Appeal, Fiji's highest court after the abrogation of the Supreme Court following the May coup. The full bench met in March, chaired by Sir Maurice Casey of New Zealand, and consisting of Justices Ken Handley of Australia, Gordon Ward of Tonga, Sir Maori Kapi of Papua New Guinea and Sir Ian Barker of New Zealand. The interim administration was represented by two Queen's Counsel (Nicholas Blake and Anthony Molloy) and the respondents by Australian legal academic George Williams and the high profile human rights lawyer Geoffrey Robertson, QC. The appearance in the court of case of such a distinguished cast ensured high drama and unusual amounts of international interest.

The court first considered the state's contention that the abrogation of the constitution was justified because the electoral system— preferential voting—had produced an outcome detrimental to Fijians, that the first-past-the-post method of voting would have given a more balanced result, that 1997 constitution had weakened protection of indigenous Fijian rights guaranteed under previous constitutions, 'so that the new government under an Indo-Fijian prime minister could disregard and erode the rights of indigenous Fijians'. On the system of voting, the court concluded that under the first-past-the-post system, one of the Fijian parties, the SVT, would have won more seats (from 8 to 17), and Labour three fewer (34 instead of 37), but overall, the People's Coalition would have won 45 seats (increased to 47 with the addition of two VLV candidates to the cabinet). 'Whichever system had been used, the voting figures would have made the FLP the largest individual party by a substantial margin'. The court similarly rejected the claim that Fijian rights could be eroded by the government of the day, noting the ironclad guarantees in the constitution. No significant issue touching indigenous concerns could be passed without the consent of the Fijian people themselves, specifically without the support, in the Senate, of 9 of the

14 senators nominated by the Great Council of Chiefs. Any 'attempt by the government to change the law in relation to land or to indigenous rights by stealth was impossible under the 1997 constitution and any suggestions that it needed to be replaced on that ground cannot be substantiated'. Nor did the court uphold the doctrine of necessity as a justification for abrogating the constitution.

Had a new legal order been created by the coup? Had the revolution succeeded? The interim administration argued that it had. It was now firmly in control of the country, it claimed that the machinery of administration was functioning, and the population had acquiesced. Fiji's continued diplomatic relations with the international community also attested to its legitimacy and authority. The court ruled otherwise. Several human rights and community organisations had presented affidavits showing curtailment of basic freedoms. The existence of emergency legislation inhibiting pubic expression of dissent was proof enough of continuing public disquiet about events in the country. 'The people must be proved to be behaving in conformity with the dictates of the *de facto* government', the court concluded, and the interim administration had not furnished convincing evidence to support its claim, thus failing the test of acquiescence. Summing up, the Fiji Court of Appeal ruled that the 1997 constitution remained the supreme law of the country. It had not been abrogated. And the parliament had not been dissolved but prorogued on 27 May for six months. But on one issue—whether the president had in fact resigned of his own accord—the court ruled that he had, contradicting Gates' judgment. Ratu Mara was no longer the President of Fiji. The vice president, Ratu Josefa Iloilo, had assumed the office of president.

The much anticipated decision of the Court of Appeal did not create the havoc in the country that some had predicted (or hoped for). Instead, the Great Council of Chiefs, the interim administration and the military, after some public misgivings about its ability to maintain law and order, agreed to respect the decision. What was the way forward? The court's decision divided the Labour Party. One faction, led by Deputy Prime Minister Tupeni Baba, preferred a broad-based government of national unity from among the members of the deposed parliament. Baba, a politician of thwarted ambition with a shaky power base, whose strident criticism of Mahendra Chaudhry's style was public knowledge, would lead that government with other Fijian parties, including the SVT. What Fiji needed, he said, was more breathing space to heal the wounds of the coup, not another acrimonious election in an heightened atmosphere of racial tension.

Chaudhry disagreed. He would never agree to be a part of any government that included people who were 'connected even remotely' to the coup (*Pacnews*, 5 March 2001). But some in the Labour Party tentatively explored the possibility of having the Christian Alliance, Speight's party, in a multiparty Labour government.[3] The national interest, Chaudhry said, 'would best be served if we were to go for fresh elections'. Accordingly, Chaudhry advised the president to dissolve the parliament after reconvening it to deal with constitutional issues raised by the opposition parties. Astonishingly, in his letter to the president, he even agreed to reconsider the alternative vote system, of which had been staunchly opposed. 'The People's Coalition has an open mind on this and is prepared to discuss changes to bring back the first-past-the-post system' (People's Coalition government media release, 7 March 2001).

The president disregarded the advice of both the factions. Instead, he listened to the senior officers of the army who met him soon after the Appeal Court's ruling. The military expected the president to observe the spirit of the constitution, but added emphatically that 'as a matter of national interest we cannot afford to have Mr Chaudhry and his group back' (*Fiji Sun*, 4 March 2001). The army, now a central part of the Fijian political equation and the ultimate guarantor of public security, could be ignored only at the country's peril. Even Chaudhry's own colleagues agreed, including his deputy prime minister, Adi Kuini Speed, who urged her former leader to 'use good sense and realise that it is going to be very unstable if he returns as prime minister. It will be very dangerous because of what has happened' (*Fiji Times*, 5 March 2001). In an act of astounding constitutional contortion, President Iloilo swore in his nephew, People's Coalition Minister Tevita Momoedonu as acting prime minister, and asked him to advise dissolution of parliament, which Momoedonu did. Iloilo accepted the advice and Momoedonu's prompt resignation, and reappointed the Qarase's caretaker administration to prepare the country for general elections. Chaudhry challenged the constitutionality of the president's action, but was unsuccessful. The announcement of elections in August paved the way for the next phase as political parties geared up for elections. Fragmentation and confusion were the order of the day. The People's Coalition fractured. Tupeni Baba resigned from the Fiji Labour Party in May to form his own New Labour Unity Party, accusing his former leader of trampling on 'dialogue, compromise and consensus', of being insensitive to Fijian concerns and problems, of an absence of 'fair and equitable distribution of power' within the party. Chaudhry, Baba said bluntly, was a 'dictator' (Fiji Labour Party campaign material). The disunity among Fijians was worse. In western Viti Levu, Apisai Tora, ever-mercurial, formed yet another political party, the Bai Kei Viti, to challenge the Party of National Unity; the party that he himself had launched to contest the 1999 elections. Competing for the same vote, on an almost identical platform, they cancelled each other out, thereby decreasing western Fijian voice in national affairs both were keen to secure. The SVT regrouped under the leadership of Filipe Bole, but it was pale shadow of its former self, unsure of its identity, uncertain about its future direction, confused about its electoral tactics and strategy, and contradictory in its political pronouncements.

The Fijian Association, under its ailing leader, Adi Kuini Speed, was divided and drifting, unable to articulate a coherent vision. The Nationalist Vanua Tako Lavo Party had its predictable agenda for Fijian nationalism and political control appropriated by other 'mainstream' political parties. Among them was the newly formed Conservative Alliance Matanitu Vanua Party, conceived on the island of Vanua Levu by supporters of George Speight and the coup. The party wanted the 1997 constitution replaced with one that gave Fijian political control. 'We can't have immigrant people run the government; political control must be related to the ownership of resources that fuels Fiji', thundered one of its leaders, Ratu Rakuita Vakalalabure (Fiji Sun, 5 September 2001). The party rejected the ALTA, demanded greater landowner control over the exploitation of natural resources (forests, fisheries, minerals), and compensation for past government projects on alienated Fijian land. It also wanted Speight and his co-conspirators granted amnesty. Speight, the party claimed, was not a terrorist but a political prisoner, not a traitor but a hero of the 'Fijian cause', a latter-day Sitiveni Rabuka.

Laisenia Qarase's Soqosoqo ni Duavata ni Lewenivanua was the mainstream Fijian 'nationalist' party. Its unabashedly pro-Fijian agenda and deep animosity to Mahendra Chaudhry, which intensified as the campaign progressed, increased its appeal among Fijian voters. The SDL portrayed itself as the party best positioned to realise the aims of the Speight coup, trumpeting the undoubted wealth of bureaucratic and technocratic talents among the rank of its candidates. It, too, would review the constitution to entrench Fijian paramountcy. It would set up a Land Claims Tribunal to investigate land claims by landowners. The Fijian Blueprint was its manifesto for the indigenous community, and the SDL committed itself to its full implementation. And the Qarase administration blatantly used the advantage of incumbency to the maximum: practising pork-barrel politics at its worst (or best), improving roads, building bridges, donating money to schools in marginal Fijian constituencies, providing farming implements, brush cutters, outboard motors and generators (*Sunday Times*, 2 September 2001). Loyalists were placed in strategic decision-making positions in the public service and statutory organisations. The powerful Methodist Church lent the party its own considerable support, 'threatening eternal damnation for those not supportive of whomever it support[ed]' (*Sunday Times*, 2 September 2001). Well funded, sharply focused, uncompromising and strident in its defence of Fijian interests, the SDL easily out-gunned its Fijian rivals.

Apart from the advantage of incumbency, Qarase was helped by the division and lack of drive in other Fijian parties. A good example was the performance of the SVT. Its new leader, Filipe Bole, a veteran politician, adopted a moderate, multiracial stance. He defended the 1997 constitution and criticised Qarase's nationalist rhetoric. Bole also saw no problem working with Chaudhry. The party's manifesto emphasised social and economic issues—health, education, jobs, infrastructure, reforming the value-added tax system, helping first-time home buyers (*Daily Post*, 29 July 2001)—making its platform virtually indistinguishable from that of its rivals.

But many in his own party did not share Bole's vision. Among them was former SVT leader, a coup-supporting nationalist, Ratu Inoke Kubuabola, for whom there was a 'Fijian consensus that the 1997 constitution does not adequately safeguard the indigenous rights and aspirations' (*Daily Post*, 16 August 2001). On Chaudhry, Kubuabola declared the Labour leader 'must accept reality; he is not a man of peace, he is for confrontation; he is trying to take what is not his for the taking. The reality should tell Mahendra Chaudhry why he just doesn't qualify to lead this country' (*Daily Post*, 24 August 2001). Mere Samisoni, the SVT candidate for Lami, was an ardent supporter of the Speight coup, supplying food to rebels at the parliamentary complex. Berenado Vunibobo, with nationalist leanings, was likewise linked to the Speight camp. He was, moreover, a member of the Constitution Review Commission that were lobbying for the constitution changed. The SVT also suffered the indignity of its sponsorship by the Great Council of Chiefs being severed on the eve of the elections. The party which had started with much promise and which had been in power throughout the 1990s was clearly hobbled by doubt about its purpose and identity, unable to articulate a vision that resonated with its primary constituency, the indigenous Fijians. That role had been usurped by the SDL. And the SVT's newly minted but generally unconvincing politics of moderation was undermined from within its ranks and attacked by other Fijian parties.

Labour's success in winning 16 seats was due to its own innate strengths as well as the weaknesses of its opponents. Baba was unable to entice to the NLUP other senior members of Labour equally displeased with Chaudhry's style and who had been reprimanded for indiscipline and purported insubordination (Krishna Datt and Pratap Chand, for example). Baba, a former academic prone to ponderous intellectualising, had no political base of his own, and Labour supporters accused him of treachery at a time when unity was imperative. The party's new style election campaign, featuring pop singers and football players, was ridiculed by an electorate demanding, and accustomed to, a more serious approach to political campaigning. Baba's handing out of food parcels to squatters and other urban poor, smacked of vote buying, similar to the tactic adopted by the SDL. Perhaps most damaging of all to NLUP's claim to be clean and transparent was the revelation that a convicted fraud, Peter Foster, had bankrolled the party's campaign to the tune of F$200,000 (*Pacific Island Report*, 13 August 2001).[4] This revelation made a mockery of Baba's call for transparency, accountability and good governance, and he paid the price. Baba lost his seat, although two of his colleagues won.

The other major threat to Labour was the National Federation Party. In 1999, NFP had won a third of the Indo-Fijian votes to Labour's two-thirds. The NFP had much ground to cover, and ultimately it was not up to the task. One problem was leadership. The retirement from politics of its long-term leader, Jai Ram Reddy, had left a huge gap. The resignation of Biman Prasad, an academic economist and newcomer to politics, just two days after being elected leader compounded the problem. His replacement, Attar Singh, a trade unionist, was unable to erase the image of a weakened, drifting party searching for a leader. The NFP's moderate and conciliatory approach, its emphasis on social and economic issues, which looked suspiciously like a facsimile of Labour's manifesto, lacked appeal in an atmosphere charged with racial tension. Chaudhry could, and did, claim the mantle of Indo-Fijian leadership.

The NFP's electoral tactic of highlighting its role in the political and economic development of the country—its role in the achievement of Fiji's independence, in the Dening Arbitration, which had caused the departure of the Colonial Sugar Refining Company from Fiji, in the negotiation of the Agricultural Landlord and Tenant Act, even its role in the successful review of the 1990 constitution—carried little weight with voters reeling from unemployment and poverty, and profoundly ignorant of history. The NFP's traditional support base had eroded over the years, captured by Labour—the sugarcane growers were with the Labour Party-affiliated National Farmers' Union, as were public servants, teachers and workers. The emigration of thousands of Indo-Fijians since the coups of 1987 had robbed the party of supporters who might have been more sympathetic to NFP's moderate stance and multiracial vision. Labour's claim that the NFP was yesterday's party, supported by rich businessmen, some of whom had allegedly supported the Speight coup, did not help. In the end, the NFP was unable to capture the imagination of people looking for a party to lead them into the future, not one harking to its past glories.

The other minor Indo-Fijian parties were similarly ineffectual. Among them was the Justice and Freedom Party, formed by Dildar Shah after the May coup. Holding the United Kingdom and Australia responsible for the introduction of Indians to Fiji and, by extension their present troubles, the party demanded compensation from them as well as permanent residence for Indo-Fijians in Australia. The plight of Indo-Fijians in the camps in Lautoka and Vanua Levu served to heighten the appeal of their position. But the single-issue tactic failed, its cause emotionally appealing but legally unsustainable. The indentured workers had come under a contract, an agreement, which entitled them to return to India at the end of five years, at their own expense, or at the government's expense after ten. Most had chosen, voluntarily, to stay on in Fiji, acquired Fiji citizenship and participated in the affairs of the country as full citizens. To be sure, indenture was a harsh, brutalising experience, but it was not slavery, at least in the technical sense. Voters sympathised with the party's cause but rightly thought its realisation impractical.

But Labour won seats not only because of the weakness of its opponents. Chaudhry was an astute, skilful politician, perhaps the most adroit in the country, and the only Indo-Fijian political leader of national stature. Many rallied to him for that reason, just as many Fijians supported Qarase. To some Chaudhry appeared arrogant and confrontational, but his supporters saw him as strong, fearless and principled. There was an enormous amount of emotional sympathy for what Chaudhry and his colleagues had endured at the hands of the parliament hijackers: the humiliation and the beatings, the imminent threat to their lives. And yet, despite it all, they had remained undaunted. As Chaudhry said at his rallies, 'they put a gun to my head and I didn't flinch. Why should you be afraid to vote for me?'.

Leadership aside, Labour's other campaign claim was its record of government. They had removed value-added tax on essential food items, generated employment (6,400 jobs) and investment (F$300 million worth of hotel projects approved), improved infrastructure, cracked down on tax evaders, achieved a remarkable 6.6 per cent of economic growth, and F$47 million budget surplus in just the first three months of 2000. They were overthrown not because they had failed but because some vested interests (and others who felt otherwise marginalised) felt threatened. Labour wanted to complete the task they had begun. They had done nothing wrong; they were the wronged party. The Indo-Fijian electorate listened sympathetically, understood the message and responded overwhelmingly in support, especially those who were desperately poor and without hope. The Fijian nationalists' shrill attack on Chaudhry stiffened their resolve.

The election produced a stalemate, with neither SDL nor Labour winning an outright majority of seats. Both parties then began negotiations with the Conservative Alliance, the moderates and the independents to form a multiparty government required by the constitution. That Chaudhry was seeking a coalition with the party whose members had masterminded the coup against his government a year earlier was full of irony, but then, in 1992, Chaudhry had supported Sitiveni Rabuka, the architect of the 1987 coups. Initially, the Conservative Alliance grossly overplayed its hand by demanding amnesty for Speight and his co-conspirators, a voice in senate nominations and, most improbably, deputy prime ministership for Speight. To their credit, both Qarase and Chaudhry flatly refused the amnesty demand. Realising their strategic error, the Conservative Alliance dropped their demands and agreed to join Qarase's SDL government; political opportunism won over political principles. Qarase also successfully enlisted two independents (Savenaca Draunidalo and Marieta Ringamoto) and New Labour Unity Party's Kenneth Zinck to his side. He had formed a multiparty government, as the constitution demanded.

That, however, was not enough. The constitution (Section 99) provides that in establishing the cabinet, the prime minister must invite all parties whose membership in the House of Representatives comprises at least 10 per cent of the total membership of the house to be represented in proportion to their members in the house. If the party declined the invitation, the prime minister could then nominate members of his own party or a coalition of parties to fill the places in the cabinet.

As the leader of the largest party in parliament, Qarase was thus constitutionally obliged to invite the Labour Party to join his cabinet. This he did, reluctantly, hoping that Chaudhry would decline the invitation. According to the formula provided for allocating the number of seats in the cabinet in the Korolevu Declaration (Parliamentary Paper 15/1999), Labour was entitled to 8 of the 20 cabinet seats and SDL 12. Qarase, who had already stated that the idea of working with Chaudhry as an anathema, argued that Labour's and SDL's policies were diametrically opposed, as they indeed were, and that Labour's inclusion in cabinet would be a prescription for political paralysis.

> The policies of my cabinet will be based fundamentally on the policy manifesto of
> the Soqosoqo Duavata ni Lewenivanua, as the leader of this multiparty coalition.
> Our policies and your policies on a number of key issues of vital concern to the
> long-term stability of our country are diametrically opposed. Given this, I genuinely
> do not think there is sufficient basis for a workable partnership with your party in
> my cabinet' (*Daily Post*, 14 September 2001).

Chaudhry, however, thought otherwise. He accepted the invitation. 'What
fool in politics would like to be in opposition when he can be in
government', he observed (*Fiji Times*, 11 September 2001). Personal
differences between the two leaders were of secondary importance,
Chaudhry wrote to Qarase. 'We believe that common conviction on
rebuilding the nation in a spirit of reconciliation must supersede all else.
The issue of policy difference can be resolved in a frank and fair
discussion designed to reach consensus and understanding' (*Daily Post*,
17 September 2001). Qarase was unmoved. He argued now that
Chaudhry had laid down conditions that he found unacceptable.
Chaudhry, he said, wanted to have a hand in the allocation of cabinet
portfolios. He wanted to act as 'opposition' within cabinet, thus
undermining the principle of consensus and collegiality. Chaudhry denied
Qarase's charge of conditionality, and pressed for urgent negotiation,
pointing out that as prime minister he had invited into his cabinet parties
whose policies, too, were different from Labour's but who had managed
to form a coherent government. When Qarase refused, Chaudhry sought
the president's intervention. But the frail president, increasingly
dependent on advisors openly sympathetic to the cause of Fijian
nationalism, refused, swearing in Qarase and his cabinet.

Qarase's intransigence was the predictable result of many factors.
Among them is his personal antipathy to Mahendra Chaudhry. Qarase
would have been able to work with another Indo-Fijian leader, his
supporters say, less abrasive, less confrontational, someone like Jai Ram
Reddy. But personality was only a part of the equation. Political survival
was at stake too. Qarase knew that if he did not deliver on his electorally
appealing but poorly costed promises to the Fijians and appease the
nationalist fringe he would suffer the same fate as his predecessors.
Qarase's main aim was to keep Fijians united and on his side. To that
end, he worked hard to co-opt all potential Fijian adversaries and
dissidents into his circle. Apisai Tora, the opportunistic western Fijian

rebel, was appointed to the senate. Ratu Tevita Momoedonu, another westerner, was appointed Fiji's ambassador to Beijing. Ratu Epeli Nailatikau, the amiable high Bau chief and a loyal deputy prime minister in the interim administration, was appointed speaker of the House of Representatives. The president of the Methodist Church, Reverend Tomasi Kanailagi, a powerful figure in the Fijian community and privately a staunch supporter of the coups, was rewarded with a seat in the senate. The nationalist chair of the Constitution Review Commission, Asesela Ravuvu, was there as well. Ratu Finau Mara, the jobless son of the former president, was made the roving Ambassador to the Pacific Islands. The politics of patronage knew no bounds.

Meanwhile, Mahendra Chaudhry filed a motion before the Court of Appeal against the government for breach of Section 99 of the constitution. When the Court of Appeal ruled in Labour's favour, the government appealed to the Supreme Court. By the time the Supreme Court delivered its verdict, a year had passed. During this period, attempts were made, notably by the Honolulu-based East West Center, to initiate dialogue through '*talanoa*' sessions of informal consultations. Nothing happened, except restatement of hardened positions. In parliament the government continued to pursue its pro-Fijian policies, while some of its ministers indulged in inflammatory rhetoric. For instance, the minister of social welfare and women's affairs likened Indo-Fijians to 'noxious weeds' but she was not reprimanded. A plea made to the chief justice to expedite the Supreme Court case fell on deaf ears. Neither the chief justice nor the Qarase government was in a hurry for an early resolution of the constitutional crisis.

The Supreme Court heard the case on 18 June 2003 and delivered its judgment a month later (Supreme Court of Fiji Civil Appeal no. CBV0004/20025, 18 July 2003). The case relied on the interpretation of Section 99 of the constitution. The section provided, among other things, the prime minister must establish a multiparty cabinet whose composition 'should, as far as possible, fairly represent the parties represented in the House of Representatives'. The parties entitled to be in cabinet should have at least 10 per cent of the seats in the house. The prime minister could invite parties with less than 10 per cent membership of the house, but the selection would be deemed to have been from the prime minister's own party. And, importantly, in selecting persons from other parties for appointment as ministers, the prime minister 'must consult with the leaders of those parties'. The government's case turned on narrowly technical grounds. It argued that the word 'invitation' created no entitlement for any party to participate in cabinet, that the prime minister's invitation was 'no more than a mandatory first step before the commencement of good faith negotiations for a multi-party government', and that the principles of Westminster system of absolute secrecy of cabinet deliberations and the collective responsibility of cabinet to the House of Representatives would be severely compromised in a multiparty arrangement where the parties did not pursue a common policy but instead contemplated opposition within cabinet and the government.

The Supreme Court ruled otherwise. The constitution was not an abstract impractical document, as the state had argued. It had been 'drawn up with an eye to political realities and likelihoods. The construction to be placed on it in accordance with its spirit should not be directed or heavily influenced by the possibility of circumstances which the framers may have discounted as highly improbable', it ruled. The prime minister was under precise, emphatic obligation to invite all parties that met the 10 per cent threshold to be part of the cabinet. The invitation was more than a 'mandatory first step'. 'This is not simply an invitation for their members to be there without any agenda or policies of their own. This is a provision which advances the central constitutional purpose of power sharing'.

Was a multiparty cabinet inherently unworkable? Again, the Supreme Court did not think so because cabinet deliberations were 'subject to the requirements of collective responsibility and confidentiality which are recognised in the constitution as aids to effective government'. Everyone accepted that. 'This may mean a more difficult cabinet to manage than a cabinet whose members belong to the same party or coalition that has worked out some consensus before its formation. But this is the kind of cabinet that is envisaged by the constitution and it cannot be rejected as unworkable in principle because of that difficulty'. Division of opinion in cabinet was nothing new, the court argued, and the constitution, in particular Section 99, aimed to 'encourage debate on contentious policies including debate across party lines'. Finally the court ruled that there was an obligation on the prime minister to 'negotiate in good faith at least to the extent necessary to ensure that his invitation is a genuine invitation and is maintained as such. An invitation issued on conditions which are incapable of satisfaction will not meet that obligation'. Political posturing that Labour had allegedly engaged in when Qarase offered the invitation was not to be construed as rejection of the offer. The spirit of power sharing which lay at the heart of the constitution had to be honoured.

The government accepted the Supreme Court ruling. The prime minister outlined three options at his disposal (*Pacific Island Report*, 24 July 2003). He could call for a fresh election, but that would not only be expensive but also would not resolve the issue at hand unless both parties agreed jointly to amend the power-sharing provision. He could 'start with a clean slate', resign and then, on reappointment, establish a new cabinet. The third option was to retain the present numbers and add to them the appointments from the Labour Party. Qarase rejected the second option because, with only 32 seats in a 71-member House, he could not be certain of reappointment. 'Politics in its fundamental form is about survival. If you don't survive, you cannot carry through on your policies and serve the people'. Nor could he jettison his other partners in the government, for that would be tantamount to political suicide. 'The political reality', Qarase said, 'is that we are not free to make changes to our policies without first consulting the members of our parties, right down to the constituency level. We are bound by the trust people have placed in us'.

He settled upon the third option. He offered 14 seats to Labour in a cabinet of 36. Labour argued that it was entitled to 17 ministers, and mounted further legal challenge only to be told that the prime minister could invite members from the upper house to the cabinet in excess of those prescribed in the formula. Qarase had observed the letter of the law, but not its spirit. He offered Labour minuscule ministries with insignificant budgets: an 'insulting offer' Labour called it. Consultation stipulated in the constitution did not mean 'concurrence', Qarase argued, with Supreme Court support, and proposed to select members from the Labour party without Chaudhry's approval. Chaudhry himself along with some of his other high profile colleagues would be kept out.

The problem in the end was not constitutional. The constitution was clear about the rules of the game. The real problem was political. Power sharing, although difficult, is achievable given goodwill and understanding and a desire to develop a common ground. But it is fraught when the major players are constantly at loggerheads about the most basic issues of public policy. Labour wanted the perpetrators of the coup to face the full brunt of the law; the government had within its ranks many who were openly sympathetic to, or actual participants in, the violence that overthrew the Chaudhry government. Labour wanted an independent enquiry into the plundering of the public purse for political purposes; the government was reluctant to probe misconduct because the politics of patronage and support for local interests aided its election. Labour wanted race-based affirmative action policies abandoned; government regarded them as non-negotiable pillar of its political agenda. The two had contrasting views on land-leasing arrangements. The list of differences is endless. Professor Yash Ghai, the eminent constitutional expert, put the issue succinctly. 'No constitution will work properly if those who operate it have regard only for sectional interests; the constitution poses a more explicit challenge than most to work in the interest of the whole nation. It speaks—are the politicians listening?' (*Sunday Times*, 16 September 2001). Evidently not.

## Notes

1 A copy of this never publicly released report is in the author's possession.
2 For a lawyer's account, see Williams 2000.
3 A senior Labour Party member has confirmed that this option was canvassed, but no formal offer was made.
4 Foster was jailed for 18 months by a British court in 1996 for a fraudulent weight-loss scheme, and fled to Australia while on parole.

# 10
## Reflections

*Peace, peace is what I seek, and public calm:*
*Endless extinction of unhappy hates.*
Matthew Arnold

Fiji is a paradox and a pity. A paradox because this island nation endowed with wonderful natural resources, a talented and multiethnic population with a high literacy rate, a once-sophisticated, but now crumbling, public infrastructure where drinkable piped water was once guaranteed, public roads had few potholes, poverty and crime and squatters were visible but contained, hospitals were uncrowded, children went cheerfully to school, and respect for law and order was assured: this nation is tragically prone to self-inflicted wounds with crippling consequences. One coup is bad enough for any country, but three in thirteen years—two in 1987 and one in 2000—staggers the imagination. And a pity because there is no genuine resolution in sight for the country's deep-seated political and economic problems as its leaders dither and the country drifts divided. The battle lines are clearly drawn in a deadly zero-sum game. The militant nationalists, happily unconcerned about the destructive implications of their actions, threaten violent retribution if their agenda for political supremacy is marginalised in mainstream public discourse. Compounding the problem on top of all this is a manifest lack of collective political will to exorcise the country of the demons that terrorise its soul.

The tragedy of modern Fijian politics has been that rosy rhetoric for global consumption has always won over the hard realities on the ground, blinding its people to the deep-seated problems that beset the country, or at least causing them a sense of slight unease in probing too deeply into the darker recesses of national body politic lest they discover some discomforting truth about themselves that they would rather ignore (Scarr 1984; Lal 1992; Sutherland 1992). If the emperor had no clothes, it was better not to find out. And so Fiji portrayed itself as a marvellous model of functioning multiracial democracy, largely free of ethnic tension and conflict that plagued many developing countries, the way the world should be, as Pope John Paul II intoned after a fleeting visit to the islands in 1985. Few publicly acknowledged intra and interethnic tensions, and the deep reservations the different communities had about the structure of power relations in the country, and the deeply contested struggle for a definition and clarification of Fijian political identity that preceded independence. The illusion of harmony and amicable understanding in the post-independence era was just that, an illusion, and just as misleading and fraught and dangerous as the impression of balance and equilibrium and harmony conveyed by an earlier metaphor of Fiji as a three-legged stool (Sukuna 1984).

The brutal truth, of course, was that Fiji never had a genuinely shared sense among its citizens about what kind of constitutional arrangement was appropriate for it. It was an issue that had bedevilled the country's politics since the late 1920s. Indigenous Fijian and European leaders, with active official support, argued for separate racial representation. For them, primordial loyalties were paramount. The Indo-Fijians, on the other hand, championed a non-racial common roll, privileging sectarian ideology over ethnicity. The issue dominated political debate throughout the 1960s, leading to boycott of the Legislative Council and tense elections and by-elections (Norton 1990; Lal 1992; Mara 1997). The communal voice won in the end, largely because of Fijian and European opposition but partly also because of the Indo-Fijian leaders' lack of genuine commitment to the idea of common roll, following the death of A.D. Patel. (Lal 1997). Their compromise was enshrined in the secretly negotiated independence constitution, which retained ethnicity as the principal vehicle of political participation while making half-hearted commitment to non-racial politics as a long term national objective (Ali 1977; Lal 1986).

Unsurprisingly, race dominated post-independence politics. The two main political parties, the Alliance and the National Federation, were essentially racially divided, the former among Fijians and general electors and a sprinkling of Indo-Fijians, and the latter predominantly among Indo-Fijians. In time, virtually every issue of public policy came to be viewed through a racial lense: affirmative action, poverty alleviation, allocation of scholarships for tertiary education, opportunities for training and promotion in the public service. The intent to create a more level playing field, to assist the indigenous community to participate more effectively in the public sector, was laudable, but race-based, rather than needs-based, policies inevitably corroded interethnic harmony. Public memory was racially archived even though the plain reality of daily life questioned the salience of race. Citizens were asked (as they still are) for their 'race' when they opened a bank account, took out a driver's licence, left or entered the country. 'Race is a fact of life', Ratu Sir Kamisese Mara, Fiji's first and longest serving prime minister, kept reiterating. Under his administration, it almost became a way of life. Political leaders on both sides opportunistically championed moderate multiracialism, but privately—and sometimes not so privately—actually played the race card on every occasion to secure power.

With time, other realities intruded, questioning the legitimacy and value of a political edifice constructed on the foundations of ethnic compartmentalisation. Forces of change, rapid in their pace, were fast eroding old, exhausted assumptions of public discourse. The television and video brought new and strange images into people's homes. Urbanisation proceeded apace, spawning problems that transcended race, and attenuated traditional social and cultural links and attachments. Improved roads speeded up communication, and cash cropping fostered individualistic values. As R.G. Ward put it, 'the combined introduction of new skills, new technology and money have weakened the functional cement which binds native Fijian village society. This does not mean that the structure has collapsed, or will do so in the near future. It does mean that the risk of disintegration exists if other factors shake the edifice' (Ward 1987:124). Decades earlier, O.H.K. Spate, R.F. Watters and C.S. Belshaw, among others, had made essentially similar points, but were dismissed as being insensitive by traditionalists afraid of change, and ignored by a colonial government too timid or too tied down to orthodoxy to embrace potentially progressive ideas (Spate 1959; Belshaw 1964; Watters 1969). An opportunity was thus missed to enable and empower the Fijians to embrace the forces of modernity engulfing their lives. For this failure, they would pay dearly later.

Things came to a head in 1987, the year of the first two military coups, when a democratically elected, nominally left leaning, Labour-National Federation Party coalition was ousted after a month in office. Some commentators saw the crisis as a straight-out 'racial fight' between the Fijians and Indo-Fijians (Scarr 1988). Others saw the conflict fundamentally as a class struggle between the haves and the have nots, Fijian commoners and Indo-Fijian working class joining hands against the dominance of chiefs and the Indo-Fijian business élite (Robertson and Tamanisau 1988). The importance of both race and class is acknowledged, as it has to be, but the coups were also an effort to turn the clock back, to fortify old structures and values which sustained them against forces of change, to shore up the importance of rural areas as well as the power of traditional leaders at a time when the new government was determined to democratise elements of the traditional order (Lal 1988). As Dr Timoci Bavadra, the deposed Labour prime minister, told his campaign rallies in 1987, the individual's democratic right to vote did not mean a compulsion to vote for a chief. It was a free choice.

> By restricting the Fijian people to their communal way of lifestyle in the face of a rapidly developing cash economy, the average Fijian has become more and more backward. This is particularly invidious when the leaders themselves have amassed huge personal wealth by making use of their traditional and political powers' (*Fiji Times*, 17 November, 1987).

These were revolutionary words in the context of the time and the place, a call to action by an indigenous Fijian no less, against a system already feeling itself under siege. They had to be nipped in the bud quickly.

The traditionalists rallied to restore the *status quo*. The post-coup 1990 constitution, decreed by presidential edict, and prepared without widespread consultation, predictably privileged rural Fijians over their urban counterparts, allocating 30 of the 37 Fijian seats to them and only seven to urban and peri-urban areas, even though nearly 40 per cent of Fijians were urban dwellers. Moreover, a candidate had to be registered in the Vola Ni Kawa Bula (the Register of Native Births) of the constituency in which he or she was standing, further entrenching provincialism in Fijian politics (Lal 1998; Robertson 1998). Provincial and regional affiliations, often opening up pre-colonial social cleavages and questioning the structure of power distribution in Fijian society, acquired an unprecedented public and symbolic significance that tested the colonially created notion of an overarching Fijian cultural and social identity. It also had the seriously deleterious effect of weakening the operation of political parties among Fijians. The provincial councils selected candidates, and their first loyalty therefore was to their provincial power wielders. Leaders of political parties had limited influence over their selection and even less power to discipline them for insubordination or breach of party discipline. The predictable result was an undisciplined proliferation of political parties among Fijians, formed by disgruntled or discarded candidates flying regional flags or conveniently camouflaging their private agendas under the guise of 'Fijian interest'.

To prevent fragmentation, Fijian leaders had the Great Council of Chiefs sponsoring a single political party to unite disparate indigenous opinion and interests under one umbrella (Lal 1998). That party, the Soqosoqo ni Vakavulewa ni Taukei (SVT), was launched in 1990 but the hope for unity was predictably still-born, as many openly questioned the wisdom of a chiefly body getting embroiled in party politics and the highly contestable assumption that Fijians were of one mind on all things political. Would a Fijian opposed to the SVT be any less 'Fijian' than one who supported it? In an ironic twist, a commoner, albeit an uncommon one—Sitiveni Rabuka—was elected president of the party over one of the highest-ranking chiefs of Fiji, Adi Lady Lala Mara. Unsurprisingly, dissension built up, opposition emerged, rival factions developed, and alternative parties were launched, such as the Fijian Association Party, privately supported by Mara, and All National Congress and later the Party of National Unity in western Viti Levu formed by Apisai Tora, the perennial chameleon of Fiji politics. The SVT was dislodged from power in 1999 by a combination of factors, but among the most important was the political fragmentation of the Fijians (Lal 2000). That trend, which shows little sign of abating, will continue to hobble party politics among the Fijians, especially now that provincialism is back in business and flourishing and Fijian leaders are seeking to institutionalise provincial administration along the Melanesian model. 'We are still coming out of provincialism', Rabuka says, 'and having that form of system will be counter to creating national cohesiveness' (*Sunday Post*, 20 April 2003). He is right, but sadly in a marginalised minority.

The party presently in government, Soqosoqo Duavata ni Lewenivanua, launched after the 2000 coup on an explicit nationalist platform to woo the supporters of the coup, was able to win power by adopting a fiercely pro-indigenous platform and by outbidding other moderate Fijian parties that failed miserably at the polls. Its effort to consolidate its position included a promise to review the constitution to entrench Fijian political control, and pursue race-based, pro-Fijian, affirmative action policies in commerce, education and the public service (Lal 2002). It also bought off potentially troublesome opposition by diplomatic postings and through other employment opportunities. Ratu Inoke Kubuabola, a key nationalist and coup supporter, is now Fiji's High Commissioner to Papua New Guinea. Isikia Savua, police commissioner at the time of the 2000 coup, and allegedly involved in it, is Fiji's Ambassador to the United Nations, and Adi Samanunu Talakuli, a known Speight supporter from the Kubuna Confederacy, is Fiji's High Commissioner to Malaysia. Berenado Vunibobo, a George Speight sympathiser, has recently handled several diplomatic assignments for the government. Several people publicly known to have supported the coup—Apisai Tora, Ratu Josefa Dimuri, Ratu Inoke Takiveikata, Reverend Tomasi Kanailagi—are in the senate. Ratu Jope Seniloli, the coup leader George Speight's choice for president, is vice president (but now serving time in jail for taking an illegal oath of office). Political patronage has yielded the government much needed short-term benefits, but what will happen when the well runs dry, when there are no more perks to be distributed, or when the purchase price for silence or compliance rises beyond reach? How will the disgruntled elements be pacified then?

The present government has made a review of the constitution a key plank in its political platform. Indeed, while heading the interim administration set up soon after the 2000 coup, Laisenia Qarase established a constitution review committee headed by Professor Asesela

Ravuvu, a known nationalist-leaning former University of the South Pacific academic, to recommend changes (Ravuvu 1992). But the committee, set up without public consultation, criticised from the beginning, and filled with handpicked men of dubious credibility (certainly in the Indo-Fijian community) lacked legitimacy and was unceremoniously disbanded after a few months. A summary of its report—the full report, although taxpayer-funded, has not been released—suggested a hardline nationalist position requiring *vulagis*—guests, foreigners such as Indo-Fijians—to accept the primacy of the *taukei*—the indigenous people, the first settlers—in politics. The fundamental nationalist argument is that Fiji 'belongs' to the indigenous Fijians, and its political leadership should therefore always be Fijian. Others can live in Fiji and work and pay taxes but should never aspire to political leadership. That acceptance, the nationalists argue, is an absolute, non-negotiable precondition for political stability.

Although that position is unpalatable to liberal democrats, many indigenous Fijians will, I suspect, broadly embrace it as a symbolic recognition of the indigeneity of the country. There was political stability in Fiji from independence to 1987 because a Fijian, who had the confidence of his people, was at the helm, many Fijians say. When his hold on power was threatened, as in 1977 and again in 1982, retribution was threatened. And when he actually lost power in 1987, violence was sanctioned to reinstate him. In other words, democracy would be viable only with an indigenous Fijian at the helm. Perhaps. But Ratu Mara led the country under a constitution forged through consensus, flawed though it was. Astute and skilful manipulation of the electoral system put the Alliance Party in power, not a constitutional requirement for an indigenous Fijian as head of government. Any constitution that breaches human rights conventions embraced by the international community will be rejected outright. That much is absolutely certain. A constitution that sanctions racial discrimination is doomed from the start—dead before the ink has dried.

There are other issues as well. Fijian society is much more diverse now than ever before. It is criss-crossed with a host of class, regional, provincial and rural–urban interests that contest the claim of unity (Dakuvula 1992). There is no one leader who commands the respect and loyalty of all Fijians as Ratu Mara once did, or Ratu Sir Lala Sukuna before him. The question is not really about having a Fijian head of government, but rather which Fijian leader would be acceptable to a particular group of Fijians at any given point in time. Dr Timoci Bavadra was a Fijian, and Fijians ousted him in a military coup. Rabuka was a Fijian, and he was defeated by indigenous Fijian votes, first in 1994 and then again in 1999. Ratu Mara was a high chief—paramount chief of the province of Lau—and he was turfed from office after the 2000 coup by a group of Fijians. Commodore Frank Bainimarama is a Fijian, but his leadership of the armed forces was challenged by Fijian members of the military in a bloody mutiny in November 2000. George Speight claims indigenous ancestry—he now prefers to use his Fijian name Ilikini Naitini, though of course a Speight by any other name is still a Speight— and he is languishing in jail for a crime whose beneficiaries are ruling the country.

Fijians of all ranks and backgrounds talk wistfully about the urgent need of forging indigenous political unity, but, as the Reeves Commission argued, that goal is now unattainable, if it ever was. In the past, Fijians lived in villages, for the most part isolated from the other communities and dependent on subsistence agriculture. They had their own 'native regulations' and programs of work under the leadership of traditional leaders. But Fijian society has changed dramatically in the years since independence. Now, over 40 per cent live in urban or peri-urban areas, participate in the cash economy, enjoy the benefits of tertiary education, and are well represented in the professions and the public sector (Prasad, Dakuvula and Snell 2001). A sizeable and rapidly growing self-made Fijian middle class is an undeniable social fact in contemporary Fiji. It is therefore unrealistic to expect one political party to accommodate and represent a whole multiplicity of complex and competing interests.

The emphasis on unity also constrains the choices available to Fijian people who will not be able to vote a Fijian government from office if it does not deliver on its promises. Fijians, like other citizens, have the same regard for effectiveness and efficiency. 'The idea that a Fijian government must be maintained in office at all costs has grave consequences for political accountability', the commission argued. 'It requires setting aside the normal democratic control on a government's performance in office. This is bad for the Fijian community as well as for the country as a whole' (Reeves, Vakatora and Lal 1996).

But perhaps, as Stewart Firth suggests, Fijian politics increasingly is not about delivering on promises but rather about taking turns at the helm balancing regional, provincial and social interests by virtue of traditional power calculations rather than competence or merit (personal communication 2003). In this equation, non-Fijians matter little. Demographic reality dictates that future direction of Fiji politics will be influenced predominantly by indigenous concerns and calculations. The projected population of Fiji in 2002 was 824,596 of which indigenous Fijians numbered 441,363 (53.5 per cent), while the Indo-Fijians, 328,059, constituted 39.8 per cent. This trend will continue with accelerating Indo-Fijian migration and a lower birth rate in the community. Provincial and regional calculations will, as they already do, determine appointments and promotions and other opportunities in public life. Commodore Bainimarama, from the Kubuna confederacy, was appointed commander of the Fiji Military Forces in part, people say, because the two previous holders of the position, Sitiveni Rabuka and Ratu Epeli Ganilau, were from Tovata. Rabuka complained how, under the 1990 constitution, under which Fijian members were elected to parliament from the provinces, he had to ensure the presence of all the provinces in the cabinet, irrespective of ability and talent. Not to do so would have been interpreted as a slight on the province's name and incur their wrath. But as Fijian numbers increase, the Fijian people will realise that good governance and not the calculations of provincial representation will serve their interests better. Many Fijians privately do, but are fearful of expressing dissent when the strident talk of 'Fijian interests' fills the air.

Leadership is a problem for both the Fijian as well as Indo-Fijian communities. Among Fijians, the era of the dominance of paramount chiefs with overarching influence across the whole spectrum of indigenous Fijian society, tutored for national leadership by the British in the post-war years, has ended. The paramounts are gone: Ratu George Cakobau, Ratu Edward Cakobau, Ratu Penaia Ganilau and Ratu Mara are all dead. These Fijian leaders brought with them practical experience of public service—Mara was a district officer in the predominantly Indo-Fijian sugar district of Ba—and had a broad educational background in

Fiji and overseas (Mara 1997). Whatever else may be said of them and their politics, they generally believed in the principles of good, accountable governance, no doubt a legacy of their experience in the colonial civil service. They also had a multiracial circle of friends, and were committed to the principles of democracy, even if it was on their own terms.

Their successors lack their broad experience and background. Many latter-day Fijian leaders went from racially exclusive provincial primary schools to predominantly Fijian secondary schools, such as Queen Victoria or Ratu Kadavulevu, their formative years uninformed and uninfluenced by any meaningful exposure to the cultures of other communities (Dean and Ritova 1988; Sharpham 2000). They are thus culturally ill-equipped to meet the leadership challenges of building a multiracial nation, embroiled as they often are in provincial and regional politics to carve out an inclusive, more embracing national personality for themselves. In civil administration, too, senior military leaders who were facing dead-end careers but were politically well connected, were plucked from the armed forces to become district commissioners, serving in areas and among people whose culture and way of life they did not understand, unlike their colonial counterparts who were expected to have some fluency in the dominant language of the area (Hindustani or Fijian as the case might have been). That trend is likely to continue in a public culture dominated by the politics of racial patronage.

Indo-Fijians have leadership problems of their own. Over the years, there has been a marked shift in the social and educational background of Indo-Fijian leaders. At the time of independence—and before—the majority of Indo-Fijian politicians were lawyers or businessmen or landlords. Now, the base has diversified, with increasing numbers coming from the trade unions and the academia and from the ranks of retired schoolteachers and civil servants looking for second careers. They, too, for the most part, are handicapped by cultural limitations similar to those of the Fijians. Few politicians, for instance, are fluent in the indigenous language, more specifically Bauan, although those from rural areas with substantial Fijian populations such as Bua, Savu Savu, Taveuni, Levuka and Nadroga do speak the local dialects. And not many of them have a direct experience of Fijian culture. Those who do are few and are not always appreciated. When a Labour parliamentarian made his maiden speech in his Nadroga dialect, there were disapproving voices among his own colleagues. The minister of multiethnic affairs, George Shiu Raj, was a fluent Fijian speaker, at ease in both cultures, but his cross-cultural skill was sadly derided. The message seems to be that you cannot be an 'authentic' Fijian or Indo-Fijian if you are cross-culturally fluent or transgress ethnic and cultural boundaries. Such is the nature of public discourse in a racially segregated society.

The trade union culture, at least the way it has evolved in Fiji, muddies the already troubled currents of national politics. That was one of Mahendra Chaudhry's most severe handicaps as prime minister. Few disagreed with his prognosis of the problems facing Fiji, but they disliked the manner in which he articulated them: forthright, testy, even confrontational, with little appreciation that the Fijian mode of both private and public discourse is allusive and tempered by protocol. In trade union politics everywhere, ends often justify the means, but in national politics, the means, articulated in the glare of intense, unrelenting public scrutiny, is probably just as, if not more, important as the end. Chaudhry often chanted the mantra of electoral mandate to justify his uncompromising pursuit of his election promises. To be sure, he had the mandate from the voters, but that, he discovered to his enormous cost, was only one mandate among many. The Great Council of Chiefs had its mandate for the indigenous community; the Native Land Trust Board had its mandate, the Fijian dominated army its own. The art of political leadership in such a situation lay in negotiating one mandate among many competing and often incompatible mandates. Chaudhry's tragedy was that he ignored this crucial fact or at least showed an insufficient appreciation of it. This did not cause his downfall, but it made its contribution.

Multiethnic societies, with divergent traditions of discourse, are prone to miscommunication and misunderstanding among its people and leaders. Fiji is no exception. Indo-Fijian politicians revel in open, robust public debate often conducted without subtlety or irony. Their sledgehammer approach is direct and confrontational, and applauded by their supporters drunk on the rhetoric of polarised politics. The Fijian tradition of public discourse, on other hand, is generally the opposite: allusive, indirect and hedged-in by cultural protocol and sensitive to person and place. In that context, sometimes what is not said is probably just as important as what is. The gap is accentuated by the colonial legacy of racial compartmentalisation, the absence of shared cultural traditions and language (except English), attachment to different faiths and, more recently, the corrosive effects of the coups. Leaders talk at each other rather than to each other, and even then often through the media. Of course, Fiji is not alone in this, but its peculiar history compounds the problem.

Misunderstandings are not only linguistic but cultural as well. Let me illustrate. Most Indo-Fijians routinely assert that Fijians have over 80 per cent of all the land in Fiji. That is statistically true, but only a small percentage of it is economically useful. Moreover, land is not owned by one monolithic entity but by thousands of social units scattered throughout the islands. Thus, some Fijians have ample land, while others are effectively landless. But these internal facts of uneven patterns of native landownership and land distribution escape Indo-Fijian comprehension beyond the most generalised understanding of their complexity. There is something more.

> To most non-Fijians, land is an item of economic utility, a basis for an income, to be acquired, used and disposed of, if the occasion arises, without much emotional wrench. To most Fijians, on the other hand, and almost every rural Fijian, it is part of his being, his soul; it was his forebears' and shall be his progeny's till time immemorial. And the Indian sees large stretches of land between Suva and Sigatoka and Nausori and Rakiraki lying idle and can't understand it. He even becomes angry and bitter when he sees his former flourishing farm is now, after he was denied renewal of his lease, bush and scrub. The Fijian does not see it that way. Sufficient for him that it is there (Singh 1988:2, see also Overton 1988 and Kamikamica 1997).

Singh's characterisation of the problem may have an element of deliberate exaggeration to underscore the difference in perception of the two communities, but the larger truth holds about two essentially competing and often incompatible notions of land as commodity and land as cultural inheritance.

But just as Indo-Fijians do not grasp the Fijians' almost mystical attachment to their *vanua* (Ravuvu 1985), indigenous Fijians have little understanding of the deeper cultural and moral impulses that inform the Indo-Fijian mind-set. The two most crucial concepts in Indo-Fijian thought are *izzat* (honour) and *insaf* (justice) (Gillion 1977; Lal 2000).

'Do what is right, not what is opportunistic', the *Bhagvada Gita* teaches. Islam sanctions *jihad* in the face of oppression. Death is preferable to dishonour. 'A no muttered from the deepest convictions is better and greater', A.D. Patel told his rallies in the 1960s, quoting Mahatma Gandhi, 'than a yes muttered merely to please, or worse, to avoid trouble', because in the end, truth will triumph *(Satyame Vijayte)*. I believe that Indo-Fijians would accept an outcome, even if it is politically disadvantageous to them, provided it is transparently fair and does not affront their sense of dignity, honour and self-respect. Indo-Fijian leaders pushed for a common roll of voting in the 1920s when they were a minority in the population. As H.L.S. Polak told the Colonial Office in 1929, 'everywhere they [Indians] stand by the principle of the common franchise as symbol of equal citizenship' (Gillion 1977:138). In the 1960s, the overwhelming majority rallied to that cause because the cause was just, not necessarily because it was politically advantageous or indeed achievable. Privately, many Indo-Fijians would probably accept a Fijian head of government if that outcome were achieved through political negotiation, but never as a constitutional right. In 1997, for example, Indo-Fijians put aside their longstanding demand for political parity with the Fijians and accepted proportionality in the reserved seats (23 Fijian and 19 Indo-Fijian) because the allocation was based on the demographic size of the two groups. It is difficult to convey how deeply offensive the words 'second class citizenship' are to the Indo-Fijians' sense of honour and self-worth.

Many Fijians feel that the Great Council of Chiefs should play a more active role in national politics (Madraiwiwi 2002). Since its formal establishment after Cession in 1874, it has been the principal advisor to colonial and post-colonial governments on matters relating to the indigenous community. In the 1970 independence constitution, its nominees in the senate enjoyed the power of veto over all legislation touching indigenous Fijian interests and concerns. The 1997 constitution, for the first time, recognises the Great Council of Chiefs as a constitutionally established institution (as opposed to one established by an Act of Parliament). Its 14 nominees in an upper house of 34 members enjoy veto powers similar to the provisions of the 1970 constitution. The General Council of Chiefs also nominates the president and the vice president of Fiji. In short, its role and authority are an important political as well as constitutional fact and, perhaps more important, beyond dispute or debate.

The council's supporters see it as an important force for good in restraining ethnic chauvinism, in facilitating ethnic accommodation, and bridging the ethnic divide (Norton 1999). Perhaps, though, the actual evidence is contestable. In 1987, the General Council of Chiefs convened to legitimise the overthrow of the Labour Coalition government, its proceedings dominated by its more hardline, violence-threatening elements. Rabuka was hailed as a cultural hero and inducted into the council as a life-member. In 2000, it similarly convened, at the behest of Speight supporters, to demand changes to the 1997 constitution–the very constitution it had unreservedly blessed—to accommodate the nationalist Fijian demand. Such inconsistency or blatant opportunism undermines the council's moral authority and legitimacy among non-Fijians. The current chair of the General Council of Chiefs, Ratu Epeli Ganilau, says he is a 'keen to involve Indian leaders in the chiefs' council to discuss sensitive issues such as land' (*Fiji Times,* 14 April 2003). That is a welcome gesture in the right direction, but it would require a consistent effort to ensure that the Indo-Fijians are able to make genuine representation of their concerns, interests and aspirations. There are, however, some Fijian chiefs such as Adi Litia Cakobau who have argued that the chiefly council should represent the concerns of the indigenous community exclusively, and that anything else would detract from its central purpose and mission.

Unfortunately, there are few avenues available for interethnic dialogue outside the political arena where talk is inevitably shrill and antennas are tuned to ethnic partisanship and sectional advantage. Religious organisations have few opportunities for regular interfaith conversation. The Methodist Church, to which the majority of Fijians belong, has been strongly nationalistic since the 1987 coups, except briefly when it was led by Dr Iliata Tuwere. In 2003, the Church was pleading for the pardon of the soldiers involved in the 2000 mutiny as a part of the reconciliation process. In the mid 1990s, the various faiths—Hindu, Muslim, Christian—were able to overcome their differences to establish an 'interfaith search' to seek common ground to pave the way for national healing and reconciliation, but corrosive effects of ethnic and religious politics have eroded its foundations (Hurley 2000). Fijians have their traditional avenues for intra-Fijian dialogue and dispute resolution through district and provincial councils, and through the machinery of the Fijian administration. But these are closed to the Indo-Fijians. The Girmit Council, an organisation of various Indo-Fijian social and cultural organisations formed in 1979 to mark the centenary of Indian arrival in Fiji, is virtually defunct, while the Indian Summit, convened in the aftermath of the 2000 coup, has vanished without a trace. Indo-Fijians have their village committees and voluntary social and cultural associations, but these are ill-equipped to facilitate cross-cultural, interethnic dialogue. What is urgently required is a proper and properly equipped forum for an exchange of views between the two communities outside the political arena (Vakatale 2000).

Perhaps in this context, a recommendation of the Reeves Commission is worth revisiting. A number of Indo-Fijian organisations and community leaders asked the Commission to recommend the creation of a representative Indo-Fijian umbrella body similar to the Great Council of Chiefs. The commission reported

> [w]e endorse the principle behind the suggestion, but think that, initially, it should be taken up informally by the Indo-Fijian community. If there is agreement about the basis for the selection of the members of such a body, and it is able to meet and work in a way that demonstrates broad support for its composition and role, consideration should then be given to providing it with a statutory constitutional base (Reeves Commission 1996:263).

But the Fiji Labour Party has already rejected the idea. An Indian Council, it says, would 'only serve to further divide the people [and] compartmentalise through the creation of racial institutions' (*Daily Post*, 24 April, 2003). That is true, just as it is true that a properly functioning council could also conceivably challenge the party's power base in the Indo-Fijian community. Be that as it may, the prospects look bleak.

The one bright light in an otherwise dim scene is the work of various multiethnic, non-government organisations. Fiji Women's Rights Movement and the Women's Crisis Centre have done much to educate the public about issues of gender and domestic violence, even though both are urban-based. The Ecumenical Centre for Research, Education and Advocacy has sponsored important research on sensitive issues of social justice (Ratuva 2002). The Fiji branch of Moral Re-armament has played its part in trying to build cross-cultural bridges. But perhaps the most important, certainly the most controversial, has been the multiracial Citizens Constitutional Forum. Formed in the mid 1990s, it has convened numerous meetings and sponsored conferences, workshops and publications to educate the public about their constitutional and human rights (Cottrell 2000; Griffin 2002). It successfully challenged the legality of the Qarase government's unwillingness to form a multiparty government with the Labour party as provided for in the constitution. The Citizens Constitutional Forum has consistently been a sharp critic of the government's race-based affirmative action policies. Stung by Citizens Constitutional Forum's criticism, the government deregistered it, but the organisation's spirit remains undaunted, and it continues its battle for a non-racial, democratic Fiji. I believe that organisations like these, which seek non-violent resolution to the country's deep-seated problems through non-racial means, have much to contribute to the difficult task of nation building.

Recent crises have severely tested the fabric of race relations in Fiji. On the surface things look calm. People play and work together, mingle in the markets, and children attend mixed schools, but the underlying tone is one of apprehension and anxiety. The government's affirmative action for indigenous Fijians, approved in some form or other by many Fijians, is resented by most Indo-Fijians because they are not transparent and based on assumptions that defy the experience of daily life: large sections of the Indo-Fijians live in desperate poverty. They look in dread at the glass ceiling in the public sector. Sugarcane growers, for the most part uneducated and unskilled, are forced to relocate and start all over again as leases expire and their formerly productive fields revert to bush, generations of effort vanishing at the stroke of the pen or an official edict. The talk of reviewing the constitution to further entrench Fijian control causes them deep anxiety. I asked a prominent Indo-Fijian lawyer married to an indigenous Fijian what the future held for the Indo-Fijians. Her response: 'There is little future for them here unless the present government changes its policies'. That looks unlikely in the short term. Unwanted and uprooted, Indo-Fijians leave. Since 1987, over 80,000 have left, and more would leave if they could, draining the country of skills and resources Fiji can ill-afford to lose (Bedford 1989; Gani 2000; Mohanty 2002). But now, more and more indigenous Fijians are leaving as well, to give themselves and their children a better future. The Indo-Fijians are caught in a bind. They are leaving because they don't see in Fiji a future for themselves and especially their children, and the government is reluctant to spend money on training and educating a group it knows will one day go. A tragic catch-22 situation, if ever there was one.

To heal the wounds, the government has set up a Department of National Reconciliation and Unity to promote racial harmony and cohesion through social, cultural, educational and sporting activities. But interethnic reconciliation is only one part of the government's effort. An important role for the department is to 'promote greater unity within the indigenous Fijian community through various programs and activities at village, tikina, provincial and national levels'. Political self-interest and survival instincts drive the reconciliation effort; the government knows that its chances of electoral success depend crucially on Fijian unity, however elusive that prospect might be. It is precisely for that reason that, however much it may wish it, and I know that members of the government at the highest level want justice done, the government cannot afford to be seen to be proactive in pursuing the perpetrators of injustice. It is for that reason that the government reportedly asked the military to be lenient on those convicted of mutiny. It is for that reason that coup supporters have been dealt with lightly, and why the government is loathe to reprimand ministers who utter racist remarks under the cover of 'parliamentary privilege'. The government recognises that having aroused Fijian expectations with ambitious but costly promises it cannot now retreat. To appear to be making compromises in the national interest would be seen as a sign of defeat. In short, the government is riding a tiger it cannot dismount at will.

True and enduring reconciliation, which all the people of Fiji want, will come only when the truth of the past is confronted honestly and dispassionately. In 1987, opportunistic leaders looked the other way when the coup took place. Sitiveni Rabuka was hailed as a cultural hero of the Fijian people—'Steve: The Hand of God' the t-shirts proclaimed. What interests and concerns supported the overthrow of the Labour Coalition government were never investigated. Fiji is again reluctant to look too deeply into the heart of its problems. Thirteen years later, Fiji experienced another, and more, violent overthrow of a democratically elected government. And if the causes of the present crisis are not investigated, Fiji will, as surely as night follows day, encounter more violent turbulence on its ill-fated journey into the future. The politicisation of the military, the police force and the public service will have to cease. The culture of corruption and nepotism nourished after 1987 will have to be confronted, the political ambitions of the 'Children of 1987' to take the front seat as a matter of ethnic right curtailed. Regard for law and order would have to be reintroduced to groups of people, often young, unskilled, marginalised in the march to modernisation and vulnerable to emotional exploitation by would-be politicians. Only then will a solid base for economic development and investment be built.

Beyond that, the people of Fiji would have to reexamine the foundations of a political culture they have inherited. It is my firm view that a very large part of Fiji's problems derives from having a political system based on race (see also Naidu 2000). An obsession with race encourages ethnic chauvinism, poisons multiethnic discourse, and hinders the search for solutions to Fiji's deep-seated social and economic problems, which have little to do with race but everything to do with colour-blind forces of globalisation. I am not saying that ethnic sentiments are not authentic or deeply felt, or that it is a 'false consciousness' that will disappear with 'modernisation'. Ethnicity has its proper place in public discourse. But I do have a problem with a discourse that sees an individual as nothing more than the sum total of his or her ethnicity, to the exclusion of every other formative influence. I do have a problem when the central pillars of state institutions are constructed solely on the edifice of ethnic exclusivity. To put it another way, if 'race is a fact of life' in Fiji, it is but one of the many facts of life. Gender inequality, poverty and social deprivation, mismanagement and corruption, the abuse of public trust, the impinging forces of globalisation, are others.

The inescapable truth is that using race as a scapegoat will lead Fiji nowhere. Indo-Fijians do not threaten the foundations of Fijian culture and traditional society: modernity does.

## Asesela Ravuvu

The new political system emphasises equal opportunity and individual rights, which diminish the status and authority of chiefs. Equal opportunities in education and equal treatment under the law have further diminished the privileges which chiefs enjoyed under colonial rule and traditional life before ... Although village chiefs are still the focus of many ceremonial functions and communal village activities, their roles and positions are increasingly of a ritualistic nature' (Ravuvu 1988:171).

## Sitiveni Rabuka

I believe that the dominance of customary chiefs in government is coming to an end and that the role of merit chiefs will eventually overcome those of traditional chiefs: the replacement of traditional aristocracy with meritocracy' (*Fiji Times*, 29 August 1991).

And so it goes. One can turn the hands of the clock back, but it won't do the clock any good, as the distinguished humanist Oscar Spate used to say. To reclaim the potential that is surely hers, Fiji will have to reject the old, exhausted orthodoxies of the past, old ways of thinking and doing things. There is no alternative coexistence. A past unexorcised of its demons will continue to haunt the country's future.

# 11
# Postscript

Fiji went to the polls in mid May 2006, the tenth time since independence in 1970. In what was widely expected to be a contest marred by internal political fragmentation among indigenous Fijians and a surge of independents—18 political parties were registered on the eve of the elections and an unprecedented 68 independents contested—the elections delivered a result that defied most predictions. The ruling Soqosoqo Duavata Lewenivanua (SDL) party won 36 seats of the 71 seats in the House of Representatives, a clear win over rival Fijian parties. The Fiji Labour Party won 31 seats, its appeal far outweighing that of its long time rival the National Federation Party. The United Peoples Party and independents each winning two of the remaining four seats, the latter joining the government to boost its numbers. Of the total 479, 674 registered voters 256,014 (53.4 per cent) were Fijians, 204, 470 (42.6) were Indo-Fijians, 5,373 (1.1 per cent) were Rotumans, and 13,817 (2.9 per cent) were Generals (that is, all those not included in any of the other categories).[1]

The voter turnout, despite early fears to the contrary, was high: 87.7 per cent compared to 81 per cent in 2001. The turnout was uniformly higher among all ethnic groups: 90 per cent in Fijian provincial constituencies in 2006 compared to 82 per cent in 2001, 89 per cent among Indo-Fijians compared to 81 per cent in 2001, an increase of 10 per cent among Generals 73 per cent to 84 per cent and from 76.4 per cent to 88 per cent among Rotumans. Of the total votes cast, 8.8 per cent were declared invalid; this is a high figure but lower than that of

2001, 12.5 per cent. Finally, the pattern of racial polarisation at the polls was evident in this election as in others in the past. The SDL received 80 per cent of all the ethnic Fijian votes and only one per cent of Indo-Fijian votes, while Labour won 83 per cent of Indo-Fijian votes and 6 per cent of indigenous Fijian votes. In the May 2006 election, the SDL's considerable appeal to Fijian voters was evident—whereas, in 2001 it had got only 51 per cent of indigenous votes. On the Indo-Fijian side, there was a similar story. The majority of Indo-Fijians rallied behind Labour, seeing it as the only political party capable of matching the Fijian-dominated SDL and adequately representing Indo-Fijian concerns and interests. Labour's rival for Indo-Fijian votes, the NFP, got only 13 per cent of the Indo-Fijian communal votes.

More significant than the low-key election was what followed soon afterwards. Before all the results were officially declared, SDL leader, Laisenia Qarase, claimed victory and proceeded immediately to the Government House to be sworn in as the next prime minister. He then invited Labour to join his multiparty cabinet as mandated by the constitution. He had done this in 2001 as well, but at that time had offered Labour insignificant ministries, a proposal that Labour had rightly rejected as 'insulting'. This time, Qarase observed both the letter as well as the spirit of the power-sharing provision of the constitution and offered Labour substantial portfolios, including Labour and Industrial Relations, Commerce and Trade, Health, Employment Opportunity, Local Government and Urban Development, Agriculture, and Energy and Minerals.

The offer caught everyone by surprise. During the campaign, Qarase had said that he 'detested' the idea of a multiparty cabinet: multiethnic cabinet yes, multiparty cabinet no. It would not work, he said, because the manifestos of the two major parties were poles apart, and he would not deviate from his own manifesto in any multiparty cabinet. His personal hostility towards Labour leader Mahendra Chaudhry was palpable. But he changed his mind after claiming victory, saying that the multiparty cabinet idea was God's plan for Fiji and he was wholly and enthusiastically committed to it. 'The undertaking I am giving to the country,' he said, 'is that the cabinet will not fail through anything I do or anything I say'. The multiparty idea was a 'possible master key to a door that had always remained closed' (*Fiji Sun,* 19 July 2006).

Qarase's offer put Labour in a quandary. At first, Chaudhry balked, saying that while the portfolios offered were substantial, they were all 'in a mess', and they would place an extra burden on Labour ministers while the SDL would oversee the most lucrative ministries. But public opinion, both Fijian and Indo-Fijian, solidly supported the concept of multiparty cabinet, leaving Labour no choice but to participate. Soon afterwards, however, the senior leaders of the party were divided over the manner in which the multiparty concept should work. Chaudhry insisted that Labour ministers in cabinet should strictly pursue the interests and priorities of the Labour Party while others, especially senior party members and ministers, including Krishna Datt and Deputy Leader Poseci Bune, advocated a more inclusive, non-partisan and less confrontational approach to making the concept work. At this writing, Labour is grappling with its deepening internal tensions and challenges.

Of the 18 parties that contested the elections, only a handful had any hope of success. The main contenders were the SDL, Party of National Unity (PANU) and the National Alliance on the Fijian side and the FLP and National Federation Party on the Indo-Fijian side.

As the party in government, the SDL had the obvious advantage of incumbency. In the previous five years in office, it had dipped into the public purse to keep its ethnic constituency intact. A classic example was the F$16 million scam in the Agriculture ministry. The Auditor General regularly reported on the misuse of public office and public funds but to little avail. The government also sought to implement its 20-year development plan to ensure effective Fijian and Rotuman participation in 'all areas of our economic development'. To that end, in its 2005 budget it allocated F$4 million for the Fiji Development Bank Interest Subsidy Scheme for Fijians, F$1 million capital grant to the Native Land Trust Board and F$8 million for Fijian Affairs Board scholarship (*Sunday Post*, 9 January 2005).

The Qarase government took a number of steps to keep its fractious nationalist junior partner in government, the Christian Matanitu Vanua Alliance (CAMV), on side. It used the Compulsory Supervision Order to secure the early release of its members who were gaoled for their role in the 2000 coup. Among those released in this manner were Ratu Naiqama Lalabalavu, a paramount chief of Cakaudrove (Tui Cakau), (currently Minister of Fijian Affairs and Provincial Development) and Ratu Josefa Dimuri (presently a Minister of State for Agriculture— Alternative Livelihood). The controversy caused by this 'abuse' of the system was ignored by the government. The move was popular where it mattered most: the politically important Fijian heartland.

Perhaps the most controversial initiative that the government mooted was the Reconciliation, Tolerance and Unity Bill, designed, its critics argued, not so much to heal the wounds caused by the 2000 coup and related subsequent events, but to tamper with the judicial system to gain the early release and pardon of the gaoled coup perpetrators and accomplices. The government denied the allegation, but the overwhelming sense in the country was that this was indeed the government's intention. The Bill provoked sustained protest across the community, who wanted to the judicial process to take its course. As an editorial in the *Fiji Sun* put it, '[t]he implementation of such a Bill is going to create a wrong impression among the people that it is okay to execute a coup or go against the security force. This is because they will bank on such a Bill to protect them' (*Fiji Sun*, 4 January 2006). Although publicly the government stood by the Bill, privately it agreed to take a more moderate stance, agreeing, for instance, to table it after the election. But the desired political result had been achieved: the perpetrators of the coup were assured that although the government's moves had been thwarted, those in power were looking after their interests.

The government's support of the Bill brought it into direct and open opposition to the military. The relations between the two had soured soon after the 2001 elections. Some in the ruling party wanted commodore Frank Bainimarama and others to be prosecuted for removing Ratu Sir Kamisese Mara from Government House at the height of the 2000 crisis and for attempting to abrogate the constitution (*Fiji Sun*, 18 December 2004). Bainimarama made no secret of his desire to have the Home Minister Josefa Vosanibola and his Chief Executive Officer Lesi Korovalavala removed; actions that the government was loath to do (*Fiji Sun*, 27 December 2005). On several occasions, Bainimarama publicly criticised the government's policies, including those which were racially lopsided in favour of Fijians. 'This government continuously brings in racist policies and programs to justify its existence to the indigenous community', Bainimarama said, adding, '[t]he military is willing to return and complete for this nation the responsibilities we gave this government in 2000 and 2001' (*Fiji Sun*, 9 January 2006). Qarase called the army's 'continual interference' 'undemocratic and unwarranted' saying the 'Commander's stated intention of involving the military in the national election campaign is a threat to peace and stability, and the conduct of free and fair elections' (*Fiji Times*, 15 March 2006). But that was as far as the prime minister was prepared to go, ignoring those who called for the commander to be reined in. The country shuddered at the prospect of another upheaval caused by military intervention

Nor would Bainimarama allow the government to nominate Ratu Jope Seniloli, former Vice President, who was gaoled for taking a wrongful oath of office but released before serving out his term, to his old office (*Fiji Sun*, 20 February 2006). The army announced that the Unity Bill would 'never' be allowed to pass in parliament. 'The RTU Bill is not going to happen', Bainimarama thundered ominously (*Fiji Sun*, 22 December 2005). On the eve of the election, Bainimarama openly urged voters not to vote for the SDL and sent teams of army officers throughout the country to 'educate' rural Fijians about the government's 'misguided' policies. The day that parliament was dissolved in March, 500 soldiers armed with automatic weapons and wearing camouflage held a parade through Suva to 'show the people of Fiji that we are here to provide security' (*Fiji Sun*, 28 March 2006) The senior officers in the army backed their commander, although there was one (unsuccessful) challenge to Bainimarama's leadership from within the ranks, led by Jone Baledrokadroka in January 2006.

The army's active intervention in the campaign caused great anxiety. Labour President Jokapeci Koroi endorsed, on television, the view that her party would welcome moves by the army to remove the SDL from power, a strange proposition from a political party which itself had been the victim intervention by the army in 1987. The army's defiant public stance against the government encouraged many voters in the Indo-Fijian community to come out and cast their votes. 'The army is with us', Labour told its rallies. 'Vote without fear. There will not be another coup'.

The government argued that the army was overstepping its boundaries, meddling in affairs that were none of its concern. It wanted the military to observe the well-established Westminster convention of civilian control of the armed forces; the army's role was to enforce the peoples' will, not pre-empt or freely interpret it. For its part, the military saw its role as being in charge of the 'security' of the nation, very broadly defined. One senior officer told me that instead of the army having to 'clean up the mess after the fact', as it had to do in the past, it was better to prevent it in the first place. Pakistan was cited as a model.

Post-election, especially with the multiparty cabinet in place, the army's public profile has been lowered and there signs of reconciliation between it and the government. How long this lasts remains to be seen. If the government moves to implement the recommendations of a White Paper calling for a reduction in the size of the army or seeks to bring the military under proper civilian control once again, relations between the two could sour.

On the eve of the election, the fear of the fragmentation of Fijian votes appeared to be well founded and SDL's prospects looked to be threatened. The unknown factor was the impact that the independents, many of whom had unsuccessfully sought tickets from the party, might have in closely contested constituencies. Perhaps the most visible challenge to the SDL was the New Alliance Party, which espoused a radically different vision for a multiracial Fiji. The New Alliance Party was headed by Ratu Epeli Ganilau, former army commander, president of the Great Council of Chiefs, son of a former president, and a high chief in his own right. Launched on the eve of the election, the party promised to remove all vestiges of racial discrimination from public policy and criticised the government for pandering to the whims of the Fijian nationalist fringe. It tried to reclaim the middle ground by advertising itself as the legitimate successor to the former Alliance Party whose leaders included Ratu Sir Kamisese Mara, Ratu Sir Penaia Ganilau, Ratu Sir Edward Cakobau and Ratu Sir George Cakobau—scions of the Fijian establishment. The party attracted favourable media attention, but failed to win a seat. Its politics of moderation was decidedly at odds with the ascendant politics of racial polarisation that the SDL practised to great effect.

The fear of fragmentation led some senior Fijian figures, including former Reeves Commissioner Tomasi Vakatora and hotelier Radike Qereqeretabua, to form a Fijian 'Grand Coalition' in August 2005 (formally launched on 15 February 2006) to encourage Fijian parties to share preferences among themselves. Vakatora argued that Fijian political unity was the prerequisite to political stability in Fiji. 'When Fijians get rattled, they rattle the country', he said. He was criticised by many, including by the National Alliance Party, because his views went against the thrust of the Reeves Commission, which recommended the formation of multiethnic alliances. Vakatora's assessment was based on a shrewd and realistic assessment of the realities on the ground as they were, not as they out to be. Even the Vice President, the widely respected Ratu Joni Madraiwiwi, said that '[m]ost indigenous Fijians believe that their interests can only be protected by Fijian political control', adding that '[n]either the constitution nor the rule of law is sufficient for their purposes because they can be impugned by whoever is in power' (*Fiji Sun*, 16 February 2006). Vakatora was essentially saying the same thing.

The idea of a Grand Coalition failed to materialise. The National Alliance rejected the idea, PANU was loosely associated with the Labour Party, the nationalist Vanua Tako Lavo Party fizzled out and the Soqosoqo Vakavulewa ni Taukei (SVT), in power for much of the 1990s as the party sponsored by the Great Council of Chiefs, was a shadow of its former self, fielding, in the strangest of ironies, only one candidate—an Indo-Fijian. The failure of the minor Fijian parties was not an accident; it was in large part orchestrated by the SDL, which campaigned as the main Fijian party and as the defender of Fijian interests. Its pro-Fijian policies were championed. Qarase stated repeatedly that Fiji was not ready for a non-Fijian prime minister, a sentiment with which many Fijians across the political spectrum agreed. The Fijian people are 'the majority community in Fiji numerically, and they are also the majority landowning community in the country', Qarase argued in justification (*Fiji Times*, 4 May 2006). Qarase's trump card was Mahendra Chaudhry. Sensing a deep distrust of the Labour leader among many Fijians, Qarase told his audiences to 'vote for me and my party if you don't want Chaudhry as prime minister'. Tupeni Baba, Chaudhry's former deputy prime minister and now a SDL candidate, said, '[a] vote for Chaudhry is a return to 2000', adding 'all of us Fijians in the Labour Party from the beginning had left him as we cannot see [that] Chaudhry will protect the Fijian interests' (*Sunday Sun*, 23 April 2006) The tactic worked. In the last days of the campaign, SDL came across strongly as a party of and for the Fijians.

Just as Fijians rallied behind SDL, so the overwhelming majority of Indo-Fijians supported Labour. A part of the reason for Labour's popularity was the weakness of other Indo-Fijian parties, especially the NFP. Its voice of moderation, calling for dialogue and consensus, fell on soil tilled for racial polarisation. The party seemed to make some inroads in the cane belts, a Labour stronghold, in the early part of the campaign, but Labour's final campaign, stating that a vote for minor political parties was a vote wasted, and that the main players in the political arena were itself and SDL, appealed to many voters. The NFP was underfunded and unable to compete effectively with its much better organised rival. The fact that the party did not have a clearly identifiable leader, but a triumvirate consisting of Attar Singh, Raman Singh and Pramod Rae, did not help matters. Labour, on the other hand, had in Mahendra Chaudhry a leader with a track record and a household name. Its list of candidates consisted of people who had strong connections with the grassroots. Its effective television advertisements focused on issues of every day concern to ordinary people: collapsing infrastructure, bad water supply, pot holes on main roads, bourgeoning squatter settlements, inadequate housing, rising poverty levels, increasing unemployment. The NFP also raised these issues, but in the media war, it could not match Labour.

With Labour and SDL emerging as the two main contestants, the campaign turned to just a handful of issues. There was no room for nuance and subtlety, no opportunity to discuss the fundamental problems facing Fiji. And there were many. One obvious issue was the fate of the country's sugar industry, hobbled by non-renewal of leases, the impending end to the preferential access to the European Union and the perennial breakdown of ancient equipment at the main mills. The government mooted a plan to restructure the sugar industry, with the assistance and advice of a technical team from India, but the topic was never seriously raised in the campaign. Equally ignored was the question of non-renewal of leases. Labour wanted leases renewed under the Agricultural Landlord and Tenant Act (ALTA), which slightly favours the tenants according to Fijian landlords while SDL pushed for the Native Land Trust Act (NLTA), which gives more favourable consideration to the interests of landlords. The NFP proposed a 'master plan' under which government would lease land from the landlords under the provisions of NLTA but then re-lease them to tenants under ALTA. But this idea, too, remained in the background. I got the distinct feeling observing the campaign that both the major parties actually shied away from difficult issues in favour of simple messages sharply delivered.

Acutely aware of the changing demographics, the SDL played the race card effectively. With the electoral system favouring ethnic voting (46 of the 71 seats are contested on racial lines), and with the percentage of Indo-Fijians in the total population under 40 per cent, playing the race card made political sense, at least in the short term. Indigenous Fijians should control political power in Fiji, the SDL told the voters, while Labour quietly told its supporters that with the army on its side and with Indo-Fijian numbers decreasing, this might be the last chance for an Indo-Fijian to become prime minister. Shorn of all the campaign rhetoric, this issue, above all others, remained at the forefront of voters' consciousness.

The campaign itself was mild, lacking the drama of some previous elections, such as the Flower-Dove battle of 1977 or the Four Corners program about Australian involvement in Fijian politics, or even the Labour–NFP battles of the 1990s. Large campaign rallies, on the decline since the 1990s, were largely absent in this election, with most of the campaigning taking place in 'pocket meetings' and in debates on radio and television. Voting is compulsory in Fiji, but voters still expect to be transported to the polling booths, given food and drink and assistance with private problems. Most candidates agreed that the cost of the campaign was between F$10,000 and F$20,000, exorbitant by Fiji standards, with most expense associated with the purchase of yaqona. Voter apathy and avarice are problems of which all political parties are aware but are afraid to take any action for fear of retribution. There were some allegation of vote rigging, especially in closely contested seats, and two cases are before the courts, but international observers from the Commonwealth Secretariat and Forum Secretariat declared the election free and fair.

As indicated at the beginning, the real drama began once the election was over and the results were known. Qarase's offer to Labour to join his multiparty cabinet caught many by surprise, most of all Labour leader Mahendra Chaudhry. The national mood favourable toward power-sharing notwithstanding, Chaudhry was wary of joining Qarase's cabinet. At first he tried to woo the two independents (Jioji Konrote and Robin Irwin) to form a Labour-led government. When that failed, he submitted nine Labour names for inclusion in the multiparty experiment, but insisted that as the parliamentary leader of the Labour Party, he should decide the allocation of portfolios for his members.

Qarase flatly rejected the idea on the sensible and entirely defensible grounds that the prerogative of deciding the allocation of portfolios should be his as prime minister (*Fiji Sun*, 23 May 2006). He had made the same point three years earlier when he had argued that the right of consultation with the opposition leader did not mean concurrence. 'I do not require Mr Chaudhry's agreement on whom I choose as ministers. The choice is the prime minister's' (*Pacific Islands Report*, 24 July 2003). Poseci Bune was moved from Labour's preferred Agriculture portfolio to Environment, Lekh Ram Vayshenoi from Local Government and Urban Development to Mineral and Energy, and Gyani Nand swapped portfolios with Bune. 'The Prime Minister is not acting in good faith', Chaudhry thundered. 'It is not a master–servant relationship' (*Daily Post*, 23 May 2006). This language was reminiscent of past politics and curiously jarring in the optimistic atmosphere of the post-election period.

Unable to force the prime minister's hand, Chaudhry sought to have himself appointed Leader of the Opposition, reportedly asking a Ba high chief, Tui Ba Ratu Sairusi Nagagavoka, to intercede with the president, his paramount chief, on his (Chaudhry's) behalf (*Fiji Times*, 5 July 2006). That Chaudhry lead the opposition while eight of his members were part of the government was a strange proposition. Attorney-General Qoriniasi Bale insisted, and the president was so advised, that by joining the multiparty system, Labour had effectively become a part of the government. Chaudhry's demand was contrary to the provision of the Korolevu Declaration of 26 January 1999, which Chaudhry himself had signed. That document provided that any party which participated in cabinet would not be deemed to be in opposition (*Fiji Times*, 23 June 2006). Chaudhry repudiated both the letter as well as the spirit of the Korolevu declaration. Finally, in a sad display of petulance, he refused to vacate the leader of the opposition's office in the parliamentary complex, forcing Mick Beddoes, the duly appointed opposition leader, to remain in his much smaller office.

These incidents, insignificant in themselves, were symbolically important—they sent the signal that Chaudhry was a reluctant supporter of the multiparty concept. His fears were real. He risked losing influence over his ministers in cabinet, losing control of the broad direction of the party, becoming a guest in his own house. He was also acutely aware of the political dangers of playing second fiddle to Qarase. Parties that had joined his Peoples' Coalition in 1999 (Christian Democrats and the Fijian Association Party) were defunct. The same fate befell the CAMV which had joined Qarase's government in 2001. Labour would not disappear; it was too big and established for that, but Chaudhry feared a diminished role for himself and his party. In his first parliamentary speech, Chaudhry drew the line. 'The FLP does not wish to be tainted with the scams, corruption, wastage of public funds and the incompetence that characterised the part Government'. He would set a timeframe and expect Labour's concerns to be addressed urgently. These included the enactment of a comprehensive code of conduct for all holders of high public office, the removal of racial discrimination from the affirmative action programs and the adoption of tough anti-corruption practices (*Hansard*, 8 June 2006).

Labour's dilemma was well summed up by Vice President Jon Madraiwiwi in his address to the thirty-fourth annual Congress of the Fiji Institute of Accountants on 23 June 2006.

> The Fiji Labour Party faces dilemma of enormous proportions. Should it continue to cooperate, conceding to the Prime Minister much of the credit flowing therefrom? Is it not better that it withdraw from the Government and consolidate its position as the Opposition? Politics is about advantage, manoeuvre and counter-manoeuvre. Given demographics and continuing high levels of emigration, its core support base will continue to diminish. There is little prospect that voting patterns will alter significantly over the next decade. Therefore, unless the FLP is able to attract significant Fijian support, it runs the real risk of remaining on the sidelines (*Fijivillage*, 4 July 2006)

Tensions surfaced early. One of Chaudhry's staunchest supporters in the Labour caucus, Lekh Ram Vayeshnoi, Minister for Energy and Mineral Resources, insisted that his loyalty lay totally with Chaudhry and that he would insist on pursuing Labour policies in cabinet. Several of his colleagues, eager to make the new concept work, demurred publicly, causing further tension. Chaudhry supported Vayshnoi: 'the FLP constitution states quite categorically that every member, whether a backbencher MP or a cabinet minister, must uphold the principles and objectives of the party. The directive here is very clear—we must be guided by party policies and principles in conducting ourselves' (*Sunday Post*, 25 June, 2006). Sitiveni Rabuka supported Chaudhry, saying that the Labour leader was

> ...right in demanding that FLP cabinet ministers remain committed to party policies. Let us remember they have gone to join a multiparty cabinet, not an SDL Cabinet. They need to work on unity rather than uniformity as they are there with the mandate of the people who voted them in on the FLP policies that appealed to them (*Fiji Times*, 1 July 2006).

Krishna Datt, Labour Minister and one of the founders of the Labour Party, disagreed, saying in parliament that those leaders—he clearly had Chaudhry in mind—who could not work cooperatively in a multiparty set-up, who wanted to persist with their old ways, 'must pass on their batons to others who are willing to try and I am very serious about that (*Hansard*, 8 June 2006). Responding directly to Chaudhry's demand that FLP interests must be given priority by its Labour ministers, Datt said, '[t]his is one of the guiding principles of the Fiji Labour Party—to work in the public interest, in national interest and that is what we, FLP MPs who have accepted the cabinet posts, are required to do' (*Daily Post*, 22 June 2006). For their part, Chaudhry loyalists in parliament boycotted Datt's speech in parliament introducing the Employment Relations Bill.

Emboldened, some other senior members began to talk about the need for Chaudhry to change his confrontational style. Said Felix Anthony, one of the rebels,

> I believe that the leadership style has to change. It has to be much more democratic in our decision making process. We need to practice what we preach to the world about transparency, democracy and accountability' (*Fijilive*, 6 July 2006).

Chaudhry rejected the suggestion outright, and reverted to his old ways of unilateral decision making. He submitted his list of eight nominees for the senate, but doing so directly to the President rather than through the leader of the opposition whose nominees they technically are. The well-regarded former Senator Dr Atu Emberson-Bain was dropped in favour of the lesser known Sachidanand Sharma who happened to be a relative of Chaudhry's. A former Vuda parliamentarian (Vijay Singh) was not included in the list even though Chaudhry had promised him a senate seat if he agreed to let Felix Anthony contest his seat. Nor were any of the senior members of the party's Management Board consulted about the nomination (*Fiji Sun*, 29 June 2006). While Chaudhry was away overseas, some of them submitted a different list to the leader of the opposition, but withdrew it when Beddoes stuck with Chaudhry's list. Some of the rebels did the unthinkable by questioning whether Chaudhry was in fact the parliamentary leader of the Labour Party, as he had not been elected to that position after the election, which is the normal Westminster convention.

With the split now out in the open, Chaudhry sought ways to discipline the dissidents. The Nasinu branch of the Labour Party expelled Datt from the party, and similar moves were afoot elsewhere. Chaudhry has promised to haul his wayward colleagues before the party's National Council, which consists largely of his supporters from the National Farmers Council. Chaudhry has many options at his disposal. He could, though with some difficulty, have the rebels sacked from the party, which would prompt a by-election. Or he could submit a new list for the cabinet, though the dearth of talent in the parliamentary Labour Party is conspicuous by its absence. There is no doubt that Labour's image has suffered a dent, for this is the first time in its twenty year history that there has been such a massive questioning of Labour leader's style and the party's direction from within its own ranks. Chaudhry is still popular with the rank and file of the party, but he is no longer viewed as invincible or indispensable.

Chaudhry's misery contrasts markedly with Qarase's position. The SDL leader is not the diffident man was he was when he assumed office in 2001. He is now decisive, confident of his political skills and in the driver's seat. He has risen in national esteem for the magnanimous manner in which he has conducted himself, and especially for the apparent sincerity with which he has pursued the multiparty cabinet. But he must resist the temptations of hubris by insisting on the implementation of his election manifesto or by bringing controversial legislation before parliament early in its term. Doing so may damage the developing amicable atmosphere in cabinet and give Mahendra Chaudhry the excuse he needs to opt out of government.

The multiparty cabinet is a novel concept for Fiji, but it has been practised in many European countries that practice forms of consociational democracy. It can work in Fiji if there is a will to make it work. Its success will require a change in the adversarial political culture spawned by the Westminster system since the advent of party politics in the 1960s. And it will require a more enlightened leadership with a genuinely overarching national vision for Fiji. The multiparty idea is Fiji's great challenge and also its great opportunity.

## Notes

[1] I am grateful to Dr Ganesh Chand and Professor Wadan Narsey for these figures, although they are available in several places. Election details are found at http://www.elections.gov.fj. and fijilive.com/elections 2006 . I have documented this piece lightly as the details are easily accessible on all major news websites about Fiji.

# References

Ali, A., 1977. *Fiji: from colony to independence, 1874–1970*, University of the South Pacific Monograph, University of the South Pacific, Suva.

——, 1980. 'Political change: from colony to independence', in A. Ali (ed.), *Plantation to Politics: studies on Fiji Indians*, University of the South Pacific, Suva:130–56.

Alliance Party, 1987. Alliance Party election manifesto (unpublished).

Anthony, J., 1969. 'The 1968 Fiji by-elections', *Journal of Pacific History*, 4:132–35.

Bain, A. and Baba, T. (eds), 1990. *Bavadra: Prime Minister, statesman, man of the people. Selection of speeches and writings, 1985–1989*, Sunrise Press, Nadi.

Barr, K., 1990. *Poverty in Fiji*, Fiji Forum for Justice, Peace and the Integrity of Creation, Suva.

Bavadra, T., 1986. Speech presented at the First Annual Convention of the Fiji Labour Party, Lautoka, 19 July.

Bedford, R., 1989. 'Out of Fiji: a perspective on emigration after the coups', *Pacific Viewpoint*, 30:142–53.

Belshaw, C.S., 1964. *Under the Ivi Tree: society and economic growth in rural Fiji*, Routledge and Kegan Paul, London.

Burns, Sir A., Watson, T.Y. and Peacock, A.T., 1960. *Report of the Commission of Enquiry into the natural resources and population trends of the Colony of Fiji 1959*, Legislative Council Paper 1/1960, Legislative Council of Fiji, Suva.

Chapman, J.K., 1964. *The Career of Arthur Hamilton Gordon: First Lord Stanmore, 1829–1912*, University of Toronto Press, Toronto.

Cole, R.V., Levine, S.I. and Matahu, A., 1984. *The Fijian Provincial Administration: a review*, Pacific Islands Development Program, East-West Center, Honolulu.

Cottrell, J. (ed.), 2000. *Educating for Multiculturalism*, Citizens Constitutional Forum, Suva.

Dakuvula, J., 1992. 'Chiefs and commoners: the indigenous dilemma', in D. Robbie (ed.), *Tu Galala: social change in the Pacific*, Bridget William Books, Wellington:70–79.

Davidson, J.W., 1966. 'Constitutional change in Fiji', *Journal of Pacific History*, 1:165–82.

Dean, E. and Ritova, S., 1988. *Rabuka: no other way*, Doubleday, Melbourne.

Durutalo, A., 2006. 'Fiji: party politics in the post-independence period', in R. Rich et al. (eds.), Political Parties in the Pacific Islands, Pandanus Books, The Australian National University, Canberra:165–84.

Elek, A. and Hill, H., 1991. *Fiji: economic reforms and performance since the 1987 coups*, The Australian National University, Canberra.

Farrell, B.H. and Murphy, P.E., 1978. *Ethnic Attitudes to Land in Fiji*, Santa Cruz Data Paper no. 6, University of California, Berkeley.

Firth, S., 1989. 'The contemporary history of Fiji: a review article', *Journal of Pacific History*, 24:242–46.

—— and Tarte, D. (eds), 2001. *20th Century Fiji: people who shaped this nation*, University of the South Pacific, Suva.

France, P., 1969. *Charter of the Land: custom and colonisation in Fiji*, Oxford University Press, Melbourne.

Gani, A., 2000. 'Some dimensions of Fiji's recent emigration', *Pacific Economic Bulletin*, 15(1):94–103.

Ghai, Y., 1997. *The Implementation of Fiji Islands Constitution*, Citizens Constitutional Forum, Suva.

Gillion, K.L., 1977. *The Fiji Indians. Challenge to European Dominance, 1920–1946*, The Australian National University Press, Canberra.

Government of Fiji, 1969. *Education for Modern Fiji: report of the Fiji Education Commission*, Fiji Education Commission, Government Printer, Suva.

Government of Fiji, 1975. *Report of the Royal Commission Appointed for the Purpose of Considering and Making Recommendations as to the most Appropriate Method of Electing Members to, and Representing the People of Fiji in, the House of Representatives.* Parliamentary Paper no. 24, Government Printer, Suva. ·

———, 1983. *Report of the Fiji Royal Commission into the 1982 General Election,* Parliamentary Paper no. 74, Government Printer, Suva.

———, 1988. *Fiji Constitution Inquiry and Advisory Committee Report,* Government Printer, Suva.

———, 1994. *Budget 1994,* Government Printer, Suva.

Gregor, E., 1980. 'Current status and development in the pine industry', *Information Update,* 7 February.

Griffin, A. (ed.), 2002. *Election Watch 11: a citizens' review of the Fiji Islands general election 2001,* Citizens Constitutional Forum, Suva.

Hurley, B., 2000. 'Interfaith search, Fiji', in J. Cottrell (ed.), *Educating for Multiculturalism,* Citizens Constitutional Forum, Suva:92–97.

Kamikamica, J., 1997. 'Fijian native land: issues and challenges', in B.V. Lal and T. Vakatora (eds), *Fiji in Transition,* Research Papers of the Fiji Constitution Review Commission, School of Social and Economic Development, University of the South Pacific, Suva:259–90.

Kermode, Sir R., 1993. *Report of the Commission of Inquiry into the Deed of Settlement dated 17.09.92 between Anthony Frederick Stephens and the Attorney General of Fiji,* Parliamentary Paper 45, Government Printer, Suva.

Lal, B.V., 1983a. 'The Fiji general elections of 1982: the tidal wave that never came', *Journal of Pacific History,* 18(2):134–57.

———, 1983b. 'The 1982 general election and its aftermath', *USP Sociological Bulletin,* 5:3–17.

——— (ed.), 1986. *Politics in Fiji. Studies in Contemporary History,* Brigham Young University, Laie.

———, 1988. *Power and Prejudice: the making of the Fiji crisis,* New Zealand Institute of International Affairs, Wellington.

———, 1992. *Broken Waves: a history of the Fiji Islands in the 20th century,* University of Hawaii Press, Honolulu.

———, 1997a. *A Vision for Change: A.D. Patel and the politics of Fiji,* National

Centre for Development Studies, The Australian National University, Canberra.

——, 1997b. 'The deconolisation of Fiji: debate on constitutional change, 1943–1963', in Donald Denoon (ed.), *Emerging from Empire? Decolonisation in the Pacific*, Division of Pacific and Asian History, The Australian National University, Canberra:26–39.

——, 1998. *Another Way: The politics of constitutional reform in post-coup Fiji*, Asia Pacific Press, The Australian National University, Canberra.

—— (ed.), 2000a. *Fiji Before the Storm: elections and the politics of development*, Asia Pacific Press, The Australian National University, Canberra.

——, 2000b. *Chalo Jahaji: on a journey through indenture in Fiji*, Fiji Museum and Division of Pacific and Asian History, The Australian National University, Suva and Canberra.

——, 2002. 'In George Speight's shadow. Fiji general elections of 2001', *Journal of Pacific History* 37(1):87–101.

—— and Peacock, K., 1990. 'Researching the Fiji coups', *The Contemporary Pacific: A Journal of Island Affairs*, 2(1):183–95.

—— and Vakatora, T. (eds), 1997. Papers of the Fiji Constitution Review Commission (2 vols), School of Social and Economic Development, University of the South Pacific, Suva.

Lal, P., 2000. 'Land, Lomé and the Fiji sugar industry' in Brij V. Lal (ed.) *Fiji Before the Storm: elections and the politics of development*, Asia Pacific Press, The Australian National University, Canberra:111–34.

Lasaqa, I.Q., 1984. *The Fijian People: before and after independence*, The Australian National University, Canberra.

Lawson, S., 1992. *The Failure of Democratic Politics in Fiji*, Clarendon Press, Oxford.

Legge, J.D., 1958. *Britain in Fiji, 1858–1880*, Macmillan, London.

Legislative Council of Fiji, 1966. *Report of the Working Committee Set Up to Review the ALTO*, Legislative Council Paper 23, Suva.

——, 1970. *Report of the Fiji Constitutional Conference*, Council Paper 70/ 1970, Suva.

Lloyd, D.T., 1982. *Land Policy in Fiji*, Department of Land Economy Occasional Paper no. 14, Cambridge University, London.

Macdonald, B., 1990. 'The literature of the Fiji coups: a review article', *The Contemporary Pacific: A Journal of Island Affairs*, 2:197–207.

Madraiwiwi, Ratu J., 2002. 'Parkinson memorial lecture', in K. Gravelle (ed.), *Good Governance in the South Pacific*, University of the South Pacific, Suva.

Mara, Ratu Sir K., 1997. *The Pacific Way: a memoir*, University of Hawaii Press, Honolulu.

Martin, L., 1981. 'Political blackmail over the green gold', *Islands Business News*, 6 August.

Meller, N. and Anthony, J., 1968. *Fiji Goes to the Polls. The Crucial Legislative Council Elections of 1963*, East West Center Press, Honolulu.

Mohanty, M., 2002. Contemporary emigration from Fiji: some trends and issues in the post-independence era (unpublished).

Moynagh, M., 1981. *Brown or White: a history of the Fiji sugar industry, 1873–1973*, Pacific Monograph Series no. 5, The Australian National University, Canberra.

Naidu, V., 2000. 'Evaluating our past and moulding our future', in J. Cottrell (ed.), *Educating for Multiculturalism*, Citizens Constitutional Forum, Suva:59–64.

Narsey, W., 1985. 'The wage freeze and development plan objectives: contradictions in Fiji government policy', *Journal of Pacific Studies*, 11:11–44.

Nation, J., 1982. 'Fiji: post-independence politics', in R.J. May and H. Nelson (eds), *Melanesia: beyond diversity*, Vol. II, Research School of Pacific Studies, The Australian National University, Canberra:601–21.

Nayacakalou, R., 1975. *Leadership in Fiji*, Oxford University Press, Melbourne.

Norton, R., 1990. *Race and Politics in Fiji* (2nd ed.), University of Queensland Press, St Lucia.

——, 1999. 'Chiefs for the nation: containing ethnonationalism and bridging the ethnic divide in Fiji', *Pacific Studies*, 22(1):21–50.

——, 2002. 'Accommodating indigenous privilege: Britain's dilemma in decolonising Fiji', *Journal of Pacific History*, 37(2):133–56.

————, 2004. 'Seldom a transition with such aplomb: from confrontation to conciliation on Fiji's path to independence', *Journal of Pacific History*, 39(2):147–62.

Overton, J. (ed.), 1988. *Rural Fiji*, Institute of Pacific Studies, University of the South Pacific, Suva.

Prasad, S., Dakuvula, J. and Snell, D., 2001. Economic development, democracy and ethnic conflict in the Fiji Islands (unpublished).

Premdas, R., 1980. 'Constitutional challenge: the rise of Fijian nationalism', *Pacific Perspective*, 9(2):30–44.

Ratuva, S., 2002. *Participation for Peace: a study of inter-ethnic and inter-religious perception in Fiji*, Ecumenical Council for Research, Education and Advocacy, Suva.

Ravuvu, A., 1985. *Vaka I Taukei. The Fijian Way of Life*, Institute of Pacific Studies, University of the South Pacific, Suva.

————, 1988. *Development or Dependence: the pattern of change in a Fijian village*, Institute of Pacific Studies, University of the South Pacific, Suva.

————, 1992. *The Facade of Democracy: Fijian struggle for political control, 1830–1987*, Readers Publishing House, Suva.

Reddy, J.R., 1980. Speech presented to the 16th Annual convention of the National Federation Party Convention, Ba.

————, 1993. Speech presented to the National Federation Party convention, Nadi.

Reeves, Sir P., Vakatora, T.R.. and Lal, B.V., 1996. *Towards a United Future: report of the Fiji Constitution Review Commission*, Government of Fiji, Suva.

Robertson, R.T., 1998. *Multiculturalism and Reconciliation in an Indulgent Republic*, Fiji Institute of Applied Studies, Suva.

———— and Tamanisau, A., 1988. *Fiji-Shattered Coups*, Pluto Press, Sydney.

Roth, G.K., 1953. *Fijian Way of Life*, Oxford University Press, Melbourne.

Said, E., 1993. *Culture and Imperialism*, Chatto and Windus, London.

Sharpham, J., 2000. *Rabuka of Fiji. The authorised biography of Major-General Sitiveni Rabuka*, Central Queensland University Press, Rockhampton.

Singh, Sir V.R., 1988. Opening address, in *Protecting Fijian Interests and*

*Building a Democratic Fiji: a consultation on Fiji's Constitution Review,* Citizens Constitutional Forum, Suva:9–14.

Slatter, C., 1989. 'The trade union movement since the coup' in S. Prasad (ed.), *Coup and Crisis-Fiji a year later,* Arena Publications, Melbourne:22–26.

Spate, O.H.K., 1959. *Fijian people: economic problems and prospects,* Legislative Council Paper no. 13, Government of Fiji, Suva.

Scarr, D. (ed.), 1984. *The Three-Legged Stool: selected writings of Ratu Sir Lala Sukuna,* Macmillan, Basingstoke.

Sutherland, W., 1989. 'The new political economy of Fiji', *Pacific Viewpoint,* 30(2):132–41.

——, 1992. *Beyond the Politics of Race: an alternative history of Fiji to 1992,* Social and Political Change Monograph, The Australian National University, Canberra.

Stanner, W.E.H., 1953. *The South Seas in Transition: a study of post-war rehabilitation and reconstruction in three British Pacific dependencies,* Australasian Publishing Company, Sydney.

Statton, M. and McGregor, A., 1991. *Fiji: economic adjustment, 1987–1991,* Pacific Islands Development Program, East-West Center, Honolulu.

Thomas, N., 1990. 'Sanitation and seeing: the creation of state power in early colonial Fiji', *Comparative Studies in Society and History,* 32(1):149–70.

Usher, Sir L., 1986. *Mainly About Fiji: a collection of writings, broadcasts, and speeches,* Fiji Times Ltd, Suva.

Vakatale, T., 2000. 'The constraints and challenges to building multiculturalism in Fiji', in J. Cottrell (ed.), *Educating for Multiculturalism,* Citizens Constitutional Forum, Suva:13–23.

Ward, R.G., 1987. 'Native Fijian village: a questionable future?', in M. Taylor (ed.), *Fiji: future imperfect,* Allen and Unwin, North Sydney:33–45.

Watters, R.F., 1969. *Koro: economic development and social change in Fiji,* Oxford University Press, Oxford.

# Index

victory in April 1977, 38
aims of, 41
problems of, 42–43
(1987 elections), 56
1994 elcetions,117–18
political fragmentation, 178
appeal to Fijians, 179
Fijian politics, divisions within,
118–19
disunity in, 221
Fijian problems, official attitudes
towards, 8–9
Fijian society, sources of change, 234
Fijian Teachers Association, view on
scholarship for Fijians, 33, 54
Fijian unity, problems with emphasis
on, 239
Firth, Stewart, 240
Fisher, Nigel, 15
Foreign policy, issues in 1987
campaign, 67 ff
Foster, Sir Robert, 22

Ganilau, Ratu Epeli, president of
New Alliance Party, 256
Ganilau, Ratu Sir Penaia, reaction to
result of 1982 general election, 27
alleged sympathy for aims of
coup, 72
post-coup actions, 73ff
Garvey, Sir Ronald, 9–11
Gates, Justice Anthony, 208, 217ff
Gavidi, Ratu Osea, 43–46, 56, 85
support for Viti Levu Council of
Chiefs, 101
1994 campaign, 118
General Electors Association, 51
General Voters Party, 91–92
divisions within, 119

George, Telford, 128
Ghai, Yash Professor, advice on
boycott options, 91
Gillion, Ken, 28
Globalisation, impact of, xi
Gordon, Sir Arthur Hamilton,
policies of, 2–3
Government of National Unity,
Rabuka's proposal for, 105–6
Grand Fijian Coalition, formation
and rejection of, 256–57
Grantham, Governor on Fijian
problems, 8
Great Council of Chiefs, powers of,
2–3
reaction to 1982 general election,
26–27
constitutional proposals of, 74
support for SVT, 83
deliberating on 2000 coup,
199–200
termination of SVT link, 223
role for, 244

Hart, Sir William, 2

Iloilo, Ratu Josefa, 219
Inder, Stuart, 47
Indian Alliance, problems in, 36, 52
Indian Council, proposal for, 246
Indian domination, fear of, 5
Indian indentured labour,
introduction of, 4
Indian problem, 8
Indo-Fijians, attitude to education, 32
discrimination in public service, 34
opposition to the abrogation of
the 1970 constitution, 73–74
political divisions amongst,

Public service, racial imbalance in, 152

Qarase, Laisenia, head of SDL, 222
opposed to sharing power with Labour, 2001, 226–27
offering 'insulting' ministries to Labour, 230
offer of portfolios to Labour in 2006, 252
post 2006 stature, 263
Qarikau, Marika, 194–95
Qeleni Holdings, 108
Qereqeretabua, Radike, founding Fijian Grand Coalition, 256
Queen Victoria School, 5
Quentin-Baxter, Alison, 129

Rabuka, Sitiveni, justifying his role in 1987 coup, 72–73
implicating Mara in 1987 crisis, 72
handing over government to Mara and Ganilau, 75
distancing himself from the interim administration policies, 80
elected leader of SVT, 83
disenchantment over his ascendancy, 83–84
invoking the Melanesian model of leadership, 84
leadership, critics of, 85
challenge to, 86–87
fight with Kamikamica, 92–93
support for prime minister, 96
dilemmas of, 99, 101–2
challenge to, 101–2
performance as prime minister, 103
pro-Fijian economic policies, 104

mooting government of national unity, 105
collapse of government, 111–12
on the motives of his critics, 113
plea to voters (1994), 116
causes of defeat in 1999, 177
alleged involvement in the 2000 coup, 198
on future of customary chiefs, 250
Race, obsession with, ix, 249
Racial imbalance in public service, 34
Ramrakha, Karam, 21, 30
resignation of, 38
role in 1977 crisis, 38
Ravuvu, Asesela, chair of review commission, 213, 238
on Fijian dilemmas, 250
Reconciliation, Tolerance and Unity Bill, 254
opposition of the military to, 255
Reddy, Jai Ram, critical of Alliance land policy, 30
criticism of PSC policy, 34
resignation from parliament, 37
role in NFP reconciliation, 39
relations with Mara, 39
explanation of coalition with WUF, 45–46
opposition to (1992) boycott, 87
on a possible government of national unity, 92
plea for fairness, 106
exposing corruption in government, 109–10
criticism of government budget, 111
popularity of, 120
advocacy of consociationalism, 122

www.ingramcontent.com/pod-product-compliance
Lightning Source LLC
Chambersburg PA
CBHW050809270326
41926CB00037B/4605